USA / *From Where We Stand*

USA / *From Where We Stand*

Readings in Contemporary American Problems

Edited by
LEO J. RYAN
Assemblyman, 27th District, California Legislature

fp
Fearon Publishers
Lear Siegler, Inc., Education Division
Belmont, California

Library of Congress Catalog Card Number: 73–116372.
Printed in the United States of America.

Dedicated to

Christopher, Shannon, Patricia, Kevin, Erin, Barry, Kari, Nick, Deirdre, Drew, Billy, Cormac, Sheelagh, Tim, Dean, Bobby, Geoffrey, Owen, Danny, Colin, Randy, Ramsey, and all the other young children who are one generation away from all the problems discussed in this book. They do not yet have the authority or status to make the decisions that will affect their lives and their children's lives when this country actually reaches the third millennium. Hopefully this book gives evidence that we are stumbling in the right direction.

Thanks

There are many people who have helped in the production of this book. Where the book is found to have some value, they share the credit. Where there is some flaw or shortcoming, the blame must be mine.

Thanks especially to my editorial assistant, Mrs. Gaye Lopez, who spent so much of her own time on this project. Thanks also to Maxine Wright, Susan Woodbury, Jan Easterday, Dennis Doyle, and Bob Caughlan.

Leo J. Ryan
Sacramento, California

CONTENTS

Introduction

FROM WHERE WE STAND

Leo J. Ryan

There is general agreement that the 1960's took one bright step forward before its promise turned to total disaster. In a political sense the decade began with two men riding down Pennsylvania Avenue in Washington, D.C. President Eisenhower, 70 years old, the commanding general in World War II, and a national hero, was giving way to a younger man–John F. Kennedy, 43 years old, who had been a naval lieutenant in that same conflict.

The general represented the solid values of the Midwest. The former lieutenant was a Harvard-educated man and the son of a multimillionaire. John Kennedy had entered the rough and bruising world of Massachusetts politics and had become one of its United States Senators while he was still in his early thirties. Amusement for the older man was a western movie at the White House or a game of pitch-and-putt golf on the lawn. For the younger man, it was inviting the Nobel Prize winners to dinner at the White House or romping on the lawn with his young children.

By the time President Kennedy took office, World War II was an event of the past. The people of the nation no longer spoke of "post-war" events. No longer did we need to struggle with the problems of the returning veterans. The nation had survived the after-shocks of that most gigantic of all wars in history and had adjusted to a peace-time economy. With that 1960 election we began to look ahead with hope. The World War II veteran had become a civilian, had gotten his education with the help of the G.I. Bill, and had bought a home in suburbia with G.I. financing. He was now employed, married, and raising kids. He looked ahead to the promise of the Good Life. The new president symbolized the style and the hope of an entire generation of young men and women whose adult years began with military service in a bloody and dangerous war.

On November 22, 1963, President Kennedy was assassinated and that new world began to come apart. With the Kennedy assassination the new momentum was disrupted, never to be regained. Five years later came the assassination of Martin Luther King, increasing the alienation of the black community. Finally, in 1968, came the assassination of President Kennedy's younger brother and political heir, Robert Kennedy.

During these years, the children of the World War II veterans grew up. Born in the late 1940's and early 1950's, they entered high school and college better prepared than any previous generation—and they were shocked by the paradoxes they saw in the world they would have to live in. In school they had learned a pledge that ended with the words "with liberty and justice for all"—but they were aware that not even a Supreme Court decision could ensure an American citizen a decent education if he was black. They studied the history of their country and learned about its past wars. They followed the war in Vietnam (in which they would be expected to serve) and found it to be a savage slaughter over confused issues and with no real agreement as to its morality or purpose or outcome.

They were aware of the furor over nudity in the theater and sex-education programs in the schools, but these things did not seem obscene in comparison to the pictures they had seen of the bloody corpses of tiny children slaughtered in Vietnam.

They listened to adults preach of the sanctity of marriage, but they knew that a substantial portion of the nation's marriages end in the divorce courts.

They heard adults condemn the Pill on the basis of morality, but they knew that U.S. population had grown from fewer than 100 million in 1900 to more than 200 million in 1970, and that no significant material effort had been made to control the excessive increase.

In church they heard sermons about loving one's fellow man, but they saw that members of those same churches seemed to ignore the massive needs of a ghetto population whose poverty was as grinding and oppressive as any in the world. They also saw that white churchgoers rarely found a place in their midst for a black man and his family.

They were aware of the uproar over the use of drugs by millions of young people, but they knew that their parents drank alcohol at cocktail parties, used barbiturates to put themselves to sleep, and amphetamines to pep them up.

In college their professors turned them over to teaching assistants or lectured them in classes of enormous size, making it difficult to ask questions or to have any answered.

In 1964 the student rebellion began on the Berkeley campus of the University of California. It spread throughout much of the world and started a revolution that still continues. This is not to say that change is unknown in this country or that it is undesirable. The story of America is a record of steady change. There is very little similarity between the Puritan world of John Winthrop three hundred years ago and our world today.

What was unique about the 1960's were the assassinations of three respected leaders–John F. Kennedy, Martin Luther King, Jr., and Robert F. Kennedy. These assassinations frustrated the normal efforts of political parties to move ahead, and the major problems of the 1960's continued into the 1970's. The war in Vietnam, civil rights, urban problems, transportation, and environmental pollution were all areas of immediate concern. The most recent elections seem to indicate that neither party has the capacity to look ahead. Neither seems to have the capacity to see the needs of the United States in the last third of the twentieth century.

This is not the first time our nation has been in this position. In 1870, for example, political leaders had little comprehension of the enormous changes that would occur as a result of westward expansion. Could President Grant foresee the effect that the transcontinental railroad would have on the shape and structure of government in new states and counties? Could he know that labor unions would become a significant force in American political life? The political parties in the last third of the nineteenth century did not look ahead. They felt no sense of urgency about the future. What followed was the most corrupt and venal era in American politics. We are still suffering from it, politically and socially, especially at the state level.

Today we have reached a similar period in the history of our country. We are led by political parties that are stalled, dead center, between an old conservatism that looks nostalgically to the past–a past that never existed in the way it is remembered (do we really want typhoid epidemics again, or a sixty-hour work week?)–and an old liberalism that still believes that labor must struggle to achieve a living wage and that all our social problems can be solved by a massive infusion of federal money. The elements of our future politics are much different from these old ideals, and the stakes are much higher: They probably involve our survival as a nation and as human beings on this planet.

How much longer, for instance, can we continue to crowd more and more people into this world? How much longer can we afford to wage senseless, destructive wars? How long can we permit the uncontrolled use of the earth's resources when there is no possibility of replacing them? Indeed, how long will it be before we have completely used up everything our lives depend on?

These issues are the politics of the future. Neither Republicans nor Democrats have begun to spell out in substantive fashion the means by which we can control population growth, environmental problems, and the conservation of our natural resources.

Having identified these areas as crucial, the political parties that will control our future will have to find ways to deal with them without the smothering heaviness of too much governmental control. They will also have to find a way to avoid the danger of allowing a small minority to disrupt and perhaps destroy the capacity of the majority to direct its own destiny. We cannot afford to allow another agency to grow up uncontrolled through lack of competition, as we have done in the case of our public school system, for example. We must allow for the element of competition in every aspect of big government, labor, and business in order to provide checks and comparisons of services that can give the individual some choice in the direction and development of his own life.

There are four changes in our present national direction that must take effect in the 1970's. First of all, we must recognize that our organizational structures have become so big that we have almost destroyed the element of competition in business, labor, and government. Even though organizations do compete to some extent, there is a sluggishness of response that inhibits vigorous competition. There is a sameness of product and a resistance to change. Why, for instance, did the Volkswagen, the MG, and the Toyota take so much of the small-car market for so many years before the major American automobile manufacturers began to produce small cars?

Second, we must develop a way to enable the individual to be heard, whether he is crying for help or making a suggestion to government or business that might improve the quality of our existence. One of the political realities of the past ten years has been the "confrontation," a desperate device usually used by a relatively small group, or even a single individual, to stop normal processes from functioning in order to bring about some kind of change in policy. It is used by people who complain that they cannot be heard by anyone in the regular structures of government or business. Whether it is a group of conservationists placing themselves in front of a bulldozer in a housing subdivision, or a group of black students occupying a school building in order to force a change in school rules, the technique is the same. It is the use of people to create change outside of the ordinary processes.

Unless business, government, and labor improve their abilities to change, the individual stands to lose even more of his identity than he already has by becoming an ever-smaller segment of our massive population. We have never had to be concerned about this problem before in this country, but we must become concerned about it now.

In the first U.S. Congress, a member of the House of Representatives spoke for about 45,000 people. Today each member represents some 500,000 people, and the total number of votes cast in his election district is between 200,000 and 300,000. In another thirty years the number of people represented by each member of the House will be at least 750,000. In business and in labor we face the same problem of dealing with huge numbers of people. For example, how can a man who lives in a thousand-unit apartment development make a complaint to his landlord? How does a man who belongs to the three-million-member Teamsters Union make his feelings known to the policy makers of that organization? Unless he can do so, he will look with distrust upon *any* organized group.

Third, we need to recognize that the capacity of the earth to sustain human life is limited. We have never had to be concerned about this problem before. Now we know that humans *can* populate the earth to the point where they can strip this planet of all the resources that enable us to live as we do. What will replace the great Mesabi iron ore range that supplied the raw material for the construction of our railroads and automobiles for forty years? It is all gone now. How will we replace the oil fields of the Southwest when they are exhausted? What about the vast forests of redwood trees that are now gone forever except for a few protected acres?

Finally, we need to build into our system the capacity to create change through competition and through the rewarding of individual excellence. The more massive our population and governmental structures become, the less recognition we pay to the individual. We need to develop the idea of positive reward instead of negative reward. We say that children fail in school, when there is good reason to believe that it is the school that has failed. How can any child do less than he can do with his own native wit? His environment can slow down his nomal learning progress. But isn't it the school's job to repair weaknesses as they are found? Again, we punish the law violator by throwing him in jail. But 95 percent of those in penitentiaries are released sooner or later. While they are in prison they are punished for their prior bad behavior—but they are not rewarded for any signs of change and improved behavior. The result is a hostile attitude when they are released, and half of them are sent back to prison.

Let us apply these four general statements for some specific problems.

We need some better means of choosing delegates to our national party conventions. Until now, those politicians who actually chose the convention delegates have not been selected by any election power in the individual states. At least one of the results of our present system was the chaos at the Democratic National Convention at Chicago in 1968.

In developing solutions to urban problems and housing problems, we need to formulate far more comprehensive plans than we now have to subsidize private corporations that are willing to build large living complexes that rise vertically rather than sprawl horizontally, and that are in *walking* distance of commercial and industrial areas. There should be room for persons of modest wealth to live in the same structures as the people with more wealth. Children who live in these buildings should be able to attend elementary school in them. There should also be strict requirements for providing large open areas among such buildings.

The churches should be encouraged through our tax structure to take a more active role in helping with the poor in a given area. Why can't the worship of God be pointed more toward solving the problems of His people, to replace at least partially the sermon and the hymns? Surely, the Bible's own comment that the greatest virtue is charity could be demonstrated in a practical fashion.

Our schools should be developed to a point where they are obliged to compete for students. Why shouldn't our educational system offer parents an alternative to the neighborhood school? Why not enable parents to shop around for a school? The availability of many different kinds of public *and* private schools would do much to provide the varied educational backgrounds that are necessary in a society that demands many kinds of work skills.

We should reexamine our national goals and ask ourselves if our national security really requires that we possess the ability to destroy everyone in the world. Our present military commitments cost us $100 billion each year. That is $500 a year for every man, woman, and child in this country. Is this the best use of this money?

One way we can work for peace in the world is to encourage the largest possible number of American citizens to visit foreign countries. With the development of the 747 jet airplane, which can carry 490 passengers, and the C5A, which will carry 900 passengers, we can look forward to a time when these planes will do for international air travel what the Greyhound bus did for national travel. There is reason to assume that the advent of mass air travel will create the same movement of people and goods on an international scale that now takes place in this country. And if mass air travel is not enough, a system of worldwide communication by television and communications satellites should light up the dark corners of the world forever. With enough first-hand knowledge of the people of other countries, the chances for armed conflict will diminish. Our foreign policy planning and our military expenditures should reflect this fact.

Finally, we should look ahead to the astounding effect that the computer will have on our economy and our way of life. The day is not far off when home communications devices combining the services of computers, television, and telephone will make it possible for us to do many things at home that we presently have to go out to do. The potential uses for such a system are great and the impact of it on our lives can only be guessed at. We can only guess–but the time when the effects of today's planning and development will be felt is only one generation away.

Chapter 1

THE URBAN ENVIRONMENT

The population of the United States doubled in the first seventy years of this century, and it will double again by the year 2000. Seventy years ago most Americans lived in small towns or on farms. Today, more than two-thirds of the population is urban. It is the city where we find our greatest problems.

If we could start all over again, would we consciously design our cities to be like those we know today? Would our housing patterns be the same? Would we create tens of thousands of separate taxing agencies? Would we design tall downtown buildings that are in use 40 hours a week and stand empty the remaining 128 hours? Would we design whole cities that are deserted after business hours–except by the very poor who live in squalor on the outskirts? Indeed, would we deliberately develop a class of people who live on welfare paid for by the middle-class citizens who daily pass through the slums on their way from the suburbs where they live to the city where they earn their living?

Since we cannot start from scratch, we can at least agree–perhaps–that the only real way to improve our urban environment is to begin to change it, keeping those things we value and removing those that are too costly or are of little worth.

In the articles in this chapter we take a hard, critical look at our cities. We try to find out where we went wrong ("No One's in Charge"), and we consider what kinds of cities we *should* have been planning ("What Kind of City Do We Want?"). We analyze our living area ("The Community: Could This Be Our Town?") and look for a way to ease the lot of the slum dweller ("How To Clean Up the Nation's

Slums"). We consider the fact that we have built our cities in such a way that we are obliged to travel great distances ("The Agony of Getting Anywhere"), and then we examine one of the possible solutions to the transportation problem ("What Area-Wide Transit Can Do for Supercity").

What human values should be considered in building a city? We examine the thoughts of Constantinos A. Doxiadis, one of the world's best-known city planners, on this subject ("Sprawl vs. Livable Cities"). And what of the cities of the future? Will they be modules of antiseptic luxury covered by plastic domes? The possibility exists ("A Smokeless, Noiseless, Trafficless City").

No One's in Charge Conrad Knickerbocker

Worrying about cities has become the most fashionable form of national self-torture, succeeding bootlegging, necking in rumble seats and the other great social concerns of the past. Mention the word "city" to thinking Americans and their eyeballs roll back in their heads. They clench their teeth and their fingers begin to twitch. "Yes," they gasp. "Terrible. Cancer in the air we breathe. Detergents in our drinking water. Entire Himalayan ranges of poptop cans. One-hundred-car freeway accidents. Thirty million people suddenly with no lights. Can't walk in the park."

All true enough, but short of the point. The bleats are pertinent chiefly to the epicenters of what cities have become, whereas—as a subject for concern—the word "cities" must take in a great deal more; not just the dense heart but also the surrounding, outspreading, gradually thinning swarm, beyond the city limits to the tiers of suburbs as well. And it must also take in the emotional calculus of American life—the frantic rhythms and moods that make our urban existence unlike anything city dwellers have experienced ever before, from Babylon down to the present.

Thinking about cities this way, a whole new set of references can be seen, deriving from the way our cities have grown up. Once, cities grew leisurely, following the natural impetus of their history and geography. No more. Now they simply explode—like a trick camera sequence in which time appears to collapse—from hamlet to metropolis. And as a result they no longer make complete sense as places. They are no longer coherent.

How then does urban man live? Norman Mailer says the cities are totalitarian. Barry Goldwater says they are violent. Readers of David Riesman's *The Lonely Crowd* think city dwellers are all anonymous consumers, devoid of self-determination and filled with anxiety because they live in a ruthless, monolithic, increasingly specialized industrial society. As evidence, those who agree point to a Saturday afternoon neighborhood stroll which reveals that urban inhabitants relieve tension by racing slot-cars and playing with Crazy Foam.

The certain truth about American city life is that it has, at last, moved beyond comprehension, that it is changing—and fast. And nobody is in charge. At last, anything can happen.

The touchstone of this remarkable new dispensation is the freedom it offers—freedom mind-staggering in its variety of choice. Freedom to build a tavern in the shape of a three-masted schooner on Boston's Route 1, or a skyscraper in the shape of a Kleenex

This article first appeared in *Life* Magazine, December 24, 1965. Reprinted by permission.

box in Kansas City. Or to live like an English gentleman on Chicago's Near North Side, or like a Roman nobleman in Beverly Hills, or a pioneering homesteader in Pittsburgh, or a Revolutionary War merchant in Tacoma. Our cities today are huge, bottomless grab bags of yearnings and styles embracing every phase of 5,000 years of Western civilization. An American city is a place where the post office looks like the Parthenon, the home of the town's richest citizen is a replica of Blenheim Palace, and everybody else lives like a Texas rancher.

No wonder the people who live in the cities tend to come unstuck. Confronted with this awesome range of life styles, they have constant trouble trying to keep fixed in their heads who they are or where exactly it is that they are living at any particular moment. In their search for sea anchors against the uncertainties of complete freedom, they nurse great visions, some of them remote from common sense and logic, and most of them as two-edged in their implications as the most prevalent vision of them all:

Mom is settin' a spell on the porch swing and fanning herself with a paper fan imprinted with the legend, "Clyde's Eats—Ho-Made Pies." Pop has just finished mowing the yard, which glistens forever green despite the summer's heat. He hooks his thumb under the bib of his overalls and says, "We got a mighty nice place here, Mom." The kids return from the ole swimmin' hole trailing a nice mess of catfish. "This is a wonderful place to raise children," Mom says. The entire family sets a spell on the front porch, drinking lemonade and singing *Old Dog Tray*. Fade out.

Nothing dangerous here, just us fools. It is an innocent vision, hallowed by three centuries of belief in the ultimate goodness of living near the *land*. Innocent but destructive. The pastoral dream may have made some sense in 1920, when nearly half of the nation still lived on farms or in small towns. But it has helped destroy the cities of today and it casts a nightmarish shadow over the city of tomorrow.

The ole swimmin' hole syndrome has already, in fact, created a nation of cities which are, in reality, not cities at all. Of the 30 great metropolitan complexes that contain at least one million residents each, many are noncities—clusters of high-rise office buildings (built as much to convince the inhabitants that "New York hasn't anything on us" as for economic reasons) surrounded by mile on mile of suburban family dormitories in which the blue light of television flickers at night and where the sidewalks are nearly always empty. Parts of New York, Boston, Chicago and San Francisco still offer city living in the traditional sense—the rich, teeming, multileveled life; the nonhomogenous swirl of smells, sights, sounds of different people engaged in a wide variety of pursuits. But the back-to-nature fixation has driven much of the rest of the nation into street upon street of meaningless, tiny symbolic "farms" stretching coast to coast.

And these farms turn out to be 60-foot frontages of crab grass. There is no front porch, and no time for anyone to set a spell. Because the junipers all died last Saturday and the garage door fell off—thanks to mass building engineered to create pastoral dreams cheaply—Pop has to spend weekends doing day labor around the place. Meanwhile Mom, who puts in 30 hours a week as a child chauffeur, uses the ranch wagon to take the kids to their judo lessons. There is no swimmin' hole—ole or new—except the kidney-shaped pools built in the backyard on the instalment plan. Instead, the quarreling residents of Grinder Switch Estates will have to vote yes or no on a bond issue to build a new colonial-style sewage-treatment plant to replace the present suicidally overloaded arrangement.

Odd—it looked so good in the commercial: hand-in-hand walks through spring meadows; a brace of silky setters; deep, satisfying drags on king-sized, menthol-flavored, triple-filtered cigarets. But pursuit of the vision has somehow failed to make life simpler. A sense of malaise infects the good, clean living. Rock-solid rural verities turn to sand in the treacherous climate of tract housing. A sports car flattens the cocker spaniel. Pretty soon, the inhabitants begin to wonder who they *are*. They go into group therapy. Later, they try a debt counselor. Finally, when things get really rough, they move somewhere else—preferably west, to Marlboro Country, where Mom says again, it's a good place to raise kids.

American urban freedom produces wild and woolly scenes. Drive down Kansas City's Main Street and suddenly there's a big airplane aimed right at the car. A crash? No, just an old plane fuselage that has been wedged into a parking lot and converted into a cocktail lounge. Only in an American city can one leap off a jetliner and 36 seconds later be shoveling quarters into a slot machine while wiser heads read self-help gambling books at the cigar counter. Only in America can one witness from a descending jet what appears to be a daily reenactment of the German gas attack at Ypres, but is merely the San Fernando Valley on a good day when everybody has his car out. Millions of Angelenos live at the bottom of this sea of hydrocarbonous gas while, above the mountains, the sky gleams a pure, cruel blue.

Look again at Kansas City and see how the style of life that has evolved there is in beautiful organic harmony with the city's history and prairie surroundings.

One of the world's first shopping centers—and still one of the classiest—is the Country Club Plaza in Kansas City, which was built in 1923 in a Spanish-Moorish style because the late J. C. Nichols, its founder, thought this architecture was "a lot of fun." And lo! A little piece of old Spain right here in the steak capital of the world! If you are rich in Kansas City, the first thing you do is build a French provincial house in Mission Hills with an enormous hand-hewn shingle roof such as was never seen in any French province. Then install a California patio for friendly outdoor living. Then learn to ski Swiss style. Then put a St. Tropez ocean-going cruiser into the Lake of the Ozarks, a semitropical, manmade lake in the middle of the state gradually filling up with empty beer cans. Then buy an English riding habit and join the Mission Valley Hunt, which rides to hounds yoicks-style and which has never run a fox to ground in more than 30 years of existence.

When the Brooks Brothers salesman from New York unpacks his sample trunks at the Town House Hotel, Kansas City swingers pour out of their nickel and dime advertising agencies and Swedish-modern insurance offices. They greet the salesman by his first name and tie up the telephone with long calls to their wives describing swatches of English worsted and flannel. Then they jump into their Porsches and go to the Irish pub on top of the Commerce Tower for a self-congratulatory lunch. The main requirement for the good life in Kansas City, as in most other places, is that it be parachuted in from somewhere else.

This holds also for culture. E-Z culture is a fashionable yearning of the city dweller. With a few notable exceptions, urban cultural undertakings are an inch deep and a mile wide. Like many communities, Kansas City tends to tolerate a cultural undertaking only if it meets two standards: 1) the art form in question must have no discomforting bearing whatsoever on one's own life; 2) the presentation must be big and spectacular, producing lots of newspaper clippings and local names in the paper. Last May, a group of the city's civic leaders, spearheaded by the country club set, organized three performances of *Julius Caesar,* George Frederick Handel's baroque, overblown opera that had rested, except for rare occasions, on the shelf for more than 240 years. The $144,000 production involved an enormous cast of genuine international opera stars, some of them imported from Italy, and massive scenery that appeared to have been left over from the filming of *Cleopatra*. Everyone, from bankers' sons to used-car dealers, donned tuxedos and packed the Music Hall to fight sleep for three interminable hours. The pain was worth it, however, because the international press took notice. Meanwhile, the Kansas City Philharmonic, a less flamboyant but more productive enterprise, is having difficulty raising funds to support the growth it should enjoy. Culture is okay—just so it doesn't happen too often.

If on one level, American cities fail to make sense as coherent places, some of them add up beautifully as moods. Take your pick. Yearn for what you will. If watching *Gunsmoke* happens to be your idea of a good time, there is a whole band of communities extending from Great Falls, Mont., south to El Paso, Texas. These cities memorialize past cowboy glories in a pseudo-Matt Dillon style that just will not quit.

Present relevance, of course, has nothing to do with it. The genuine Wild West has definitely gone and Albuquerque, for instance, owes much of its current thrust to energies of the Sandia Corporation, a nuclear systems complex. With all this local brain power concentrated on extending the frontiers of science, one might expect Albuquerque to show signs of developing into an amazing new city of the future, uncrippled by the myths that hobble the rest of the country. But no, the minute a stranger hits town, he buys a Billy-the-Kid kit like everyone else and begins collecting Indian blankets.

Ed Pennybacker, an Albuquerque radio newsman who was last year's president of the Rio Grande Horse Association, reports that there are 250,000 horses within easy automobile commuting distance of the city—nearly one for every man, woman and child in the Albuquerque area. When the residents are not rehearsing the horseback pursuit of Cochise, they are off in some gulch camping out overnight. The combination pickup truck and aluminum camper has become an Albuquerquean status symbol. It is driven to work to show off in the company parking lot. The really snazzy models have a rifle rack hung in the rear window. Some fast-draw artist is always shooting himself in the leg. Transplanted Easterners stagger across the burning desert like Gabby Hayes looking for the Lost Dutchman Mine. They are, in reality, seeking a few slivers of turquoise for their rock hound collection.

Scientists at the Sandia Corporation tend to devote their lunch hours not to egghead discussions of a larger future, but to passionate declarations on the art of lawn-growing. As in Greenwich, Bloomfield Hills and Bel Air, the Albuquerque lawn is ranch, spread, farm and virility symbol all in one. The difficulty of raising Kentucky blue grass in the New Mexico desert presents a red-blooded challenge, the kind our homesteading ancestors faced. Hence, a successful Albuquerque yard looks like one of those gardens the Moors used to create in the midst of the Sahara with the aid of hundreds of slaves.

Not long ago Albuquerque also was the scene of a brief but spirited skirmish involving culture. William Weinrod announced one day that KHFM, his radio station, proposed to abandon an all-classical music format in favor of popular tunes. A barrage of letters and telephone calls from distraught college-educated housewives, among others, changed his mind. The good life in the American desert requires—marvelously—*both* Bach and Billy-the-Kid kits, and in Albuquerque vacuum cleaners are still run to the tinkle of *The Well-Tempered Clavier*.

Outdoor living, as everyone knows, has magical, soul-enlarging properties. Hence, entire cities declare, as their prime spiritual reason for being, their proximity to mountains (Denver) or a desert (Tucson) or water—both salt and fresh—(Seattle). No one can find the good life (the *really* good life) at the foot of a concrete canyon. So, these noncities have managed to become no more than points of departure–true bedroom communities–because the locals invest all their energy maneuvering to get away to the mountains, the desert or the shore.

Everybody at the Country Club, a suburban community of 16 expensive homes on Bainbridge Island in Puget Sound, gathers at the clubhouse for tea on Saturday afternoon in Seattle's wholesome air. On Sunday night, the clubhouse bell rings and they get together and sing hymns. Seattle and its environs is a haven for good guys who cannot buy the hyped-up versions of urban life peddled in the great cities of California or the East.

Larger Seattle, in fact, is the good-guy cities of America all rolled into one. Here, as in Cleveland, Des Moines, Dallas or Spokane, the past has no bearing. In the core city the bums cluster on the hard benches of Pioneer Square around a fading Indian totem pole, the sole remaining emblem of a rip-roaring time when the place was one vast Skid Road. Nowadays Seattle offers the perfect middle-class vision–lots of ranch-style living, free repertory Shakespeare in the parks, op art in the department store windows, and the future is expected to bring only bright, uncomplicated views of Mount Rainier. No sad, old guys need apply.

"If you're a real he-man, you'll never leave Seattle," John E. Steiner, chief project engineer of the Boeing 727 jetliner, told a visitor recently. "This is *great country*," he said, clenching his fist. It was suggested that the Seattle area might be a good place to raise kids and Steiner whipped out photographs of his children kneeling over catches of salmon and holding aloft braces of pheasants. Every evening the canoes, hydroplanes, water skiers, motor boats, sailboats, and yachts careen around Lake Washington as though they were headed toward the rescue of an army at Dunkirk.

"Seattle has few rich, few poor, no eccentrics, and no bohemians," says Irving Clark Jr., an attorney who conducts a local radio and TV talk show on the side. "We have a large, prosperous middle class. Indeed, we are the most nearly classless community in the country. We are strikingly friendly to outlanders. We are everlastingly healthy."

Existence in urban Seattle, as in many cities of its kind, is also without major horizons or challenge. The citizens harbor no rancorously divergent viewpoints nor do they debate great issues. Nor do wild and invigorating ambitions spur them. There is no climate of dissent nor, for that matter, assent. Seattle possesses its fair share of organizations purported to be concerned with the city's future, but about the most these groups can come up with is the annual Seafair, a 10-day water-centered binge involving parades, aquatic shows and speedboat races. Under the circumstances, souls tend to go stale.

"Besides being rosy-cheeked," Attorney Clark admits, "Seattleites are also unhappy. The other day I counted up 26 people I've known who have committed suicide. Those are too many to blame on the weather."

Architecturally and spiritually, Los Angeles was the first city to say the hell with it as a place; better to be a state of mind in which any life style goes and it is still the pluperfect example of its kind. Driving from Hollywood to Burbank, one passes Persian minarets, Turkish palaces, Venetian *palazzos*, stately English homes, Tudor cottages, French monasteries, Arabian gardens, Spanish adobe haciendas. In Los Angeles, you can be anyone you want to be, if you can pass the physical.

Not everyone out there operates in overdrive. What seems like 80% of the folks came out of the heartland beginning a quarter of a century ago, fleeing from 160-acre hog-and-corn farms with too many kids near Dexter, Iowa, or Mankato, Kan., or Kingfisher, Okla. In 1946, they scraped up enough for a down payment on a $10,000 bungalow in Glendale. They took such good care of their bent-grass lawn that every three years a realtor convinced them to sell the place at a profit, and they moved on to a slightly better house in one of those Los Angeles suburbs with a name like Sun Valley. Today they live in a $38,000, seven-room stucco ranch-style with a den and a jet-powered kitchen, elaborate as a missile silo, in which one can actually do the outdoor barbecuing inside. The place is so clean and bright it squeaks. Their backyard contains three apricot trees, two pet chickens they won at a supermarket opening and two land tortoises from the desert near Bakersfield, where their son is engaged in real estate. Last month their daughter, who was going to be a kindergarten teacher, ran off with an Italian hairdresser from Wichita Falls, Texas.

They have no desire to lead the fast life and the closest they come to it is an economy weekend once a year in Las Vegas, where "a $5 steak out there you get for $1.50." The only way you can tell they came from Iowa is that he still calls his wife Toots, just as he did when she was a cheerleader back at Dexter High. They wave occasionally to their neighbor, an elderly woman who claims she is Mae West's sister. Mainly they talk about a cousin who arrived in 1943 with $700 in his pocket and who went to work at a bomber plant in Long Beach. Last week he sold one of his apartment houses in Hollywood for $140,000.

But there are plenty of those in Los Angeles who *do* want the sweetly influential existence of the new swingers—the 10%, the creative minority across America. They can be found all over the sprawling city—around the canteen wagon in the lot at the Color City, the NBC-TV studios at Burbank, for instance, drinking coffee and eating a Danish. The door of the wagon truck reads "Ben's Catering Service," and a sticker on the bumper says "U.N.C.L.E. Agent." The fringing mountains, which still bear the faint scars of the trenches dug for old World War I epics, stand brown-gray against the hydrocarbonous horizon. All morning the young stagehands with their peroxided sideburns come and go, muscular in their tight, faded chinos and tennis shoes. The executives call their wives Mommie and project a John Huston briskness. Their suit coats buttoned at the bottom, they walk importantly through the studio doors as trucks from Mark IV Messenger Service, "radio dispatched," deliver bales of neat brown envelopes filled, one presumes, with new scripts from Malibu.

In the studio, the lofty corridors are stacked with props and scenery, a dream dump containing all the furniture of America's off-hour obsessions—gaudy panels to dress up television shows with names such as *Paradise Bay, Let's Make a Deal, You Don't Say,* and *PDQ.* The script girls, unit managers, technical directors, account executives, copy writers and sound engineers wear the guarded expressions of floorwalkers about to make a fabulous sale of distressed merchandise. Unimpressed by the omnipresent inventory of props—the harps, the wheels that say Barnyard Roulette, enough escritoires and armoires to fill Versailles, what seems like enough rigging for a three-masted schooner, a complete Texas saloon, an entire Kentucky race track complete with ante-bellum stable—they stride toward the shoeshine stand or the machine that dispenses fresh apples. The pale skins of the young actresses crawl with smog under their tan make-up. Smoking languidly, they lounge outside a set depicting a Lucite penthouse, waiting to deliver lines that sound like "Carlos, never again expect me to make good on your gambling debts."

At the very top of the Los Angeles heap, lie clusters in the hives of Sunset Boulevard and the Beverly Hills Hotel. In the hotel's Lanai Restaurant, with its decor of cruise-ship moderne, the old ladies in their long heavy dresses sit about, their watches and bracelets barely visible in the fat of their arms, their hair glowing with subtle mistints. They flash enormous sets of dazzling false teeth. Their husbands—tanned, barrel-chested croquet players–talk with the terrier brightness of Jack Warner. The place has a faded Franchot Tone elegance, reminiscent of the big night club scenes in circa 1937 movies in which the young men carried cigaret cases.

Around the bar in the hotel's Polo Lounge, the slightly puffy announcer, out here to do commercials, pats his shining toupee, which is always perfectly in place. Miss 1953 of an important European country has her third Bloody Mary of the day. Every few minutes, the captain pages the new names – Marty Ransohoff, Dick Sarafian, Joey Heatherton, Dodo Denney. Large special-delivery letters for Phyllis Diller pile up at the desk.

In the struggle for the tan Bentley Continental Park Ward coupé convertible and the Marimekko girl to go with it, high-flying dreams can sometimes collapse with intolerable swiftness. Over coffee at Ben's Wagon, one hears an epitaph: "I used to work steady, but my agent landed Lee Marvin and now he never calls me. So no more jobs." No more sweet times at Whisky à GoGo, The Trip, or It's Boss. Perhaps not, but the balloon still has a lot of altitude left.

On the other hand, far, far away in downtown Los Angeles near the bus station, an indifferent young man in motorcycle boots, with red hair and heroin eyes, blows a popcorn whistle and stares at a pile of fried chicken wings displayed in a smarmy window. And in the doorway of an arcade, an old man in baggy pants cries out, "The end, the end!"

The old man is wrong. It is not the end. In the random clutter of American city life, there are fragments that *do* fit together. A quiet young educator buys a 19th Century bowfront town house in Boston's decaying South End and fixes it up. His friends do the same thing and pretty soon the neighborhood is not going to pieces any more. An energetic Chicago housewife creates a shopping center tenanted solely by artists and craftsmen displaced by urban renewal. A greeting card executive helps organize the Kansas City Lyric Theater, an unpretentious but solid forum for young opera singers who otherwise would have to go to Europe for the same training.

So much for The End. Generalize about the American city, and the specifics will prove you wrong. Watching a pretty girl with electric-blue contact lenses striding by the handsome traditional structures of Boston's Newbury Street, or leather-faced ranchers in shiny black suits murmuring quietly in the lobby of San Antonio's capacious Gunter Hotel, or courtly old ladies nodding to each other on the verandas of New Orleans' Garden District, it begins to make sense–sometimes. Sometimes–here and there–the crazy energy of the city takes the best of the past and joins it with the present to make the future more accessible.

But the odds are against the tidy dovetail. The nature of the city–its very open-endedness, the wondrous possibility of all things–makes it so. City dwellers may be nervous and irritated by expectations far exceeding their capacities; obsessed with antique myths while demanding more of everything new; noisy, yet mute and lonely–always lonely–unable to articulate who they are because they are moving too fast to know. They have more freedom than they know what to do with. But if this freedom of choice is sometimes stupefying, it is also exhilarating. A man with a weathered face atop a button-down collar leans into a dry Manhattan at a smart New York restaurant and says, without the least trace of regret: "When I am here, I wish I were on the farm. When I'm on the farm, I wish I were here." Change is all-pervading: outdoorsman today, lover of Handel tomorrow; the sports car rallyist and suburban sheep rancher earns his living as an electronic-data-processor–anything to be other than what grandfather was: a grocer in Waco.

American city life has never stood still for more than a nanosecond. It is always in the process of becoming. If the past has little influence, the future is thereby closer. Americans have not so much built their cities and their noncities as assembled them from do-it-yourself kits. Conformity, hell. "The reason I left Rochester is because my old man never made it there" sums up the unprecedented range of individual choice that American cities offer. In *The Great Gatsby*, one of the best novels of city life ever written, F. Scott Fitzgerald tells the whole story: "Gatsby believed in the green light, the orgiastic future that year by year recedes before us. It eluded us then, but that's no matter–tomorrow we will run faster, stretch out our arms farther. . . . And one fine morning–"

What Kind of City Do We Want? Nation's Cities

Our suburban problems would be hard enough to solve in a static urban economy with a static urban population, a static racial and social mix, and a static transportation method and system—but our urban economy and population are anything but static. On the contrary, our urban economy, society and technology are all undergoing great simultaneous changes; our urban population is doubling to a projected 1999 level well over 250 million-plus, and before 1999 our urban wealth will at least quadruple, as the average income of twice as many families doubles to a projected $15,000-a-year-plus-of-today's-purchasing-power. And even now, before these increases, our urban transportation system is already near the breaking point.

So within the next generation, our cities will have to be almost completely rebuilt twice as big and, we hope, at least twice as good. Within a generation we will have to erect and find the money for more new urban homes, business buildings and facilities than we have built in all the years since Jamestown and Plymouth Rock. We will have to replace at least half of all today's urban dwellings because they will no longer be good enough for anyone to want to live in when the average family has sufficient income to qualify for a $25,000 FHA-financed house. (This means we should build at least half as many new homes to replace decaying housing inside or close in to our cities as we add on the outskirts.) And we will probably have to replace half of today's business and industrial buildings because they will no longer meet the vastly different needs of 1999 business.

In addition, many of our cities will almost certainly have to be restructured to fit some new and radically different means of transportation. High-density cities like New York are finding that the additional facilities needed to bring in just one more car per day during commuter hours will cost $21,000; low-density cities like Los Angeles are finding the cost, in money, time and space, of relying solely on the automobile equally bad.

They are stuck with far more than their share of the costs created by national problems like education, poverty and segregation. Their municipal costs are climbing twice as fast as their local tax base.

They are choked by obsolete political boundaries that (1) encourage both people and industry to seek tax havens in the suburbs and (2) make coordinated planning difficult and often just plain impossible. They are losing prosperous families and their money to the suburbs almost as fast as they are herding more poor families and their costs into the slums. They are losing blue-collar jobs to the outskirts almost as fast as they can add new white-collar openings downtown. They consume four times as much land as they use.

From *Nation's Cities*, April, 1967. Reprinted by permission.

They are stuck with a tax system that penalizes improvements and subsidizes obsolescence, blight, sprawl and the spread of slums, and they are stuck with a concept of landed property that lets landowners capitalize for their own private profit all the economies and advantages of urbanism, so city dwellers must pay twice over for the multibillion-dollar values they themselves create living close together—values they have already paid for once by an enormous investment of both public and private money. . . . The former president of The American Institute of Architects adds a word of urgent warning:

> We cannot remake our cities without solving their painful social problems. As blight, congestion and lack of good-enough schools drive middle-income residents from our urban centers, the poor move in, the gap between the rich and poor grows, and the suburban noose draws tighter. If the present trend continues, the untrained and undereducated poor will become the dominant population group in almost all our major cities within the next few years. The consequences of allowing our cities to become the poorhouses of America had better be recognized while there is still time to avoid them.

We Will Spend Trillions

To meet this challenge and seize this opportunity, our cities will need all the help they can get—from architects and planners, from the upper-income families who have fled to the suburbs to escape the cities' problems, from the state governments and from the federal government, of course.

All of us applaud and welcome the growing interest in urban problems shown by the federal government, but, alas, this interest is still finding expression more in words than in dollars. . . .

In 24 years the Housing and Home Finance Agency and its successor, the Department of Housing and Urban Development, has not kicked back to the cities a nickel of taxpayer money for housing and urban development; in every year but two, its receipts from insurance and other nontax sources have exceeded its expenditures. For fiscal years 1966 and 1967, HUD actually budgeted *minus* $100 million of tax money for housing and urban development. City dwellers pay most of the federal taxes, but the farmers still get back from Washington eight times as much money as the cities; by some calculations, 13 times as much. And most of the money the cities do get back is earmarked, not to ease the cities' present financial burdens but to encourage new municipal spending by offering to share the increased cost of meeting responsibilities the cities are not yet meeting.

This is no time to think small about the money our cities will need. It will cost not billions but *trillions* of dollars to correct what is wrong with our central cities today, while they are doubling their metropolitan populations and their more-and-more affluent citizens are doubling their demands for better everything.

Between now and the year 2000, someone will have to put up close to $1,500 billion for new and renewal nonfarm housing alone (nearly half of it urban replacement housing); someone will have to put up at least another $1,000 billion for new and replacement commercial, industrial and utility construction; and someone will have to put up at least another $1,000 billion for all the new and better community facilities needed to go with the new and better housing: new streets, highways, parking; new and better schools and colleges; new park attractions, playgrounds, transportation; new smoke controls, sewers and sewage treatment, water supplies; hospitals, etc., etc., etc. (Metropolitan New York alone projects a need for 61 more college campuses for 1.3 million more students, 100 more hospitals with 45,000 more beds, etc.).

Over 33 years, the money needed to build and rebuild our cities twice as big and twice as good will average out to over $100 billion a year, and even in tomorrow's far more affluent economy, it is just plain nonsense to hope that even half that annual amount will be provided by any government: national, state or local. Governments will be hard pressed to find enough tax money to meet the $30 billion-a-year need for more and better community facilities.

The rest can be found only by harnessing the profit motive, much more effectively than now, to urban renewal and urban improvement, and making as much as possible of this enormous enterprise attractive and profitable for the investment of private capital. Private capital will get its money's worth only if we make good planning, good design and good building more profitable than bad. And it will be a lot easier to interest private capital in urban betterment if the local tax system is modified to encourage new construction and better land use, instead of (as now) penalizing improvements and subsidizing blight, slums and sprawl.

With our fast-growing affluence and our fantastically expanding technology, there is no earthly reason why American cities should have to be dull or ugly or dirty or polluted or traffic-choked or expensive to live and work in.

There is no reason why cities should sprawl far out beyond their boundaries to blight the countryside with leap-frogging and premature subdivision.

There is no reason why cities should let slums and other inadequate, obsolete or decrepit buildings clutter and pre-empt most of their good close-in locations.

There is no reason why our cities should waste most of their land, most of their streets, their parks, their open space, their waterfronts, their rooftops.

There is no reason why cities should waste most of the third dimension that could multiply their convenience and their livability at much less cost than sprawl.

There is no reason why people who like high-density living should not also enjoy open-space recreation quite near at hand, nor any reason why people who prefer low-density living should not enjoy it much closer to where they work and shop.

There is no reason why good urban planning should constantly be frustrated by obsolete political boundaries.

There is no reason why city governments should be kept too broke to make their services good and desirable instead of just cheap and tolerable.

There is no reason why our cities should not be good places to bring up children, with good schools and provision for safe outdoor play nearby.

There is no reason why our central cities should be abandoned to the poor and the disadvantaged, or why they should be stuck with so much more than their share of the problems of poverty and segregation.

If we accept the simple mathematical fact that for most people, urban living has to mean living close together, and *if* we focus our planning and spending on practical ways to make living close together more rewarding and less expensive.

If we stop looking backward and dreaming that tomorrow's urban life could be more like yesterday's village life, and relinquish the notion that low density is somehow better for everybody.

If we make good use of the new tools offered by today's fantastic new technologies—new tools so numerous that we can mention only two:

1. Airconditioning, which the ex-vice president of the National Association of Home Builders calls "the greatest improvement for indoor living and indoor working since we brought the toilet indoors," an improvement that makes cities as livable in summer as in winter.

2. The electronic elevator, which—almost unnoticed—is changing the potentials of urban living almost as much as the automobile.

If we make sure the city has a vibrant downtown to draw people and business from far and near to live, work, shop and have fun.

If we restructure our biggest cities as radiating clusters of high-density land use.

If we persuade or compel city people and city industry to stop trying to get something for nothing at other people's expense, i.e., stop trying to save a little of their own money by choking the city streets, polluting the city water, polluting the city air, etc.

If we harness the profit motive forward instead of backward to good land use and good planning, so private enterprise will find it profitable to assume, without subsidy, most of the cost of rebuilding our cities bigger and in every way better.

If we stop letting landowners make city living expensive by capitalizing, for their private profit, all the benefits of today's huge urban investment of other people's money.

If we stop waiting for massive state and federal aid before tackling all the little jobs that need doing first.

If we can find a cure for the problems and costs of segregation and one-class neighborhoods.

For people, this means living closer together to maximize their freedom of choice in housing, career and employment opportunities, direct personal contact and confrontation, meeting people and making more kinds of friends. This closeness also increases freedom of choice in places to shop, and places to pursue leisure-time cultural and recreational activity.

The more people who live close together, the greater their variety of choices should be and the greater their chance of being able to get what they choose to want. . . .

Cliff dwellers and suburbanites alike are drawn to the city to enjoy advantages only close-in living can offer, and most suburbanites wish they could enjoy their kind of living without traveling so far each day to get it.

For business, minimizing the handicaps of distance means easy access to more abundant and more specialized labor, to a greater variety of supporting services, to government offices, to low-cost mass transportation, to supplies in greater volume and greater variety, and to more customers and bigger markets.

For business as for people, the consequence of closeness and concentration should be greater efficiency, greater economy and lower costs.

Some kinds of business have to locate closer to the center than others. Some must locate downtown for maximum access to markets, to clients, to supporting service or to a great variety of labor. Other kinds of business are more self-contained and so find it more profitable to trade maximum access for greater space—to accept less accessibility on the outskirts in order to get more space than they could afford at the center. Still others may find easy access to a freeway more important than easy access to downtown.

But once again, the difference is only one in degree. The advertising agency downtown and the factory in the suburbs are both drawn to the city for advantages only closeness can offer, and most suburban industry would relocate closer to the labor center and the transportation hub if closer-in land were cheaper. . . .

It is no longer necessary to go to the transportation center for so many kinds of shopping, or to find employment in those kinds of industry that are least dependent on quick access to markets or supporting services (notably big factories).

But however their pattern may change, the reason and purpose of cities remains unchanged and unchangeable—the same today as in the railroad age, the canal-boat age, and the stagecoach age—to bring people and businesses together for ease and variety of access and contact.

The Community: Could This Be Our Town? Wolf Von Eckardt

The first residents are about to move into what promises to be one of the first modern communities in America worthy of the name. It is a comprehensively planned new town, named Reston, located 18 miles west of Washington, D.C., on a wooded Virginia hillside. By 1980, if plans work out, it should have 75,000 inhabitants, most of whom will not need to commute because they will have shopping, education, cultural inspiration and, most of all, their jobs practically within walking distance. Reston may well point a way toward arresting America's hideous urban sprawl that consumes our land at a rate of one million acres a day and that is hardly, as someone has put it, "a healthy soil for the growth of our civilization."

The countryside is uniquely beautiful and the first buildings already show equally unique architectural charm and excellence. But the bulldozers are still tearing into the red earth and the workmen are still clambering about the scaffolding and construction debris.

By next summer, however, Reston's first village–the plans call for seven such neighborhoods plus an urban town center–should be coming to life. Its artificial 35-acre lake, surrounded by lovingly arranged clusters of townhouses, should be filled with boats and swimmers. Already stocked with fish, its clear water will mirror the shops and community center of a bustling waterfront plaza and a handsomely sculptural 16-story apartment tower that heralds the town from afar.

People will walk to this village center through the woods and townhouse plazas on walkways and overpasses and underpasses that are dramatically lit at night and no automobiles will get into their way. The children will, of course, also walk safely to their new school, designed for the latest needs of modern education with the help of Ford Foundation experts. Cars have their own roads and are parked away discreetly so they don't clutter up the townscape.

Reston already has a champion golf course and architecturally intriguing club house, designed by Charles M. Goodman. By summer it will also have tennis courts, a riding stable, a boat marina, an art gallery, adult education courses, a youth center, numerous playgrounds with enchanting, modern equipment designed by sculptor Gonzales Fonseca, and probably a little children's zoo where the tots might try milking a cow.

By summer, too, developer Robert E. Simon, whose initials form the first syllable of the name of the town he launched almost singlehandedly, will know. He will know whether free enterprise can do better than build sleezy suburban subdivisions which, with their cute neo-Williamsburg or Cinderella "homes," all their kitchen gadgets, barbecue patios and useless front lawns, cater at best to fashionable market expectations of "gracious living," as though living consisted only of consuming the products of manufacturers and television producers. He will know whether we can house our burgeoning population other than in "residential areas" as though residence were an activity in itself separate from exercising body and mind, from doing and experiencing things, from working, shopping, playing and spontaneous sociability.

And Mr. Simon and the rest of us will know whether the American consumer is actually willing and ready to live in real communities. If his thoughtful community planning helps us translate the high American standard of living into a higher standard of life, it is only because he feels he can sell homes and industrial sites better if he enhances them in a beautiful setting with civilized amenities and diversions close at hand. He believes the market ripe for, as his sales brochure puts it, "a self-respecting admixture of aloneness and togetherness." He is building Reston for profit.

But to reap profits you've got to seed investments. And that, one suspects, is still tougher than Simon cares to admit to an inquisitive journalist. The bankers and investors have misgivings about tightly clustered townhouses in the country where cars are parked as much as a hundred yards from the kitchen entrance. They doubt that Americans will care to live so close to shops that they might actually see them from their bedroom window even if they also have a splendid view over lake and trees and an architectural ensemble resembling a modern Portofino. And it remains to be proved that Americans will voluntarily rent the apartments Simon offers above his row of stores. He wants people and life on his village center plaza at night, even after the shops are closed.

The new town idea is, of course, nothing new. Ebenezer Howard, a London court stenographer, had originally inspired this cause at the turn of the century with his idea of emptying the slums of London and transplanting their wretched dwellers to self-contained "garden cities" of limited size surrounded by a greenbelt. The garden city movement, rallying around Sir Raymond Unwin's battle cry, "Nothing Gained by Overcrowding," offered many important solutions to the problems of housing people in an industrial society. The American branch of this movement, led by people like Lewis Mumford, Catherine Bauer Wurster and Clarence Stein, vigorously fought for "decent, safe and sanitary" housing and inspired the greenbelt towns of the Roosevelt days. But when, with the postwar housing boom and the rush to suburbia, its great opportunity came, the movement seemed spent. England, after decades of searching national debate, passed her New Towns Act in 1946 and there are now 18 new towns in Britain at various stages of completion. But what is left of the élan of America's old "housers" of the thirties has now moved from the barricades to bureaucracy.

What's in It for Me?

"The long hair boys have been of no help to me whatsoever," says Simon. "They are sympathetic, that's all. The ones within the government write letters with a lot of questions, the answers to which are already in their files."

Nor is Simon particularly sorry that, for lack of support from "housers" and the home-building industry alike, President Johnson's new town proposal failed, although the rest of his housing bill passed in remarkably good shape. Without advance notice, let alone national debate or political preparation, the President, last January, unexpectedly asked for federal funds to assist local governments to comprehensively plan and acquire land for "the orderly growth and development of new communities." The proposal didn't say "new towns," but that's what was meant. The new program was to be put under FHA, the most stodgy and private developer-minded of all the agencies. People within that agency spoke of the idea with little knowledge and less enthusiasm. Its builder-promoter friends reacted intensely against it. Their opposition was joined by the mayors—even the more liberal ones like James H. J. Tate of Philadelphia, John F. Collins of Boston, and Raymond R. Tucker of St. Louis speaking for the U.S. Conference of Mayors. They fear, as Mayor John F. Collins of Boston put it, that the new towns "might make rebuilding of the central city more difficult." They are afraid that the new towns might compete for urban renewal funds and lure industry away from their realm. "It was a disgrace," said a Congressional aide who watched the proposal go under. "There is no longer a lobby for housing, for a decent home for every Amercan. Even the liberals lobby only for their own little bits, their special pork barrels."

The opposition of the bankers, investors, builders and promoters is understandable. They have built suburbia at untold profits and are still spreading their subdivisions and housing projects all over the countryside at a frightening rate. Because of government mortgage insurance, the bankers and investors run practically no risk. The builders and promoters themselves invest little more than their judgment on where and what to put up. The "where" is easy—on the cheapest possible land near the most crowded metropolitan concentrations. It may not make sense to crowd them still further but the county governments are happy to welcome them and present them with the most essential sewers and local roads. Most county councils are dominated by people whose main cash crop is land. Once the land is built up, let the new residents worry about paying for the necessities as they spread ever-lengthening distances to work and dream Thoreau dreams of rearing the kids in the bosom of Mother Nature—or a postage-stamp-size piece of it without sidewalks, playgrounds, trees.

The "what" is answered with clever packaging and public relations. Wrap a shoddily built house in a fashionable façade, stuff it with gadgets, put a gaslight or something in front for that extra bit of nostalgia, give it a romantic name and you'll have the suckers beating a path to the sales office. What the customers are primarily looking for is a good "housing buy," a nice home of their own. If they have three kids they'd like to have four bedrooms and no traffic jam in the bathroom. Try and pay for that in the city, nowadays. Even the rent for a small apartment is apt to be twice as expensive as the monthly mortgage payment on a subdivision house. So the builder-promoters sell them that shelter, gift wrapped with that gas lamp or rickety carport, sell it hard and fast and get out.

Only a few insurance and other large companies have themselves built and assumed a continuing responsibility for the housing developments they invested in. But lately they've shied away from this. The kind of building that they can invest their prestige in is becoming increasingly expensive. The new requirements for racial integration might make them unpopular. As one corporation bigwig told Albert Mayer, an architect-planner, big companies prefer to hide behind the builder-promoters as they prefer not to have "high visibility."

Eggheads in Suburbia

The system, substantially aided by government programs like FHA, which makes sure that the pipes won't burst and the mortgage money keeps flowing, has thus pretty well met the middle-income housing shortage right after World War II. The home-building industry feels that it has earned the nation's gratitude. And the system still works. What slack the egghead disenchantment with suburbia might have created is taken up by urban renewal's new bonanzas downtown.

And is the egghead disenchantment with suburbia really justified?

No—if we're talking in terms of a verdant environment *versus* asphalted city blocks.

Yes—if we look at subdivision suburbia today which, to the extent that it is planned at all, is planned for buildings, land use and zones but not for people.

To the suburbanite who has just tired himself out manicuring his front lawn and is getting ready for the three-mile drive to the bowling alley, some erudite magazine article deploring the ugly monotony and Miltown boredom of his environment reads like sheer poppycock. His wife might deplore the hours she must spend driving to a monopolistic supermarket and the kids to their lessons and birthday parties, but that is a price she gladly pays for a better and newer school than the city offers. And since, when her exhausting chores are done, she prefers to do nothing in particular, it doesn't occur to her that looking at people from a nice bench on a nice urban plaza, boats on a nearby waterfront, gushing water in the fountains of a gala shopping mall, or exhibits in an art gallery, makes doing nothing in particular a lot more fun. After all, most likely she hasn't heard of, let alone seen, the town centers of Farsta, near Stockholm, or Tapiola, near Helsinki which have this kind of thing within easy walking of every home.

Sociologists and psychologists say they simply don't know much about the effect of environment on the human species. Herbert J. Gans, of Columbia University, says the talk about a suburban pathology is simply a myth. What problems exist, he says, are those people brought along with them when they moved out. "Most of the effects described by the myth of suburbia either can be traced to factors other than the move to suburbia, or do not take place at all," he has written. Developer James Rouse, who is now building a new town somewhat similar to Reston between Washington, D.C., and Baltimore, and who has given the problems of community building considerable thought, has a more convincing answer. "There is absolutely no dialogue in the U.S. today," he has been quoted as saying, "between the people who have developed knowledge about people—the teachers, the ministers, psychiatrists, sociologists—and the people who are designing and building cities."

Fractured Communities

But much is evident, whether it has been researched or not. Restlessness in suburbia, not as drastic as in the city ghettos, to be sure, but restlessness nevertheless, is a fact. For instance, Montgomery County, Maryland, at the edge of the nation's capital, is a nice place to live and far from the worst of postwar suburbia; on the average it is the wealthiest and best-educated county in the nation; it used to have one of the best school systems. Yet, there is, even amidst this rather homogeneous community of doctors, lawyers, scientists and high level government experts, rampant juvenile delinquency, which everyone used to think was a disease of poverty. Kids from good homes with all the "privilege" our society can offer smash windows, throw home-made bombs into libraries, race about in stolen cars and crash parties. A frightening number of their parents crowd the waiting lists of the psychiatrists and the county's woefully inadequate psychiatric clinic. Perhaps we would have the same problems in the city, as Mr. Gans argues. But non-planned subdivision suburbia doesn't ameliorate them.

In the 1962 election, Montgomery County rebelled against non-planned subdivision suburbia, or rather the effects of it. Its good citizens were fed up with steadily rising local taxes to pay for catching up with services, notably school buildings, that sound planning should have built right with the first houses. So they elected the subdividers, builder-promoters and their rabble-rousing friends to their county council. The new council is merrily and noisily wrecking the good school system, cutting down on school construction and other already insufficient services and deliberately castrating what little planning there was.

It's happening all over suburban America with the subdividers fanning the rebellions and, with the powerful help of the real estate boards, the mortgage bankers, the National Association of Manufacturers and the Chamber of Commerce, fighting any restraints on their lucrative operations.

But despite all this Bob Simon is optimistic. He has managed to get interim financing for the exciting beginning of Reston that is now evident in his Virginia woods. He's got 6,750 acres of them, the site for his entire town. His superb master plan and architectural designs have electrified planners and architects all over the world. The construction of that first village is assured. All of Reston's currently available lots for individuals and builders who want to erect their own detached houses are already sold. The design and appearance of these houses is carefully controlled by Reston's architectural board. Although he only just started advertising them, Simon has already sold a number of the clustered townhouses ranging from $23,000 to $46,400.

And, most importantly perhaps, there is already assurance that Reston will not be another dormitory community. Six industrial enterprises have, as of this writing, already contracted to locate in Reston's industrial park which comprises 14 percent of the town's total area. A federal government agency may follow soon. A building that provides a pool of meeting rooms, cafeteria and a printing facility for the industrial park is being built.

No one could possibly in this country tamper with free enterprise in the building or any other industry even if he were idiotic enough to want to do so. Large-scale government housing projects are apt to be deadly, as our public housing has shown. And even the much touted, socialistically built new Swedish communities near Stockholm, though a vast improvement over run-of-the-mill American subdivisions and well planned, have not been able to overcome an institutional tedium. . . .

How to Clean Up the Nation's Slums?

Newsweek

The building is 443 Manhattan Avenue, Harlem, New York. It is a yellowish-brown obscenity, scrawled with lesser obscenities. It is both an affront to the mind and an assault on the senses.

In front, the areaway is clogged with piles of putrid-sweet garbage, whose only containers—paper bags—have long since burst. On the fragile wooden stairs inside, grime, sweat and urine smells are strong enough to be tasted on the tongue. The skin itches as rat holes yawn in the half-lit gloom: rat holes everywhere; a patient inspector has counted exactly 502. Out back, roaches and flies crawl over mounds of "airmail," garbage tossed from windows above. And in a four-and-a-half-room apartment on the first floor, Earl Weldon, a quiet, unemployed Negro, sits roped in by electric wires running everywhere from a single living-room outlet, two broken windows at his back, staring absently at his hands. A week ago, part of the bathroom ceiling in the $44.90-a-month apartment, which Weldon shares with his wife and three little girls, caved in onto the toilet, washstand and bathtub. But the apathetic Weldson hasn't bothered to clean up this latest disaster. Rats might fall out of the ceiling hole anyway, he shrugs, "so now we uses a neighbor's john."

This article appeared in *Newsweek*, August 28, 1967.

Tangible Symbol. The life-sapping degradation of Manhattan Avenue is its own best argument for cleaning up the nation's slums—and if that isn't enough, four years of worsening riots have provided reasons just as ugly. To be sure, better housing offers no panacea for the problems of the urban poor, about half of whom are Negroes; it will not in itself raise incomes, provide better education and medical care or furnish cultural standards for people who have never known them. Yet to ghetto dwellers, says Anthony Downs, an economist and Federal consultant in urban affairs, bad housing is the most tangible, immediate symbol of all their problems, and "hence they want relief."*

Not everyone in the ghettos, of course, is as badly housed as the Weldons. But in spite of the fact that public-housing projects across the land now hold nearly 2.5 million people, the stark fact is that almost no progress has been made in reducing the number of slum dwellings. Even the Census Bureau admitted recently it did not know exactly how many truly dilapidated housing units existed in the U.S. and that the 1960 census figures, showing that totally unfit housing had declined dramatically over the preceding decade

*In a Louis Harris survey of the causes of the riots (*Newsweek*, Aug. 21), ghetto dwellers themselves said lack of decent housing was the greatest single reason for their discontent.

from about 3.9 million units to 2.3 million units, were wildly inaccurate.

Migrant Flood. The bureau's best guess now is that there are almost as many families living in officially uninhabitable homes and apartments as in 1950. In addition, another 9 million of the nation's poor families are living in dwellings that are classed merely as "substandard"—shabby, uncomfortable, deteriorating, but not a clear menace to life, safety or health.

One key to the persistence of the problem has been the sheer tide of migration to the urban slums. Rural Southern Negroes and Puerto Ricans have been flooding into the central cities, accelerating the white middle-class flight to the suburbs, at a rate that has made a mockery of existing programs. Between 1950 and 1960, the last census figures available, a crushing 5.3 million of these largely unskilled rural immigrants arrived seeking a better life in the city. "There has been," says Harvard-MIT urban planner Chester Hartman succinctly, "just nowhere near enough money to do the job."

And with the migration has come collapse of the private-housing system. For years, it was fashionable to blame the slums on the "slumlords"—men whose greedy exploitation and neglect of their property condemned the poor to lives of misery. Certainly, there were many such. But in cold economic terms, literally no one else has yet offered a way to house a family of ten for what slum dwellers can afford—$40 to $50 a month. Even such crusaders as Charles Abrams, the pioneer who launched the nation's first public-housing project in New York, concedes that the slumlords are paid a premium to perform a dirty job that other businessmen—and society itself—want no part of.

In recent years, even this often sizable premium has lost its attraction. "The slumlord is not a villain in this piece; there are no real villains," says Abrams. For one thing, cities are enforcing their building codes much more strictly than before, which costs landlords money. At the same time, experts say, ghetto dwellers as a group have become increasingly irregular payers of rent, rising vandalism is increasing costs, and restless Negroes are changing dwellings so fast that profit-draining vacancies are high. Paradoxically, slum conditions have grown so bad that they are accomplishing the age-old reformer's dream of "'taking the profit out of slums."

Payoff. Even the reformers are reassessing the slumlord cliché. The Citizens' Housing and Planning Council, a nonprofit civic group in New York which wanted to prove decent slum housing could pay, purchased two tenements, renovated them, and found that it had to raise rents from a truly low average of $23 a month to $60 a month. Turnover averaged 80 per cent a year, and rent delinquency hit 30 per cent; annual maintenance costs and vandalism repairs came to $30 per room. Three years later, the council no longer believes that such activities can be profitable. Though he used to consider himself a liberal, executive director Roger Starr sourly remarks that "all my liberal friends feel the riots are attempts at self-assertion. To me, they are an expression of instability and viciousness."

Ups and Downs. But if the private system has failed, Federal public-housing projects have been almost equally inadequate. As a matter of "slum clearance" policy, public projects knock down an existing housing unit for each new one they provide—hardly a solution for overcrowding. The bulldozers destroy whatever semblance of neighborhood the slum retains and scatter its inhabitants while new buildings are going up. In operation, housing projects notoriously dump the worst problem tenants back onto the private market; in Philadelphia, for instance, authorities reject dope addicts, alcoholics, the disabled, people with police records and unwed mothers of two or more children. And with few exceptions, residents who manage to improve their incomes are evicted —a process that weeds out leadership, talent, energy and any hint of inspiration for those who remain.

Urban renewal, the second major Federal approach to the problem, has actually destroyed much more low-income housing than it has built. In effect, city planners have abused the program for the unspoken purpose of "Negro removal." Stockton, Calif., for example, scattered thousands of slum tenants into the countryside and razed 32 Negro churches in an urban-renewal project that resulted mainly in commercial buildings and middle-income or luxury apartments almost entirely inhabited by whites.

A major problem in all government programs is the fantastic amount of red tape. Inserted by Congress as a safeguard against corruption, the procedural steps prescribed in several programs are so time-consuming that many local agencies and companies simply refuse to try to use the programs. The Federal Housing Authority, for instance, has a special program for granting long-term, low-interest loans to local nonprofit agencies that are interested in sponsoring low-income apartment construction. A synagogue in Malden, Mass., applied for a loan to build a 108-unit project more than two years ago. Though it has received basic approval from the FHA, a final okay is still lacking. In the meantime, construction and other costs have risen so steeply that the project will now be forced to raise its monthly rentals from $89 a unit to $109.

New Deal. For all their faults, housing projects alone are providing shelter for nearly 650,000 families. But these days, very few individuals think that this type of development is the total answer to the slum housing problem. And in the past two years, government and private industry as well have developed a wide range of experimental and pilot programs that would appear to offer real hope for the future.

The new programs incorporate two major shifts in emphasis. First, they are turning increasingly to rehabilitation of existing dwellings rather than the bulldozer approach. And second, Federal officials are trying to turn all their projects, as far as possible, over to industry for execution. "If we can get the private sector involved and show them they aren't going to be strangled in red tape," says Don Hummel, head of housing and renewal assistance for the new Department of Housing and Urban Development, "we'll get some real competition again."

A bigger private share is the core of HUD's new "turnkey" construction program. Traditionally, the government has acquired land, hired designers and then picked a contractor to build each housing project, keeping the whole project under strict surveillance. Under the new approach, builders with land and designs need only get one approval of the plan, and can build the project with almost no bureaucratic interference. The system promises to cut the average time needed to build a public project literally in half, to two years. And in fact, the first turnkey project, the ten-story Claridge Towers building in downtown Washington, D.C., did even better than that, opening last January just a year after approval was granted. The time savings cut the cost of each apartment unit to $15,500 from an estimated $18,000 under government supervision. With such results, President Johnson last week ordered an extension of the turnkey approach, ordering housing authorities to lure profit-seeking private real-estate companies to operate public housing projects after they are built.

The rehabilitation approach also promises lower costs; in Philadelphia, officials have found they can buy and restore a typical three-bedroom unit in a sturdy but dilapidated row house for as little as $12,300. Even more important, rehabilitation takes less time than new construction and can tap a supply of housing that Federal authorities estimate at 9 million dwellings.

Practical Plan. Action-Housing, Inc., of Pittsburgh, a nonprofit civic agency that has been working at low-cost renovation since 1958, has come up with a particularly imaginative scheme to exploit the Federal government's new policies. The agency proposes to form a limited-profit corporation (earning no more than 10 per cent on its investment) that would buy houses for renovation, arrange a contract with a building renovator, split the risk with the Federal Housing Administration on a low-cost mortgage and then sell or operate the rehabilitated property. Action Housing has already obtained half the financing for the new corporation from Alcoa, Westinghouse, U.S. Steel, Pittsburgh Plate Glass and Rockwell Manufacturing. Furthermore, it has a firm commitment from the FHA that the agency will systematically slash red tape, and it has even worked out concessions from the local Building Trades Council that will eliminate jurisdictional disputes, speed construction, cut some kinds of overtime pay and "substantially reduce costs." "In cooperation with government, using all the Federal tools now available," says Action chairman J. Stanley Purnell, "[the new corporation] can create a new profit-motivated industry. At the same time, it would fulfill a well-documented social and physical need."

As the Pittsburgh project indicates, literally dozens of private companies are becoming interested in the low-cost housing field. Firms as various as Armstrong Cork (building materials) and Smith Kline & French in Philadelphia, Lockheed Aircraft in Burbank, Calif., Warner & Swasey (machine tools) in Cleveland and Union Carbide in New York have all tested the prospects, either by renovating one or more slum dwellings or by trying to develop new products for the rehabilitation market.

New Project. U.S. Gypsum, probably the most active single company in the field, has demonstrated the uses of its construction products in renovating 120 apartments in six Harlem buildings. The company is now working on 200 additional Harlem apartments, will soon start another project in Cleveland and has tentative plans for Chicago and fifteen other cities. Civic spirit is undoubtedly a factor in such involvement, but there is also the lure of profits; with the injection of enough Federal money, slum renewal could be expected to develop into a $50 billion market.

But that kind of money is a long way off, and profits are even less sure. In hard economic terms, producing good housing that is cheap enough for literally every slum dweller is beyond the dream of nearly all the experiments thus far. Yet one ingenious Philadelphia project, just getting under way at the suggestion of Charles Abrams, promises to house almost the lowest-income tenant—and make him a homeowner, eventually, in the bargain.

Abrams found that the current slump in values of slum housing has driven prices of hundreds of livable, two-bedroom, single-family units to $3,000 or lower. A city-backed agency has begun to buy these buildings and sell them to slum dwellers on a down payment of $100 or less, with carrying charges, including taxes and insurance, of about $40 a month. Skeptics abound, but Abrams thinks similar opportunities exist in many U.S. cities.

Still a Gap. For the most part, though, a gap seems sure to remain between what slum dwellers can afford and what operators must charge for new or rehabilitated housing. It was to bridge this gap that the Administration last year began its "rent supplement" plan, under which the slum dweller pays up to 25 per cent of his income to his landlord and a government subsidy makes up the difference. The plan, funded last year at $32 million, ran into severe trouble in Congress this summer when the House rejected an increase to $72 million. But the President still hopes the Senate will vote the full increase—a prospect considerably enhanced this month when Minority Leader Everett Dirksen reversed his previous stand and said he would vote for the bill.

In the wake of this summer's rioting, new proposals for slum housing are surfacing almost daily. In the United States Senate alone, there were 38 bills pending at last count proposing ways to improve America's ghettos. Included among them was a proposal by Republican Sen. Charles Percy of Illinois to create a $2 billion National Home Ownership Foundation, which would make low-interest mortgage loans to enable slum dwellers to buy their own houses. New York's Robert F. Kennedy, in another major bill, proposed that Federal loan subsidies be paid to private developers who go into slums, with substantial tax credits added as another inducement. The Kennedy bill had more support than Percy's, but neither, given a currently cost-conscious Congress, seemed to have much chance of passing this year.

Distant Dream. In the long run, some version of both ideas—ownership subsidies and tax incentives—seems likely to be adopted. Ultimately, too, thinkers both in the White House and on campuses hope to get slum dwellers out of the ghetto by building integrated, low-cost new towns in the suburbs.

But this, to housing experts, is no more than a distant dream. After all, they point out, the nation has yet to make a serious commitment even to the projects that are now in force. Spending on slum housing is now running at a total of about $400 million a year; Harvard urban planner Chester Hartman argues that real solutions would need spending on the order of $7 billion to $8 billion a year for decades to come.

And in the end, even these huge outlays would not really wipe out the slums. Slum housing, after all, is simply one rat in the rathole of discrimination, deprivation and despair. All the problems must be solved together, or there will be no solution.

The Agony of Getting Anywhere Newsweek

In Washington, the snow came just about the time that city of transients was dispersing for the long Christmas holiday weekend. Inexorably, the snowball rolled its vicious circle: local streets iced over, which stalled private cars, which blocked the intercity buses, which left travelers stranded down the line, which placed added demands on the airports, which had to close runways because of snow drifts, which delayed passengers already holding tickets, which caused a scramble for cabs, which were stuck on the icy streets . . .

What happened in Washington over the Christmas weekend might have happened in any large U.S. city on any given day–stormy or clear. For most city dwellers, snow and rain only intensify the year-round agony of getting anywhere.

At almost any hour that urban Americans are on the move, there is an anthem of gnashing teeth. Automobiles choke the expressways; and as soon as more expressways are built to relieve the congestion, the new road space fills up with more cars. In the air, passengers jet across half a continent in two hours, then spend half as much time traversing the few miles to their downtown hotels. And the once-great railroads have, with a few exceptions, turned their backs on the commuter.

Lyndon Johnson's Great Society, in the words of Rhode Island Sen. Claiborne Pell, "is fast becoming an immobile society."

What's wrong with the U.S. transit system? The trouble is twofold. Historically, it never was a system; and currently, the auto is king. U.S. transit is a collection of competing modes that were created, not to provide public service, but to provide a living for the operators. The modes that grew the fastest were the moneymakers, like the early railroads; and when the profits collapsed, so did the modes of transportation. On top of that, road builders too long ignored the cities' special problems while they hustled the farmer off to his market on interstate highways. "It is no coincidence," says Robert Nelson, director of the U.S. Commerce Department's Office of High-Speed Ground Transportation, "that the Bureau of Public Roads used to be in the Department of Agriculture."

Private Riders. The ascendancy of the auto only complicated matters. In no other society has man deployed so many wheels: they enable him to live in one place, work in another, and vacation anywhere he chooses. And typically, when he travels from place to place, he uses his own private car: eight out of ten of the nation's commuters travel by auto.

In fact, the increasing use of motor vehicles for personal transportation in the U.S.–from 34 million of them in 1946 to 90 million in

1965—is a fairly accurate measure of the extent to which rail transit has declined over the same period (from 790 million rides in 1946 to 299 million in 1965). Urban mass transit has suffered a similar fate. Between 1950 and 1960, according to a study by Northwestern University, the mass-transit industry lost 45 per cent of its customers and suffered a 25 per cent cut in net revenues.

Recently, however, two developments have occurred which may revive the moribund mass-transit industry and stem the American's flight from subways, buses and trains to the comfort—and sometimes convenience—of the private car.

The first development is political. At long last, responsive politicians, like New York's Mayor John V. Lindsay, are beginning to pull the various modes of transportation together under a single administrative umbrella. In Washington last fall, Congress established the new Cabinet-level Department of Transportation (DOT) to get traffic and transit moving.

Regression. The second development is social—a growing, nationwide revolt against autos and highways. "We've repeated with the auto all the mistakes we made with the railroad," complains Lewis Mumford, the dean of urban philosophers. "The railroads plowed right through the city to dump their loads in the freight yards in the center. Now, the same kind of thing is being done on an even greater scale by the motor car. What people don't realize is that throughout the Northeast in the 1920s, there was a vast trolley network. With transfers, you could go from New York to Portland, Maine. But when the auto took over, the system collapsed. All over the country today are stranded towns."

Mumford represents a growing body of opinion—a sort of Greek chorus—that views the ubiquitous auto and the superhighway as usurpers of the good life. In addition to the fact that automobile accidents killed 49,000 persons in 1965, there is a growing suspicion that automobile exhausts contributed to the deaths of thousands more. And open space for the living is fast being covered by concrete. In just two years—from 1962 to 1964—the interstate highway system took 39,000 urban acres off local taxrolls.

The anti-auto fight takes many forms. In New York City the imaginative parks commissioner, Thomas P. F. Hoving, has banned cars from Central Park on Sundays, and is planning to turn a proposed Staten Island highway route into a hiking trail.

Revolt. In Los Angeles, science-fiction author Ray Bradbury, who owns no car and rides an English racing bike to his Beverly Hills office, recently joined with architect Frank Lloyd Wright Jr. to form PRIME, Inc. (Promote Rapid Transit and Improve Metropolitan Environment). PRIME's movers are beating the drums for $2 billion worth of rails and rolling stock. In San Francisco the board of supervisors forfeited $250 million in U.S. highway aid by vetoing two proposed freeways, and the half-completed Embarcadero Freeway stands abandoned beside the Bay, as a stark symbol of the revolt. Another symbol: the Bay Area bumper stickers that read, "Having trouble parking? Support Planned Parenthood."

The auto won't go away that easily. The car carries more than people: it supports the economy. Out of a total of $140.5 billion spent on transportation in the U.S. in 1965, nearly half the sum reflected investments in roads and automobiles—a chrome-plated 10 per cent of the entire gross national product. Dependent on the car are seven of the nation's ten largest corporations (three auto manufacturers and four petroleum companies); more than 12 million U.S. workers employed in the manufacture, distribution, maintenance and commercial use of motor vehicles; the rubber and steel industries; cement and asphalt companies, motor clubs, highway officials, contractors and parking-lot owners.

This powerful Establishment intends to defend the auto's right of way. Says Henry Ford II: "The critics would have us believe the automobile is a monster that has run out of control . . . The fact is that for most travel purposes, no vehicles have yet been developed or are even in prospect that equal the automobile for speed, comfort, convenience, privacy, economy and other qualities that people value."

Since Ford sounded that battle cry, other industry spokesmen have served notice that they intend to resist any federal transportation policy that might favor rails over rubber.

Divisions. LBJ's choice for Secretary of Transportation, Alan S. Boyd, 44, faces opposition of another kind. Even before he was officially tapped for the job, the House of Representatives refused to shift the Maritime Administration and the Corps of Engineers—two sacred cows—to DOT's jurisdiction. And the most tangled, neglected segment of the entire industry—urban mass transit—remains within the Department of Housing and Urban Development (HUD).

This leaves DOT and Boyd basically responsible for intercity rails and highways (now under Commerce) and commercial airlines (under the Federal Aviation Agency). But DOT can hardly plan a high-speed, ground-transportation system for the Boston-Washington Northeast Corridor, for example, without considering the end points in its scheme. And HUD will have a hard time deciding at what point urban transit ends and intercity systems begin, especially in the Northeast Corridor where cities merge in one elongated megalopolis. The two departments hopefully will patch this illogical division of authority within the year.

Even with what he has, Boyd faces the possibility that his new department could be torn apart by modular factionalism. Rail proponents are covetously eying the highway trust fund, which pays out to the states $3 billion to $4 billion a year and is replenished by 4 cents every time a motorist buys a gallon of gasoline. When the interstate highway program ends in six years, they argue, some of the trust fund moneys should be diverted to building rapid-transit systems. Sen. Joseph D. Tydings of Maryland has proposed that the fund be tapped even sooner.

Heresy. The very idea of building railroads with highway-user taxes is heresy to such advocates of the open road as Federal Highways Administrator Rex Whitton. Whitton, 69 and about to retire, believes the fund—after 1973—should be used to build more highways around cities and parking facilities to accommodate the cars new roads would attract.

Boyd, however, is confident there will be no factional bickering in his new agency. "All of these groups seem to understand now," he says, "that the future demands for transportation are going to be so great there will be a need for all of them." After all, he adds, "the public should have a choice of alternatives."

Few travelers have real alternatives. People in New York seem to prefer their cars over rapid transit. For example, private researchers investigated the habits of 14,800 auto commuters bound for Manhattan from Westchester County, N.Y., and Fairfield County, Conn. Both counties are served by rail lines terminating at Manhattan's Grand Central Terminal. After subtracting those whose jobs were more than twenty minutes away from Grand Central by subway and those who needed personal autos in performing their work, the investigators decided 2,000 commuters had every reason to use the railroads—but didn't.

Success. Chicagoans apparently felt differently. When the Chicago Transit Authority began running trains to suburban Skokie as an experiment in 1964, it estimated the run would attract only 1,500 passengers a day from cars. CTA carried 3,900 the first day, and its weekday average now is 7,000.

Most commuter transit systems fail by

ignoring what happens to the passenger at either end of the trip. The highly successful Chicago & North Western Railway doesn't. Under the aggressive leadership of Ben Heineman, the North Western has installed "commuter cruisers" that boat passengers from the downtown terminal up the Chicago River to the east side of the Loop, and it is planning an enclosed, block-long "Northwest Passage," between the terminal and a nearby el station, complete with escalators. With such touches, Heineman is finally proving that rails can serve the public as well as turn a profit—the North Western showed a $1.3 million net income last year.

The advocates of the auto see the city's salvation in better roads—and more roads. Most city planners concede that many urban communities lack adequate highways, but they also point out that new expressways aimed at the central business districts often generate more traffic than the downtown areas can reasonably handle—and sometimes more than even the expressways themselves can handle (Chicago's Congress Street Expressway, designed for 96,000 cars daily, was saturated with 115,000 before it was fully completed). Moreover, cautions Stanley Tankel, planning director of the private, nonprofit Regional Plan Association in New York City, "Every time you increase one of the three basic facilities for automobiles—freeways, approaches or parking—you put pressure on the other two."

The most violent debate between transit boosters and highway advocates swirls quite naturally around costs. The transit camp argues that urban expressways are exorbitant, and indeed some are: the 52-mile Delaware Expressway through Philadelphia will cost $353 million, only $26 million less than the 313-mile Keystone Shortway through exurban Pennsylvania. And a 3,168-foot stretch of expressway in Philadelphia will cost $58 million—$30 million for the right-of-way, $28 million for construction.

"It doesn't cost President Johnson one red cent to build roads," counters Ford's top economist, A. J. Goldenthal. "All highways are built on a pay-as-you-go basis out of highway-users' taxes."

'Box on Wheels'. Still, Detroit is not blind to public-transit needs—and to its own key role as a manufacturer of buses. But the buses may have to change radically. As HUD's Assistant Secretary Charles M. Haar defines them, "They are still boxes on four wheels." HUD currently is looking into new designs and has already farmed some out to communities for actual testing. One of the most promising demonstrations is the minibus, a 138-horsepower vehicle which provides short-haul rides for a nickel in downtown Washington. In Peoria, HUD stepped in and put a deficit-ridden bus system back on its tires with such features as guaranteed seating, zone fares and revised schedules.

But the true test of transit plans is not so much how they work in Peoria (pop: 127,000) but how they work in a megalopolis. Into the 8.6 square miles of New York City's central business district (CBD) each day pour 3.3 million commuters. A quarter of them come in cars and taxis, rolling along at an average speed of 8½ miles an hour. Even between rush hours, Midtown Manhattan traffic never lets up. "We have approached the limit," the Regional Plan Association announced last year. "No significant increase in automobile capacity can be provided in the CBD . . . except at exorbitant expense in money and disruption of heavily built-up areas or mutilation of badly needed parks."

Towing. As a result, the Lindsay Administration has been dreaming up ways to scare off the commuting motorist. The first move was to put policemen in tow trucks to haul illegally parked cars off to a crumbling Hudson pier. Violators protested bitterly, then begrudgingly paid for the tow as well as the ticket. Now Lindsay is considering the merits of doubling parking fines—some to as high as $30. And Transportation Administrator Arthur Palmer Jr. is weighing the possibility of higher midtown commuter parking rates (from $3.50 for 8 hours to $7). Another unofficial scheme would require statewide adoption: taxing motor-vehicle registrations according to size rather than weight. In effect, each motorist would be paying for the space his vehicle occupies. A less punitive deterrent has been proposed by Traffic Commissioner Henry Barnes. He wants to build more low-rate parking lots near subway stations in Brooklyn and Queens. By increasing parking facilities outside the CBD, says Barnes, "We can reasonably tell the motorist to keep his car out."

But the New York City Transit Authority, operator of the world's largest—and perhaps most unattractive—passenger railroad, isn't at all sure that adding extra bodies to their crowded underground trains even approximates reason. "It's ridiculous," says Transit Commissioner John Gilhooley. "We can't go around telling people to keep their cars out of the business district. They're just not going to tolerate being pushed around in a subway."

With HUD looking into the possibility of 80 mph speeds for tomorrow's subways, several U.S. cities are pressing ahead with plans for entirely new systems. Atlanta has selected 1984, of all years, as the deadline for completing a $437 million, 66-mile system that will carry 1 million riders a day in electric trains operating at subway, ground and aerial levels. Washington hopes to begin a $430 million, 25-mile subway system next year; and in Boston, the Massachusetts Bay Transportation Authority is developing a master plan for $346 million worth of extended track, 200 new cars, 25 new stations and 19,000 commuter parking spaces.

SF Express. The most expensive plans have been developed in California. San Francisco's $1 billion Bay Area Rapid Transit (BART) is already a-building. By 1970, commuters from a dozen communities will be riding lightweight aluminum cars at an average speed of 50 mph (existing U.S. commuter transit systems rarely average better than 20 mph).

The majority of U.S. transit planners seem satisfied with the current state of the art, as reflected in BART, Toronto's twelve-year-old subway and the brand-new Montreal Metro (a rubber-wheel train). But now and again there is a loud dissent; and the latest comes from William L. Garrison, director of Northwestern University's Transportation Center. "The mass-transit system is a dog," snaps Garrison. "Cities are making a big mistake by plowing a lot of money into existing subway technology. We've got to break away."

Skybus. Breaks are being made. In Pittsburgh, for example, Westinghouse Electric Corp. has unveiled and tested its new "Transit Expressway." Sometimes called the Skybus, the system consists of 30-passenger, rubber-tired cars on an elevated guide rail. For smaller cities with medium-volume transit problems, the Skybus may be a solution.

Industry is also polishing up some futuristic modes of personal transportation between suburban and downtown areas. Cornell Aeronautical Laboratory's Urbmobile (undeveloped) and Alden's StaRRcar (undergoing tests) are basically the same: small cars operated either manually on the street or by electrical guidance on an automated highway. Both share a common disadvantage: slow on the street.

Most large U.S. cities might not be too receptive to the idea of guideways, tubes and conveyor belts crisscrossing their inflexible surfaces. Streets, bridges and buildings are where they are and cannot easily be shuffled to accommodate some new appurtenance. For this reason HUD is searching for new and inexpensive methods of tunneling. One possible means: the use of laser rays to weaken rock, as demonstrated recently by two MIT students.

Shoe Leather. "We must put the mechanical things underground," says Regional Plan's Tankel. "The sun, the sky and the trees belong to men." And in an increasing number of cities, planning and transportation decisions are taking into account the fact that yet another mode of travel must be considered—shoe leather. Says Edmund Bacon, the Philadelphia city planning director whose downtown master plan features malls and subway stops at sunken plazas: "Part of the battle to make transit more attractive is to get people off their backsides and onto their feet."

The battle for better intercity rail systems has a different aim—high speed. Thirty years ago the fastest train-run from New York to Washington was three hours and 35 minutes. Today, it is not a minute faster (and often slower). But the DOT cadre at Commerce holds that high-speed ground transportation lies just around the next realigned bend in the track.

Right now, engineers in the Northeast Corridor Project are aiming at a top speed of 150 mph, which could bring the New York-to-Washington run well under three hours. Two demonstrations are in the works. One involves 21 miles of track on the Pennsylvania Railroad right-of-way near Trenton, where four souped-up Budd electric railcars will soon be tested at speeds up to the desired 150 maximum. And next October, 50 new 110-mph electrics will be running between New York and Washington to gauge public response to fast trips and more luxurious accommodations.

Improving the Wheel. Beside the demonstrations, Commerce has $4.5 million this year to invest in technological studies of the next generation of intercity transportation hardware—200- to 500-mph systems that would propel vehicles down an electric track, suspended on cushions of air and fire them through pneumatic tubes. Industry is pursuing its own research and development. Britain's Hovercraft Development, Ltd., has already demonstrated a 6-foot model of an air-cushion vehicle electro-magnetically propelled. Near Paris, engineer Jean Bertin's six-seat experimental Aerotrain (also an air-cushion vehicle) has been whisking observers over 4.2 miles of concrete guideway at 120 mph; by April 1968 the French hope to have a full-size system—for 84 passengers—completed between Paris and Orléans. And General American Transportation is working on an auto-toting train: commuters drive mini-autos right on a flatbed and are hauled to their stops. But tube-flight vehicles and hovercraft don't impress traditionalists like Lewis Mumford. "These things are new but they're not better," says Mumford. "It's very hard to improve on the wheel."

It is also hard to improve on the wing, but man has done it, and transit expediters are looking to V/STOL's (vertical and short take-off and landing) aircraft. Tilt wings and tilt rotors would allow planes to use launching pads about the size of a city block. Some members of the Commerce team still believe a fleet of V/STOL's, carrying 80 passengers each at 500 mph, could be developed for the Northeast Corridor by 1980—and with fares comparable to buses.

Like the small two-seater runabout in urban traffic, V/STOL conceivably could serve man best by relieving some of the congestion at conventional jet airports. Air passenger miles in the U.S. have increased 182 per cent in just ten years. In fact, FAA administrator Gen. William McKee estimates that by 1970, the nation will need at least 200 additional jetports. There are, after all, only 1,440 minutes in a day. Yet one day last September, Chicago's O'Hare International handled 2,006 take-offs and landings. V/STOL's might come in on short-haul flights. In the New York area, half the traffic at the major airports is short-haul. V/STOL's flying from short runways on piers in the East

River conceivably could reduce the number of take-offs and landings at conventional airports by 50 per cent.

Help on Earth. Moreover, the 747 jumbo jet, which will fly in three years with 490 passengers, and the SST, which will be flying in eight, are bearing down fast on the modern airport. Facilities by then may be saturated, not simply because of the maze of silvery wings stacked up in holding patterns above, but because of the airport's inability to process passengers and baggage quickly once they land on the ground. And beyond the airport lies the long, anguished journey downtown and crosstown.

The anguish is particularly acute for the motorist who pauses, in the thick of the hub-bound traffic, to consider the progress of transportation in space. In the time it takes to drive home from the airport, an astronaut could have circled the world. As President Johnson himself said on signing the High Speed Ground Transportation Act of 1965: "The same science and technology which gave us our airplanes and our space probes, I believe, could also give us better and faster and more economical transportation on the ground. And a lot of us need it more on the ground than we need it orbiting the earth."

If America gets it, then even commuters will be able to boast: "All systems are go."

What Area-Wide Transit Can Do for Supercity

Piero Patri

Despite all the wasteful and destructive consequences which have resulted from almost total domination of transportation by the motor vehicle, we have created an untapped resource of tremendous value in the process. By attempting to feed the insatiable hunger of the public for more and more facilities for the automobile and truck, we have laid out street and highway systems which account for 20 percent or more of the land in our urban areas. This system is owned by the public and constitutes by far the greatest single land resource available in our developed areas. In a region such as the Los Angeles Basin, the value of this resource is astronomical.

But before we proceed to develop this idea, let's make a few personal observations about human nature and the city. Aside from man's basic economic needs for survival, he has many behavioral requirements which the city must satisfy if it is to remain or develop into a desirable place to live. Above all, there seems to be a need for a choice of alternatives of action and experience for the individual:

He must have the opportunity for both sociability, in a world of increasing alienation, and privacy, in a world of increasing aural and electronic intrusion.
He needs constructive outlets for aggression rising from growing frustration in an ever more complex society.

From *Cry California*, Spring, 1968. Reprinted by permission.

He needs involvement in the processes which strongly affect his life.
He appears to have need for a clearly defined physical territory with which he can identify.

Variety seems to stimulate him and he is, in varying degrees, responsive to beauty, either manmade or natural. An unchanging, uninteresting or ugly environment seems to dull his sensitivity. The ugly, unpleasant environment which characterizes too much of our urban scene has made us insensitive.

One of the things we're generally unaware of is the extent to which a city's transportation system determines our life style. While there are many other forces at work shaping urban form and environmental character, a city's total transportation system has always been an integral and significant part of the city's history and will continue to be. The system directly and indirectly affects the physical character of the environment.

The degree of mobility a transportation system provides is not just the quantitative aspect of the number of persons, for example, who can arrive or leave downtown at peak hours–it affects the quality of life by limiting or expanding choices available:

It determines whether the commuter returns home exhausted and irritable or not;
It dictates whether the housewife has an opportunity occasionally to escape the intermittent tedium of home life;

It dictates whether a resident of Watts is able to find a job across town;
It dictates whether the elderly retired person is able to visit an old friend in another neighborhood;
It dictates whether the schoolchild can enrich his education through visits to interesting but distant areas;
It may even dictate whether or not a troubled teenager, because of marked inconvenience, drops out of high school.

In a large, recently developed city, such as Los Angeles, it goes almost without saying that the freeway-only solution to transportation is self-defeating, if we are concerned about anything more than moving people and goods in privately controlled vehicles from one point to another. To keep the automobile, we are spending our wealth and giving our lives, and in the process destroying the quality of our cities. Alternatives to auto-freeway transportation are going to have to be created. The problem is to develop ways of diverting part of our great urban land resource–the street rights-of-way–from the automobile to other forms of transportation and other land uses.

We must embark on a program to materially reduce the size and other objectionable characteristics (noise, fumes, safety hazards) of the urban automobile.

Take into account existing and anticipated modes of urban transportation, including high-speed trains, automated freeways, dial-a-buses, mini-cars, coin-operated autos, elephant trains, moving sidewalks and other systems which will give great flexibility. And while we may assume, as a point of departure for this article, construction of a simple grid transit system similar to the Babcock Plan, many of these recently developed and anticipated modes will have to be integrated into the network if we are to have a truly comprehensive system.

Under these assumptions, the major components of the new transportation system could be existing and proposed freeways (which roughly form a four-mile grid) and the transit system which will form a one-mile grid, with stations approximately a mile apart. The balance of the existing street system could be adapted to several uses: limited-access greenways, arterials, local streets and pedestrian ways, as well as an occasional grand boulevard. It would appear that, while many people might be willing to walk a quarter or half mile to a transit station, it would still be necessary to provide a mini-transit system which would serve the very young and the elderly, the handicapped, the package-burdened shopper, and the general population in rainy weather.

Although the term "grid" may suggest a rigid system, this isn't necessarily so. Flexibility must be a basic characteristic of any modern transportation system. While nominally a one-mile grid, the transit spacing could vary to a certain extent. The grid is a concept, not a firm geometry. It must be responsive to both natural and manmade variations of the landscape; hills, bodies of water, parks, historical landmarks, and in many cases, present-day concentrations of activity.

But further than this, the system must be designed with functional flexibility. It must be conceived so broadly that it will permit adaptation to expanded transportation demands and opportunities. We cannot afford to build hundreds of miles of subsurface and elevated transitway if this system is so inflexibly designed that it cannot serve anticipated but unpredictable technological advancements.

Given, then, a system of this scope and potential impact, what are the options, what are the opportunities for change and renewal, for infusion of elements of variety, excitement, and beauty?

The first is the creation of nodes of activity, the transit stations, the natural foci of human traffic. Here lies the possibility of recreating what was the function of, in other times and places, the plaza, the town square, the marketplace, the Greek agora. This is the primary opportunity.

A second opportunity is the chance to recapture a significant part of the street system from the auto and return it to the pedestrian. By attracting residential and commercial clustering at transit stops, we can then, if we choose, return to green-belt and park use part of the land now exclusively devoted to housing and asphalt.

Furthermore, many of the streets currently given over to through traffic will not be needed once the other elements of the proposed system begin functioning–the transit lines and greenways, will, presumably, diminish the number of vehicles on the secondary and tertiary streets. Perhaps as much as half the remaining streets need no longer be open to traffic, and this will give us the wonderful opportunity to create microneighborhoods by converting streets within areas varying from three to six blocks to pedestrian, perhaps microtransit, or, at worst, to limited motor-vehicle use.

One of the most important facets of this approach to restructuring urban form is its apparent practicability. Obviously, it will take many years to implement the overall system, but it will not be necessary to demolish the city in the process. By taking advantage of existing street patterns and by careful planning and phasing, the conversion can be accomplished without wholesale disruption. Where disruption is inevitable, the project may be combined with major redevelopment which could constitute substantial and constructive urban changes.

Obviously, a program undertaken on this scale will cost many billions of dollars to bring into being, and the inevitable question is, how can we pay for it? In the first place, much additional livability and amenity will result from utilization of an existing public resource, the street system. But in addition, with construction of the transit grid, great increases in land value at and near the nodes will provide not only a higher future tax base, but potentially the basic source of construction funds as well. There is no insurmountable obstacle to public purchase of sufficient land around the transit stops that could allow the public to reap material benefits from its own expenditure. If the increase in land values which will accrue from public spending are allocated to the public which creates the values, the kinds of changes we are considering can become reality.

If we are to create cities which fulfill human needs, the needs of young and old, families and single persons, rich and poor, black and white, it's going to take bold thinking, massive public funding, and a depth of understanding and staying power to meet our growing and tremendously complex urban socio-economic, as well as environmental, problems. If we fail, our citizens will continue doing what they have already started to do: flee the cities or burn them down.

Sprawl vs. Livable Cities

George H. Favre

Not many Detroit citizens are aware of it, but the way their city and suburbs will look to their grandchildren may have been shaped 2,400 years ago in ancient Athens.

The connecting link is trim, silver-haired Constantinos A. Doxiadis. The Greek city planner's ideas of what a city should be grew out of pondering what had turned his ancient native city of Athens from a self-contained, livable town into a modern, sprawling, anti-human metropolis.

Perhaps the best-known city planner in the world, Dr. Doxiadis is sowing his old-new ideas of city planning across four continents. Through 22 branch offices around the world, Doxiadis Associates acts as consultant to major cities not only in the United States but in Pakistan, Iraq, Syria, Jordan, India, Ghana, Brazil, and other countries.

Whether it is his headquarters city of Athens or industrial Detroit, Dr. Doxiadis sees the modern metropolis as a formless, ever-growing, thoughtless happening.

This distresses his Greek heritage of love for rationality, order, law, and democratic process. He insists that sprawl need not happen. While "natural forces" determine the broader outlines of city development, men can and must control that growth before it destroys human values, he says.

This interview with Constantinos A. Doxiadis appeared in *The Christian Science Monitor,* December 26, 1967. Reprinted by permission from *The Christian Science Monitor,*

The key to such control he finds in ancient Athens: human scale.

Interviewed here in his New York office, which looks out over the United Nations building, Dr. Doxiadis spelled out his views of what has happened in Athens and in every other great city of the world.

Quick to illustrate his ideas with paper and pencil, he draws three small circles in a triangle.

"This is the ancient city," he says in richly accented English. "Each is independent and self-contained." Then he draws a series of concentric circles. "Now we see what happens. The town grows outward, always getting bigger and bigger. Enormous pressures are exerted on the center, which then becomes suffocated and dies. This becomes a slum."

As this process continues, Dr. Doxiadis forecasts extinction of human values and of the good life, unless city growth can be brought into an orderly growth pattern.

Demographers predict a "realistic average" of around 30 billion people in the world by the year 2100, he notes. With the continuing trend for them to cluster in cities, he says we are moving into the time when megalopolis will spread out to become "ecumenopolis"—a global city.

Swiveling in his armchair and enveloping Manhattan in the sweep of his arm, he says: "The world of ecumenopolis is now under construction. This must be understood. The average lifetime of even a prefabricated house is at least 30 years. If you open now a new road here, this remains for centuries—not the pavement itself, but the conditions it creates."

Natural forces, says Dr. Doxiadis, shape a city. These are: existing cities; major lines of transportation; and aesthetic considerations.

"We cannot change these forces," he says. Take the existing city. Can a new town counteract that? "To do so you would need an equal investment. How long would that take? How much money? How many billions of decisions?

If the forces cannot be counteracted, he says, then "we must exploit them to the benefit of man."

This is what he is attempting to do in Philadelphia, Washington, Miami, Detroit, Islamabad, and in Zambia, Libya, Ghana, and the Canary Islands.

The existing city is an organism that will continue to grow, he insists. Isolated new towns cannot resolve its problems.

Small cities, says Dr. Doxiadis, in the superpopulated world of the future, are "unrealistic, unjustified, and an attempt to reverse the trend. The trend is for higher development, higher productivity. The big city makes for greater freedom, greater democracy, greater choice. If you accept personal freedom as the goal of humanity, for good or for bad, then the imperative conclusion is the very big city."

On the other hand, says Dr. Doxiadis, "we know that this city (waving his hand again toward Manhattan) is a failure. And any extrapolation we make shows that the failure is going to become bigger and bigger. We struggle with more and more pollution, noise, and congestion."

Dr. Doxiadis's solution is to maintain the human values of the small city within the larger context of ecumenopolis. "We must build a city which is extrahuman in dimension and numbers and pressures, but by units which are human."

This is where ancient Athens—and Florence, Paris, London, Constantinople, and other ancient capitals as well—come in. His studies show that the old cities never exceeded a square of 2,000 yards. That meant a maximum of 10 minutes, walking from the center to the city edge at any point.

If megalopolis, later ecumenopolis, is allowed to grow by such units or cells—much in the way nature causes organisms to grow—then Dr. Doxiadis says the city, whatever its ultimate size, will always retain its human scale.

Which direction these cells take will be subject to the larger natural forces. They will move outward from existing cities, following the lines of transportation and seeking the most aesthetically satisfying areas. Thus rivers, lakes, seacoasts, valleys, and plains will gradually fill in with these humanly scaled cells, each of which may contain up to 50,000 people.

Between these complexes of cells will remain the hills and mountains, the forests, the inaccessible and inhospitable regions, greenbelts set aside for recreation, and agricultural lands.

What's more, Dr. Doxiadis insists that democratic expression with freedom of choice and variety of development can best be fostered through such orderly planned growth.

Dr. Doxiadis is a champion of metropolitan government—within well-defined limits. He admits the need for control at a higher level for such matters as policing, water, sewage and waste disposal, and zoning of land use.

But within the individual cells, he calls for the maximum of free and democratic choice. "People should have administrative responsibility for their own sectors, without interference from anyone on the outside. Why should the citizens of the neighborhood, who want to put a statue in their local park, have to go to a city council which represents millions of people and get the decision of several administrative bodies?"

Dr. Doxiadis also wants to keep automobile traffic within each cell to a minimum. Each cell, he says, should be bounded by major high-speed traffic arteries that connect with every other unit. But within each cell, foot traffic should be separated from the wheel.

If such concepts are not exactly new, neither are they much practiced. And Dr. Doxiadis has certainly done as much as any one man to give them whatever currency they now may have.

In his work with the Urban Detroit Area and other cities for which he is a consultant, Dr. Doxiadis uses what he calls the IDEA system. The acronym stands for "isolation of dimensions and elimination of alternatives." All that means in everyday language is that his firm considers all the factors in the city—such as population growth, economy, location of major centers, industry, etc.—and figures out the best alternatives for future growth.

Using computers and what he calls "a very objective" approach, he presents what he considers the best of all alternatives to the city. If the community does not like it—if they disagree with any of the assumptions—they can insert their own assumptions. "In 20 minutes of computer time and 24 hours of drafting," says Dr. Doxiadis, "we have the new solution."

Thus the people can determine how their city will grow, in accord with their likes and dislikes.

By this method, Dr. Doxiadis believes, "we have, for the first time since cities were small enough for people to meet in the square and discuss their problems, a way for them to make all the decisions. We are only agents."

Dr. Doxiadis emphatically disagrees with those city planners who go on the assumption that eventually widespread use of videophones will eliminate the need to go to the center of the city to talk face to face for business or personal visits.

"Don't forget," says Dr. Doxiadis in one of his frequent colorful observations, "that half the human race is male and half is female. You cannot court by videophone. Electronics cannot replace the contact between a parent and child or between friends."

"This is a basic principle of ekistics," he says, "that modern technology adds dimensions to our lives; it does not subtract values."

Ekistics is the Doxiadis term for the broad-stroke approach he takes to planning. It involves economics, mathematics, social sciences along with engineering and architecture. It is systems-oriented, using computers as its basic tool.

In addition to his planning firm in Athens, Dr. Doxiadis runs his own Athens Technological Institute and the Center for Ekistics, at which he lectures in the summer. And in Los Angeles he recently teamed with Systems Development Corporation to form the Doxiadis Systems Development Center.

The Athenian planner has been criticized by some as being flamboyant and glib (he has been called the Aristotle Onassis of the planning profession). But most city planners, traditionally anonymous, acknowledge the spadework he has done in bringing their activities out of obscurity. The Doxiadis energy and flair make him newsworthy, and the planning profession benefits.

Many planners would also take exception to some of Mr. Doxiadis's ideas which, stripped of their Greek packaging, seem routine enough, and sometimes even backward. Dr. Doxiadis's insistence, for example, on the merits of the much-maligned American traditional grid system is anathema for planners enraptured by wrap-around roads and cluster housing. A pragmatist, Dr. Doxiadis sees the simple grid as the most direct answer to the problem of transversing a city. But to the old grid idea he adds the contemporary one of separating pedestrians from cars.

Eastwyck, a planned "city within a city" in Philadelphia, is an example of a Doxiadis comprehensive plan that apparently works but has won no honors for breaking new barriers in city design. Reynolds Metals Company, developer of the 25,000-acre urban-renewal site, hired Mr. Doxiadis for the job. It used his master plan, but yielded to criticism of the architectural merits of the Doxiadis houses, and hired Hyman Korman, Inc., a large home builder to do the job.

To Dr. Doxiadis architecture is subordinate to other considerations. In Eastwyck he set up a grid with superblocks, but included no through streets. Squares and streets are all inward-looking, away from the heavy industry that crushes in on the development. The prime effort was to create an aesthetic environment that would help residents forget the drab industrial surroundings.

A sense of neighborhood, of community, of human scale—these are the major elements which he believes can make tomorrow's ecumenopolis habitable.

A Smokeless, Noiseless, Trafficless City Walter Sullivan

Throughout the world today the great migration is toward the cities. Yet, it was argued last week, the cities themselves are utterly obsolete. That was the theme of the "Distinguished Lecture," given on Wednesday at the annual meeting of the American Association for the Advancement of Science. The speaker was Athelstan Spilhaus, president of the Franklin Institute in Philadelphia and former dean of the Institute of Technology at the University of Minnesota.

Dr. Spilhaus and such figures as Buckminster Fuller, designer of futuristic domes and other structures, and General Bernard Schriever, former head of the Air Force Systems Command, are working on plans for an Experimental City, to be built from the ground—or rather from underground—up. Their thesis is that to remake existing cities, taking full advantage of new techniques of transport, construction, communication and organization, would be a hopeless task.

Science and technology, coupled with the methods of systems analysis that have been used to great advantage by the Air Force and large corporations, have, say these men, made possible the construction of cities of beauty and joy, of health and intellectual enrichment. Such cities would be free of air pollution, street excavations and traffic congestion. They could be managed on a contract basis, Dr. Spilhaus said, much as large government enterprises are today.

In fact the government has already turned to a private corporation for the construction and operation of a small city—Oak Ridge, Tenn., developed by Union Carbide early in the atomic weapons program. Pan American World Airways fulfills somewhat the same role at Cape Kennedy.

Because of modern transportation and marketing methods, commerce no longer needs the city to the extent that it did in the past. Dr. Spilhaus cited the prediction of Mr. Fuller that the chief role of the city will ultimately be "metaphysical," offering a forum for the exchange of ideas, learning and culture, rather than goods.

When Dr. Spilhaus drew attention to the congestion and disorganization of modern cities his remarks fell on receptive ears, for the audience crowding the ballroom of the New York Hilton had fought its way through holiday crowds and traffic so choking that some Broadway shows began a half hour late. The actors had not been able to reach their theaters.

The trouble, said Dr. Spilhaus, is that the big cities get bigger and bigger, even though the reason for their being where they are—a harbor or rail center—no longer plays a major role in their life. Yet many industries, Dr. Spilhaus said, are moving out of the cities.

This article appeared in *The New York Times,* December 31, 1967.

Indeed, he said at a press conference before his talk, dispersal, not urban renewal, is the answer to the problems of the city. The government, in spending large sums on new housing in slum areas, is merely taking over the role of the slum landlords, he added. Ultimately, when experimental cities are available to handle slum dwellers from the overcrowded centers, he would demolish the slums and leave green areas in their place, thus thinning out the bigger cities.

The Experimental City would permit no discharge of smoke or fumes into the atmosphere. Automobiles and trucks entering from outside the city would travel by tunnel whose air would be drawn out through "fume sewers" to air-cleaning plants on the edge of town. Travel within the city would be by some revolutionary form of public transport—possibly in small pods that would carry a few people, via an automated rail system, from their homes to whatever destination they selected.

Buildings would be constructed of lightweight material, such as prefabricated panels that could be delivered underground and assembled into a multitude of configurations. All wires, pipes and other utilities would be routed through underground tunnels and ducts so that street excavations would be unnecessary.

Such extensive use of underground facilities will be possible, Dr. Spilhaus said, because the city will be designed and built for it. There will be no need for zoning since factories will not be allowed to generate noise or pollution. Schools, theaters, libraries, homes and places of work will all be intermingled, minimizing transport needs.

Through closed circuit television and similar devices students will be able to study art at the local art museum. Their science classes will be presented at a science center. They will study business on-the-job at some local enterprise. Dr. Spilhaus cited the prediction of Dr. John R. Pierce of the Bell Telephone Laboratories that many people will "communicate to work" instead of commute to work.

The idea of dispersing the heavy concentrations of population is not to blanket the countryside with "suburban sprawl," in the California manner, Dr. Spilhaus said. Rather people would be concentrated into numerous cities of 250,000 or 500,000, each surrounded by some 40,000 acres of open country. In view of the annual population growth of three million, a dozen new cities would have to be built yearly.

Each city must be economically viable and must be adapted to the region in which it is situated, he said. Nuclear plants that can desalt seawater and provide cheap power make it possible to build such cities in arid regions. Dr. Spilhaus envisioned a first generation of 50 Experimental Cities, one per state, to test new ideas in adaptation to local conditions and needs.

Some cities should be covered in part with giant domes. A transparent dome two miles in diameter could be built for about $80 million, he said. The laboratory city would provide a testing ground for such devices which, Dr. Spilhaus believes, would pay for themselves in ten years through savings in snow removal and heating.

The total cost of the first such city would be about $4 billion, Dr. Spilhaus said. Three Federal agencies and ten Minnesota industries have so far put up about $300,000 for preliminary studies. The first such city is projected for the Minnesota farming country.

Dr. Spilhaus suggested that the counterpart of a Federal Housing Authority loan could help get the project started. He argued that large sums are now being invested in projects that will benefit only a few and will further degrade our environment. As an example he cited the development of a supersonic transport which, he said, "will carry 100 people in a hurry and keep millions awake."

The current crisis in urban affairs was reflected in the number of sessions of last week's meeting that were devoted to the cities and their transport problems. Constantinos A. Doxiadis, a Greek engineer and technological prophet, predicted that intercity travel, as well as transport within cities, will go underground, with streets reserved for pedestrians only.

Traffic on streets in many city centers moves no faster than in the days of horse-drawn carts, he said. Yet techniques now available could enable one to reach any part of a city within ten minutes.

Not only will wastes be removed via pipe, Mr. Doxiadis told the meeting, but goods will be delivered in this way. Homes will be on a vast plumbing system through which goods will travel, coded for switching and shunting from store to home. Ultimately, he said, travel times to all parts of the world will be pared from hours to minutes until the planet becomes the universal city of man—what he calls the "ecumenopolis."

Chapter 2

POLITICAL STRUCTURES

In this chapter we take a look at several aspects of our political system. We have included a speech by former California Assembly Speaker, Jesse M. Unruh, ("Effective Local Government") and a newspaper article on how our nation's largest legislative body is hidebound by ancient practices that make it slow to respond to national needs. We consider the politics of protest, the popular rejection of national policy ("A Fail-Safe Line for Dissent"). We consider some of the attitudes toward radical political elements ("Virus X and the Body Politic") and in another article, the role of colleges and universities in American politics ("Campus or Battleground?"). Finally, we explore some of the assumptions about the individual's role in national politics ("Five Myths about Modern Politics").

Effective Local Government

Jesse M. Unruh

I want to talk about the future of your city—the city for whose present condition and future prospects you have accepted responsibility.

I am especially concerned that California's cities have adequate financial and governmental resources to cope with the problems and crises which are coming our way. As you are aware, these crises are precipitated by California's unprecedented growth. As you are also aware, the magnitude of that growth will be particularly acute in our urban areas. And in Los Angeles County it will rise to frightening dimensions.

Within the next ten years population densities in our communities will multiply several times over. Thousands of new residents will confront practically every one of your city councils with their demands. And they will demand not only "bare bones" services, such as police, fire and sanitation, but also programs for education, recreation, human relations—and others neither you nor I have yet thought of.

For the present, our most important single goal must be to bring order to the chaos and fragmentation caused by overlapping and uneconomic special districts.

In complex urban communities special districts have a number of disadvantages. There is little public awareness of their existence. Many do not even have regular elections because there is frequently no contest for seats on the district board. When elections are held, voter turnout is woefully low, rarely reaching thirty percent of the eligible voters. Board meetings are infrequently attended by the public. And actions of district boards are seldom reported in the press.

Last year, special districts raised and spent over $45 million from property taxes and an additional $45 million from fees and service charges. The existence of these districts has a marked effect on each of your cities. An unwise or shortsighted decision by a district board, uneconomic administration of district functions, or an unnecessarily high district tax rate can alter the entire fabric of the urban community. In short, it changes the environment in which your city is free to grow, to extend its tax base, and to provide space for homes, apartments, and businesses.

I confess that the Legislature, especially during the decade of the fifties, was not particularly responsive to your needs and to the needs of our urban communities. In 1963, however, under my authority as Speaker of the Assembly, I drastically reorganized the Assembly Municipal and

Mr. Unruh served as Speaker of the California State Assembly for many years. This speech was delivered to the Los Angeles County Division of the League of California Cities on July 16, 1964.

County Government Committee so that it would better reflect urban areas and be more responsive to the problems confronting our cities.

It was that committee which rejected the concept of a state agency which would review proposals for annexations, new districts, and new cities. And in that committee a concept unique in all fifty states was developed and embodied in legislation—the concept of a review of such proposals by city and county representatives who are closest to local conditions.

Today, some nine months after the local agency formation commissions were organized in each county, they appear to be working well. The thrust of the formation commissions, for the present anyway, is directed only toward curbing new sprawl. Overlap of special district functions, minority control of special district organization and administration, and other instances of inefficiency and duplication lie outside of the jurisdiction of the formation commissions. But these problems must be faced too, and now.

Considerable research has indicated that many of the causes of existing sprawl are directly traceable to situations involving archaic, uneconomic, or administratively unsound districts.

1. In one San Francisco Bay Area county, two fire protection districts are adjacent to an incorporated city. Each district continues to resist attempts to be annexed to that city. Neither district owns any capital plant or equipment itself. Instead, both districts levy a tax—in one case one dollar per hundred—to support an elected board and an administrative structure. The sole function of the district boards and their administrative staffs is to purchase fire protection from the adjacent city.

2. For over eight years one park and recreation district in this county has had parts of four cities within its boundaries. Each of these four areas pays taxes to support two recreation programs—that of the district and that of the city. In at least three of the four city areas sentiment runs high for withdrawal from the district. The district directors, however, have complete discretion over calling a withdrawal election. To date they have not done so. (I understand that negotiation is currently in process to work out some method of withdrawal, but in the meantime city residents continue to pay double taxes.)

3. In another northern county, a park and recreation district recently appeared before the local agency formation commission to protest a proposed annexation which allegedly would "divide the district's service area." As it turned out, the recreation district, although six years old, had never gotten around to providing *any* services to its residents.

4. There is also the case of two fire districts adjacent to one another which have resisted consolidation for a number of years. The boundary line between the two runs down the center line of a major street. Thus, businesses on opposite sides of the street are in different fire districts—districts which have never concluded a mutual assistance agreement. The insurance rates of businesses along that street reflect the cost of such needless fragmentation.

I need not multiply examples. Obviously there is need for reform wherever such situations exist. Even if the cost of special district government can be reduced by only a fraction, the aggregate will amount to a significant overall tax saving. Consider the magnitude of district investment revenues and outlay. In fiscal 1962-63 over 3,300 special districts reported the following:

1. An assessed valuation of nearly $130 billion.

2. Receipts of over $225 million from property taxes alone; (an increase of 6.5 percent over the previous year).

3. Total revenues in excess of $480 million; (up 12.8 percent over the previous year).
4. Total expenditures in excess of $470 million; (up 8.1 percent over the previous year).
5. Aggregate long-term indebtedness up $1.65 billion, of which almost $1.2 billion represent general obligation bonds; (up 10 percent over the previous year).

At the very minimum, local governments and local residents ought to have the means available to eliminate inefficient, costly, and duplicating special districts. I also suggest that at present there are two major obstacles to this goal.

First, it is unusually difficult and complicated to initiate the consolidation or dissolution of a special district. Each type of district has its own particular provisions for consolidation and dissolution. Usually an excessive number of signatures is required to petition the district board to call an election. In many instances a district board retains complete discretion of action and may ignore a petition.

I suggest that we need relatively simple consolidation and dissolution procedures, which may be easily initiated by local residents and by local governments. I suggest that there is no reason why a single consolidation procedure, a single dissolution procedure, and a single withdrawal procedure could not be made applicable to all special districts.

On the other hand, simplified procedures are of little assistance by themselves. There is also an overwhelming need for a precise knowledge of the places in which such procedures can be used, and of the appropriate circumstances in which they may be used.

Both cities and counties possess broad authority to guide and direct land use. Your planners develop and maintain long-range land use plans. And you yourselves regulate and specify the uses to which property may be put through your zoning authority.

I propose that similar planning be applied to the structure and organization of local districts. I suggest that the local agency formation commissions in each county be empowered to study and to inventory existing special districts.

In those cases in which dissolution, consolidation, or withdrawal of territory appears to be in the best interest of the community, the formation commission should submit its report to the governing bodies of the districts together with the cities and the counties.

Such recommendations perhaps need not be binding on district boards. District boards might retain the authority to reject these recommendations. The significant point is that such a review procedure would put local residents and other local governments on notice. They would be aware of opportunities for dissolution or consolidation. They would be aware of tax savings which might be achieved by such action. And thanks to the simplified procedures which I proposed a moment ago, they would have the means to initiate an effective course of action.

I believe most residents and taxpayers will choose a course of action which permits a reduction in their tax rates. They must first be aware of that choice. The formation commissions in each county are ideally suited to spark that awareness.

If voluntary action does not do the job after a reasonable trial period, then other means may have to be considered. But I would prefer to try the voluntary approach first.

I believe we ought to be able to better define what home rule really is. Home rule is not a megaphone with the principal purpose of magnifying the discordant voices of a few nearly self-appointed leaders. It is a concept of involving as many people as possible into governmental decision making. A 12 percent to 30 percent turnout of registered voters is hardly a fulfillment of this belief.

Today the future of your city cannot be

decided in isolation. The wave of the future is already upon us. And it embraces the entire urban community, of which your city is a part. Thus your obligation to guide and control the destiny of your city extends with equal force to the larger community.

Tomorrow's community necessarily is built upon that of today. Only as you act today to remedy the deficiencies of today can you truly say your voices, your interest, your hopes are shaping the future destinies of your community.

How Congress "Keeps House"– Badly

Joseph W. Sullivan

Adam Clayton Powell and Thomas Dodd notwithstanding, most Congressmen try hard to keep their individual houses in order. Collectively, however, they're probably the messiest housekeepers in official Washington.

From the Victorian accounting methods still employed on their $200 million budget to the comical diffusion of responsibility for moving furniture, household management on Capitol Hill is anything but deft. Most of the untidiness can be laid to inattention or intramural rivalry, but a few Congressional practices at least suggest imprudence.

While there's a move on to sweep away a number of the cobwebs, few lawmakers have time or inclination for an overhaul of the disjointed management system that is to blame for their formation. Indeed, far from endeavoring to set a good example for the bureaucracy, Congress conspicuously exempts its own operations from many of the fiscal and fidelity checks it's long applied to the rest of the Government.

In the preparation of its fast-growing yearly budget, for instance, Congress' many little fiefdoms decide their fund needs unhindered by questions from the Budget Bureau or any other critical overseer. In checking how the money's spent, the watchdogging General Accounting Office is largely forbidden the interrogative audits that Congress demands of it for detecting abuses or inefficiencies elsewhere. When there are buildings to be built or office supplies to be procured, moreover, the lawmakers' standards are far less strict than those for Executive-Branch procurers in the General Services Administration.

There's been no attempt to set job qualification standards for even the most technically demanding of Capitol Hill's 12,000 duty posts. Top-paying House management positions are still patronage plums for big-state Democratic delegations, whose criteria for filling them don't always include prior experience in the field. A modest 1964 start at sorting the House's once-amorphous work force into job categories and salary grades is ironically imperiled now by a Congressional "reorganization" bill that's already passed the Senate and is nearing action in the House. "Commingling of a civil service system with a patronage appointive system" is "inherently defective," the reorganizers aver.

"Most Congressmen think they're too busy with legislative and home district work to pay much attention to how the Capitol's affairs are run," muses a long-time Capitol hand. "But if they took enough time to determine just how vulnerable Congress is leaving itself, I think they'd spend a good deal more."

This article appeared in *The Wall Street Journal,* April 25, 1967. Reprinted by permission.

In the absence of tighter external controls, and with internal lines of authority often muddled, it's probably remarkable that Capitol functionaries manage as well as they do.

Certainly the work force is as honest and conscientious on the whole as any other of comparable size.

Where shortcomings clearly exist, moreover, Capitol apologists contend they're mostly inherent in a milieu where all men are equals rather than links in an executive chain of command. "We've got 435 chiefs and no Indians running the House," says Rep. Thomas Steed (D., Okla.), former chairman of the Appropriations subcommittee that handles Congress' budget. "There are obviously some inefficiencies, but as soon as you start to change something you get a hundred different ideas on how to go about it."

The one man who comes closest to speaking with finality on housekeeping matters in the House is Speaker McCormack, and in several respects he gets high marks. "The Speaker has a great sense of the traditions of the House, he's extremely interested in the well-being of all the members, and he's willing to spend unlimited time looking after the House's and the individual members' interests," attests Rep. Charles Goodell (R., N.Y.).

But the Speaker tends to become entangled in time-consuming trivia. By several accounts, he recently served as a grievance committee of one on behalf of Congress' 11 lady members, who had been denied access to the swimming pool in the Rayburn House Office Building gymnasium. The terms of his settlement with male lawmakers, who do their swimming in the buff: A ladies' swimming hour three mornings a week. Another McCormack project, reportedly the subject of several hours' involvement already, aims at locating a car-wash company willing to man the hoses in two Congressional garages.

To the 75-year-old Speaker's growing corps of rank-and-file critics, his strong sense of tradition is more of a hindrance than a help. Especially outmoded, in the critics' view, is his approach to Capitol Hill employment. "Massachusetts politics in McCormack's heyday was built on jobs and personal loyalties, but when it comes to finding a payroll slot for every old contemporary who's down on his luck, I say that's extending personal loyalty too far," complains one junior Democrat.

Adam Powell might not have thumbed his nose at Congressional convention quite so long had he not obligingly overloaded his Labor Committee staff with well-paid old cronies of both Speaker McCormack and the chairman of the subcommittee that checks Congressmen's expense vouchers. The Speaker's "pensioner" was Thomas M. Burke, a former Veterans Administration and Labor Department lawyer in Boston and a depression-era Massachusetts state senator. A 68-year-old widower who suffers from emphysema, Mr. Burke came to Washington last spring in need of one year on the Federal payroll to re-establish Government pension rights he'd allowed to lapse in the 1940s. Mr. Powell, upon request, was glad to take him on as a $15,438-a-year committee counsel.

But when Carl Perkins (D., Ky.) acceded to the committee chair in January he nixed the deal, despite several appeals from the Speaker. "I'd never even heard of the man until we went over the committee payroll and then started hearing about him from the Speaker," Rep. Perkins says. Finally, "sympathy for the old gentleman" moved the Kentuckian to take him on his own office staff for three months at one-third his committee pay.

Archaic is the word for the House's payroll and other data-processing operations. Paychecks (involving more than 2,000 pay rates, compared with no more than 200 in most Federal departments) are prepared on accounting machines so old that new House Clerk and former Congressman W. Pat Jennings is hard pressed to find spare parts. As one result, the House can meet its payroll only once a month; emergency part-time help was needed in February to hand-type employe tax-withholding forms.

"Payroll accounting, employe records, inventory controls, you name it . . . unless Congress adopts automatic data processing techniques very soon it's heading for a quagmire," asserts former Rep. Billie S. Farnum who, after four years as Michigan's auditor general, came to Congress for one term in 1965 and has remained in Washington on the Democratic National Committee staff.

Probably the major contributor to Capitol inefficiency is blurriness about who's responsible to whom for what. The House and Senate each elect three $26,000-a-year housekeeping supervisors: Clerk, doorkeeper and sergeant at arms. And each of their six loosely drawn domains intertwines with that of the $30,000 Capitol architect (a misnomer; he's chiefly a superintendent of buildings and grounds).

The $217 million budgeted for Capitol Hill operations in the year ahead includes uncoordinated fund requests from all these plus money for Congress' own $30,000 salaries, the independently run Congressional printing and postal operations, the Library of Congress and–biggest item of all–the lawmakers' office and committee staffs. House and Senate Appropriations Committees do go over the budgets. But over the past five years, in the process of lopping slightly more than three per cent (nearly $20 billion) from Presidential requests, they have trimmed less than one half of one per cent (under $3 million) from their own share.

Current Chairman George Andrews (D., Ala.) of the House Legislative Appropriations subcommittee enjoys recalling last year's skirmish over 70-cent hamburgers in the members-only dining room. But he shows scant concern that the two House Office Building cafeterias lose more than $200,000 yearly while those of nearly every Federal agency operate in the black.

Not only is there no chain of command among the chief housekeepers; it's not always clear whose direction they must follow. A 25-member Administration Committee nominally oversees the House work force. But some of its directives were openly spurned by Ralph Roberts during his 16 years as House Clerk (he was deposed in January).

To Mr. Roberts, the Administration Committee's 1964 decision to classify House employes by function and pay grade made no sense; according to committee sources, he blacklisted any worker seen giving information to the classifiers. The former clerk, for his part, accused them of malicious mischief in placing a House gymnasium masseur directly under him on the organization table. (Each side, of course, denies the other's charges.)

Because most functionaries are chiefly beholden to the Congressional delegations that picked them, staff supervisors have trouble bossing their work forces, too. The $25,000 job of House disbursing clerk, for instance, "belongs" to New York State Democrats. When this payroll management post last came open, according to one New Yorker, delegation leaders owed a favor to Erie County Democratic chiefs and invited them to pick a man. Their selection, Harry M. Livingston, had been doing maintenance work for the Buffalo Parks Department. While Mr. Livingston surprised skeptics by his determination, he incurred the wrath of Mr. Roberts, his nominal boss. Unable to replace him, Mr. Roberts assigned another man, at $22,000 a year, to run the payroll operation. (Now, with several more years' experience, Mr. Livingston is in charge again.)

The numerous straw bosses mostly maintain friendly relations. But their pursuit of harmony has prompted some astonishing deployments of the Capitol's non-union work force. To move serving tables from a Capitol storage area to a Senate Office Building reception room, a crew under the Senate sergeant at arms first hauls them to the mouth of a connecting tunnel. From there a Senate Office Building work team lugs them to the reception room. To set them up, a crew is called in from the Senate restaurant, which is under the Capitol architect's direction.

The pending Congressional reorganization bill attempts to sand down a number of these rough edges. Staff chiefs would be given clear authority to dismiss or reassign workers, or direct them to take training courses. There's also provision for a new office of personnel management to centralize hiring and record-keeping functions that now are dispersed; the House's tangled pay system would be greatly simplified.

Meantime, moving on his own, new House Clerk Jennings is also striving to simplify business operations. With counseling from former Rep. Farnum and others, he's in the market for modern data-processing gear. And there's been considerable personnel shuffling since he took over. "We found quite a few square pegs in round holes and vice versa, but I think we're getting them sorted out," he says.

Resorting little pegs is not the total answer, though. The foundations are also in need of realignment.

A Fail-Safe Line for Dissent

Robert Theobald

The Democratic convention [in 1968] transformed the political mask of America. The key issue is no longer peace in Vietnam but the acceptable limits of dissent. The visible threat is a police state: the basic question which all politicians must answer is the acceptable limits of force.

There can be no doubt that this transformation is widely welcomed. It is welcomed among the young because they feel that the events of Chicago, widely viewed on television, have radicalized much of the nation and given them the scope for massive dissent in the streets and the universities.

It is welcomed among reactionary politicians because they feel that they will win if disorder becomes massive and widespread.

But it is also clearly welcomed among many who do not fall into either of these two obvious categories. We can only understand this phenomenon when we realize the immense frustrations of living in a world of grays and half-tones and the desire of many to return to a simpler world.

The issue of law and order apparently provides the opportunity for simplistic rhetoric. Slogans such as, "We must make the streets safe for our women and children," can be met with "Dissenters have the right to make their views known regardless of their unpopularity." Both sides find it easy to reject the other as totally evil.

In addition, it seems as though the idea of a police state can be clearly visualized both from past experience and from the science-fiction nightmares of Orwell's *1984* when the communications media were totally controlled and the human race was brutalized. The liberal, as well as the radical, can feel a real sense of purpose as he fights against such desperate developments.

Unfortunately, however, for this desire to return to simplified analysis and simplified answers, the successful imposition of an Orwellian police state is impossible. I am not denying the ability of the state to control the media, nor am I denying our capacity to corrupt the human race although the views of the young throughout the world and the courage of the Czechoslovaks must give us hope.

But I am arguing that any continued thrust toward a police state would lead to the destruction of the world as we now know it. The most critical consequence of a police state today is not the limitation of individual freedom but the fact that it destroys any chance of intelligent policy development. The first casualty of any police state is the truth: not only for the public but for its leaders. Nobody is willing to provide a dictator, petty or great, with the truth if he fears that the dictator will not find it acceptable.

This article appeared in *The Los Angeles Times,* September 19, 1968. Reprinted by permission.

Without accurate movement of information, we cannot possibly create the new policies required as we move out of the industrial phase of the agricultural era into the cybernetic era. The process of socio-economic breakdown now so clearly evident will continue and intensify.

This process of breakdown due to failures in policy-making will become even more rapid as the radical fringe groups now so clearly evident increase in numbers and as their desperation over the situation intensifies.

The power of disruption available to a desperate fringe group in our complex society is phenomenal. It would be irresponsible to suggest what could be done: a consideration of just one widely suggested step—that of putting LSD or bacteria in the water supply—shows the vulnerability of our present system.

It has been argued that successful revolution is impossible in a modern society. But this half-truth has disguised a critical development: that desperate men now possess almost unlimited potential for disruption and destruction.

The real danger today is that our society will become ungovernable because of a breakdown in its culture and norms. We face the possibility of a total breakdown in moral authority which is necessary for government even in an apparent police state.

The United States has given up its moral authority in Vietnam: the Russians lost theirs in Czechoslovakia. The Catholic church gave up moral authority with the encyclical on birth control: the Protestant church has not possessed it for many decades. The Democratic and Republican parties confirmed in their conventions, each in its own way, the fact that they had lost their hold on their members.

Societies cannot be controlled by force alone. In the past the mystical bonds of religion and historical heritage bound nations together: so long as these norms were appropriate to actual conditions, the society survived. When they became inappropriate, the society collapsed.

Today, our challenge is even greater. There is no mystical or religious authority to whom most of us owe allegiance. We can only survive if we create for ourselves a set of norms which we are all prepared to respect.

This requires, of course, that we eliminate the conditions of powerlessness in which many citizens are trapped. It is not reasonable to expect people to consent to live in a society in which they are deprived of rights available to others.

The drive for law and order is only a symptom of our troubles, just as the war in Vietnam is only a symptom. If radicals, liberals and conservatives continue to neglect the hard task of imagining new social institutions which could work in the communications era we are now entering, they will reinforce the trend they profess to deplore.

We need new norms and new values, new structures and new symbologies. Until we achieve them both national and world orders will continue to fall apart: the interruption and disruption of free discussion and dialog will only hasten the process. There are no simple issues left. The human race must accept the full complexity of the world which it has, itself, created if we are to have any chance of survival.

Virus X and the Body Politic

Stewart Alsop

There is no more dismaying experience for a political writer than being confronted with an important political phenomenon he really doesn't understand. I had this experience on a Wednesday afternoon during Chicago's hell week.

That afternoon, wandering about Grant Park, I had heard a lot of youthful orators denounce "the pigs"–the Chicago police–and make much use of a four-letter transitive verb, in such brief declarative sentences as "(verb) Johnson," "(verb) Franklin D. Roosevelt," and even "(verb) America." But the whole scene–the grass, the mild weather, the oddly dressed, long-haired young men, the girls in their miniskirts and pressed hair–seemed pleasant and good-humored, rather like a huge picnic.

Then two young men rushed a flagpole beside a bandstand, and began hauling down the American flag. As the flag hit the dirt, the police charged, releasing canisters of tear gas, and bashing out blindly with their billy clubs.

There was nothing very puzzling about these events. The police obviously had orders not to allow the flag to be lowered, and the young men who were running the show obviously knew it. That was why the flag was lowered. The young men wanted a "confrontation"–meaning televised pictures of brutal cops beating up unarmed youngsters–and that was what they got.

As the flag was lowered, I looked around at the young people all around me. They were all cheering, or laughing, or smiling, with obvious pleasure. At this point I scribbled in my notebook, "generation of jerks." But this was merely an expression of the dismay and frustration of a middle-aged journalist, faced with a phenomenon he did not at all understand.

It is a major political phenomenon, for the emotion that produced those cheers, laughs and smiles has made possible the really remarkable achievements of the "New Left." The young self-styled "revolutionaries" who lead the New Left have clearly proved themselves far more effective revolutionaries than the Communists of the Old Left. To judge by what they write and say, there seems to be no basic ideological difference between the New Left and the Old Left. The real difference is one of style.

The New Left eschews both the turgid Marxist prose of the Old Left, and the rigid "party discipline"–meaning Soviet discipline–and these are two good reasons why the New Left is so much more effective. A more important reason is that it has captured the imagination of the young. An admirably succinct sentence which appeared in a New Left flyer in Chicago is typical of the style: "All power to the youth and (verb) capitalism."

The leaders of the New Left are perfectly

Mr. Alsop is one of the nation's leading political commentators. This article appeared in *Newsweek*, September 16, 1968, soon after the 1968 Democratic National Convention.

serious when they call themselves "revolutionaries." They candidly intend to use the proved techniques of "confrontation" and "disruption" to render the United States ungovernable, as the prelude to an American "war of national liberation." This sounds rather silly, until you consider what the New Left has already achieved in disrupting two great universities, for example, or in last year's march on the Pentagon—and above all, in Chicago.

Tom Hayden, a brilliant young leader of the New Left, defined the Chicago objective —that "this whole city be so disrupted it begins to charge around like a dog gone mad." That objective was fully achieved. It could not have been achieved—at least not so fully—without the enthusiastic cooperation of Mayor Daley's police. Enough of them behaved like mad dogs to play right into the hands of Tom Hayden and his friends.

But the objective could not have been achieved, either, without those kids who cheered when the flag was lowered. They were the New Left's cannon fodder—or billy-club fodder. One of Washington's most perspicacious columnists wrote that "those were our children in the streets of Chicago, and the cops beat them up." Surely these young people who hate American society and all its trappings enough to cheer when the flag is lowered, or when an orator cries "(verb) America," and enough also to risk broken heads to make Chicago "act like a mad dog," are a minority of "our children." But there are a lot of them, all the same, and this is the phenomenon that needs explaining.

The war in Vietnam has been the catalyst, of course—loathing for the war has been transformed into loathing for the American President, the American political system, even America itself. But the war cannot be the whole explanation—there have been unpopular wars before.

A kind of inverted idealism—a bitter disillusion with the humdrum grubbiness of life —is part of the explanation, but idealism in the young is no new thing. Neither is the "generational conflict"—the desire to put stupid old dad firmly in his place goes back to Oedipus Rex and beyond.

There are two genuinely new experiences to which the young have been exposed. One, of course, is television. It has been estimated that the average American child who reaches the age of 18 has passively watched a television screen for some 22,000 hours. So prolonged an exposure to inanity, gun-slinging violence, and the hard sell might be enough to drive a laboratory rat nutty. And there was a certain nuttiness in the air in Grant Park. "A lot of these white kids are just here for kicks," an amiable Negro protester remarked. The little screen's unreal kicks no doubt engender a hankering for such real-life kicks as flag-lowerings and even police charges.

Affluence—the fact that young, educated, white Americans really do not, for the first time, have to worry about making a living—is the other new experience. But a certain relationship between national wealth and national decay is not something new—*vide* the Roman Empire. As Oliver Goldsmith wrote: "Ill fares the land, to hastening ills a prey, where wealth accumulates, and men decay."

Yet there must also be something more—some political poison, some Virus X—which has caused this deep loathing for American society, and even for America itself, among many of the young. Perhaps Virus X is beyond the capacity of the middle-aged to understand, or the young to explain. But one thing seems certain. In time, Virus X will work greatly to strengthen, not the New Left, but the extreme right. In Chicago, for the first time in my life, it began to seem to me possible that some form of American Facism may really happen here.

Campus or Battleground? Robert Hessen

A larger-than-life portrait of Karl Marx dominated the entrance of a classroom building; a red flag flew from its rooftop. Chains barred the doors of other buildings, and chanting mobs roamed across the campus. The scene might have been the University of Havana or Peking. It wasn't. It took place just a few express stops from Wall Street, at Columbia University, where, from April 23–30 [1968], student leftists seized and occupied five university buildings.

The siege tactics which disrupted Columbia and brought its normal activities to a halt represent the latest assault by a revolutionary movement which aims to seize first the universities and then the industries of America. The rebels are members of Students for a Democratic Society (SDS), a nationwide organization with chapters on over 250 campuses.

Originally, when SDS began as an outgrowth of the socialist League for Industrial Democracy, it repudiated communism as an authoritarian system and excluded communists from its membership. However, in 1964–65, SDS sought to broaden its power base by forming a united front with communist youth groups. Although SDS continued to describe its objectives in such murky phrases as "participatory democracy," the real tenor of its philosophy can best be seen in its intellectual heroes, Marx and Mao; in its action hero, Che Guevara; and in its slogans scrawled across the embattled Columbia campus—"Lenin won, Castro won, and we will win, too!"

SDS' hard-core membership at Columbia is fewer than 200 out of 17,800 students. But after it seized campus buildings, barred faculty and students from their offices and classrooms, and held a dean as hostage, its ranks were swelled by several hundred sympathizers, including many outsiders. SDS launched its assault on Columbia after failing peacefully to attain two of its political objectives on campus:

1) The severing of Columbia's connection with the Institute for Defense Analyses, a government-sponsored consortium which performs research and analysis relating to national defense and domestic riot control. SDS complained that Columbia's affiliation was aiding America's "imperialist aggression" in Vietnam, while at home I.D.A.'s studies in riot control were designed to suppress demonstrations by antiwar groups.

2) A halt to the construction of a new gymnasium in Morningside Park, which adjoins Harlem, on land leased to Columbia by the City of New York.

SDS claimed that Columbia was guilty of "institutional racism," that the university was poaching upon the territory of the adjacent

Mr. Hessen is an instructor at Columbia University. This article appeared in *The National Observer,* May 27, 1968. Reprinted by permission.

Negro community, and that the separate entrance for the part of the gym set aside for use by the neighborhood children constituted "Gym Crow."

In fact, the Columbia gymnasium had been warmly endorsed by over 40 Harlem community groups when it was announced eight years ago. It would occupy only two of the 30 acres in Morningside Park. Its presence would create an atmosphere of safety in an area which is now the territory of muggers and addicts. Separate entrances would be necessary because Columbia students would enter from the Heights on which the university is located, while Harlem residents would more conveniently reach the gym through the park which lies some 200 feet below. The issue is not one of bigotry but of geography.

SDS spokesmen claimed, truthfully, that they had sought to arouse the Columbia community into opposing the gym and the I.D.A. links. They admit that their campaign was a failure, which they ascribe to student and faculty apathy, and to the administration's refusal to hear and to heed their policy recommendations.

SDS rebels then resorted to their ultimate political weapon: the initiation of physical force, believing that they had a moral right to do so because they were "acting in a good cause." In the past, they had released many trial balloons to test this technique: they had obstructed N.R.O.T.C. graduation ceremonies; they had staged sit-ins in the offices of university administrators; and they had prevented recruiters for business firms and the C.I.A. from interviewing on campus. In each case, the consequence had been a polite rap on the knuckles, a verbal reprimand devoid of significant penalties such as expulsion or criminal prosecution.

On April 23, after trying to block construction at the gym site, SDS demonstrators and their militant Negro allies, members of the Student Afro-American Society, returned to campus. At the urging of their leaders, they marched on Hamilton Hall, the main classroom building of Columbia College. They were determined to barricade themselves in until the university met their demands. An unexpected fissure occurred within the ranks of the rebels who claimed to be united in their opposition to racism: the Negro militants ordered the whites to get out, and SDS complied. SDS then proceeded to capture a base of operation of its own. The rebels first seized the administrative offices of President Grayson Kirk in Low Library, and later three more classroom buildings.

Most students reacted with bewilderment and outrage. They demanded to know why the campus police had not been called in, and why the rebels were allowed to receive reinforcements of manpower and food. They witnessed caravans of litter-bearers marching across campus with cartons of supplies, as if their destination were a country picnic. Many students also wondered why the administration had not ordered the cutting off of electricity, water and telephones inside the buildings held by the rebels, since it was known that they were making Xerox copies of President Kirk's letter files and formulating strategy with outside allies by phone.

The administration's failure to take prompt action evidently sprang from a number of motives: fear of bad publicity; uncertainty about the morality of using the police to uphold law and order; reluctance to make a decision which might prove unpopular with some of the faculty, students or alumni; anxiety that members of the Harlem community might march on Columbia if police were used to clear the buildings; and the delusion that if they took no punitive action, the rebels would recognize them as men of good will. An SDS leader later admitted that if President Kirk had responded within the first hour, or even the first day, by sending in the university's own security police, the rebels would have "folded like a house of cards." By its inaction, the administration gave the rebels time to organize their resistance, bolster their morale and mobilize sympathizers and supplies from the outside.

Members of the senior faculty attempted to mediate between the administration and the rebels. But their efforts were futile, since they were faced with an impossible assignment: to devise a peace formula ambiguous enough to satisfy both sides—which meant that the terms of settlement had to both promise and refuse amnesty for the rebels. The faculty mediators labored under the belief that the rebels would be willing to negotiate for a peaceful solution to the mounting crisis. What they discovered, however, was that every concession made by the administration only produced escalated rebel demands. SDS' ultimate demand was that they be granted total amnesty as a pre-condition for negotiation.

It grew increasingly obvious that the rebels would not withdraw from the buildings until forced out by the police. They wanted blood to be shed, so that they could raise the cry of "police brutality," acquire the aura of martyrdom, and thereby win the majority of students and faculty to their side. Regrettably, President Kirk played right into their hands, by waiting until the sixth day of siege before calling in the police. The only other alternative open to him at that point would have been total capitulation, a final act of appeasement which would have served as an engraved invitation to renewed rebel demands in the future. The proper time to have acted against the rebels was at the outset of the siege, when a few dozen campus security officers could have achieved what it later took nearly 1,000 city police to do, at a price of over 100 injured rebels, spectators and policemen.

The aftermath of calling in the police was an upsurge of sympathy for the rebels. Their allies on campus called for a general strike by students and faculty to protest the use of police and to demand the ouster of President Kirk for having called them in. One mark of the effectiveness of this strike is that Columbia College, the undergraduate division of the university, voted to end all classes for the rest of the semester, which was scheduled to run another month. The strikers also won support from those who disapproved of both the tactics and objectives of SDS, but who wished to take advantage of the strike to bring about what is cryptically described as "restructuring of the university."

Even those most sympathetic to SDS, however, do not deny that the issues of I.D.A. and the gym were merely pretexts to justify the resort to force. SDS' short-range objective is to achieve "student power," which means total control over the university. They seek student veto power over appointment and tenure of faculty, admission of new students, courses offered by the university, degree requirements and the disposition of university funds. They propose to "radicalize the faculty," which means to purge it of conservatives and of law-and-order liberals who oppose the initiation of force to achieve political ends. As befits socialists, they regard the university as just another natural resource awaiting their expropriation.

But the long-range objective of SDS is even more sinister. As a sympathetic article in The New Republic (May 11, 1968) states: "The point of the game was power. And in the broadest sense, to the most radical members of the SDS Steering Committee, Columbia itself was not the issue. It was revolution, and if it could be shown that a great university could literally be taken over in a matter of days by a well-organized group of students, then no university was secure. Everywhere the purpose was to destroy institutions of the American Establishment, in the hope that out of the chaos a better America would emerge."

The rebels have no patience for any slow process of change. They are tired of "just talk"—they want "action now." They will tolerate no opposition. They are indifferent to the fact that their tactics will destroy Columbia University by driving out the best minds, just as Nazi terror tactics drove the Jewish intellectuals out of the universities of Germany. But there is a crucial difference now. While men like Einstein could escape to England or America during the 'Thirties, SDS will try to close all avenues of escape. The use of intimidation and force will spread until there will be no sanctuary for men of reason within the academic world, or, ultimately, within the nation. One need only consider the fate of conservatives and liberals alike in countries which have been overrun by SDS' intellectual mentors: Mao's China and Castro's Cuba.

Since SDS tactics have succeeded in crippling a great university, the next targets can be City Hall, the State Capitol, or even the White House. If this prediction seems alarmist, consider the fact that SDS sympathizers known as "Yippies" already have announced plans to intimidate and disrupt the Democratic National Convention in Chicago this summer, in order to extract concessions on platform and candidates.

Whatever the final outcome of the Columbia strike, one thing is certain: the methods used at Columbia will be embraced by other student leftists on campuses throughout the country. Those who resort to force will justify their tactics by the same arguments advanced by the Columbia rebels and their apologists. If this national menace is to be checked, it is imperative that one know how to answer them.

1) Some rebels claim that none of their tactics involved the use of force. This was true only in the narrow sense that they did not shed blood. But force was inextricably involved in every act that they perpetrated. They held the Associate Dean as hostage against his will—that was force. They barricaded faculty and students from their offices and classrooms—that was force. They seized property which was not rightfully theirs and refused to release it until their demands were met—that was force. Each of these is punished as an act of force under the civil laws of our society. They are the crimes known as false imprisonment, criminal trespass and extortion.

If these acts were perpetrated by a lone individual, their criminal character would be obvious. If a single felon had held the dean hostage, or seized the office of President Kirk, rifled his desk and copied his files, no one would have confused him with an idealistic, "committed" crusader. On an individual basis, if someone demands that you grant him wealth or power that he has not earned and which he can only obtain by threats of violence, one does not doubt for a moment that he is an extortionist. The act of a lone thug does not become legitimatized when he teams up with other hoodlums. As Ayn Rand noted in "Capitalism: the Unknown Ideal," no individual can acquire rights by joining a gang. "Rights are not a matter of numbers —and there can be no such thing, in law or in morality, as actions forbidden to an individual, but permitted to a mob."

2) Other rebels admit that they used force, but claim that force is justified when peaceful tactics fail. The fundamental political principle that all men must respect is that no individual or group may initiate the use of force for any purpose whatsoever. To accept SDS' alternative amounts to carte blanche for violence, and invites the complete breakdown of the rule of law.

To understand the grotesque irrationality of SDS' argument, consider the following. Imagine that there were a student chapter at Columbia of the Ku Klux Klan, which was protesting the proposed use of the new gym by Negroes. They tried, through campus rallies and petitions, to arouse the students, faculty and administration to support their demands, but their peaceful tactics failed. If this group then proceeded to seize university buildings and hold members of the administration as hostages, would anyone have condoned their use of force, or have called for negotiations and compromise? The principle is the same: the initiation of force to achieve one's political objectives is both immoral and illegal, regardless of whether the initials of the aggressors are KKK or SDS.

3) The rebels claim they were justified in using force because the administration had refused to give them a hearing on their demands for change. A university, like a well-run business, should be interested in knowing whether it is satisfying its customers. If it provides students with incompetent faculty, or poor laboratories or libraries, or supports political policies which they oppose, it is in the university's self-interest to maintain open channels of communication so that grievances can be expressed and remedial actions considered. Students who are dissatisfied with any aspect of a university's policies have a right to peacefully protest and petition, and even, in extreme situations, to boycott classes or organize a student strike.

Five Myths About Modern Politics

Stephen Hess

Since presidential nominating conventions were invented in 1831 there have been only 66 major party nominations for President, hardly a very large sampling. Yet every fourth year, just as the delegates head for the exits, politician-watchers rush into print with a new set of generalizations. Recent events, however, have pushed over into the category of myth some of these well-worn shibboleths.

First: The Myth of the Favorite Son

". . . When a favorite son enters a presidential primary in his own state, he is generally given a free ride; out-of-state candidates usually steer clear. Ex-Sen. William Knowland, a man who once had presidential aspirations, summed it up accurately when he said: 'It is always a dangerous maneuver to enter a state where there is a favorite-son candidate . . . Ordinarily one avoids a contest in a candidate's home state, partly out of courtesy and partly out of risk of defeat.' For this reason, as a strategy to slow down the front-runner, lagging candidates try to promote favorite-son candidacies in states that hold primaries."

This assessment of the favorite son is from a study called *Hats in the Ring,* which I wrote with Malcolm Moos, and which appeared in April, 1960.

Yet virtually as our words arrived in the book stores they were being disproved by John F. Kennedy, who was then out-maneuvering two favorite son governors, Pat Brown of California and Mike Di Salle of Ohio, and defeating Sen. Wayne Morse, another favorite son, in the Oregon primary. In both California and Ohio Sen. Kennedy's threat of a contested primary proved sufficient to force the governors to come to terms.

In retrospect, the bloodless capitulation of Brown and Di Salle may well have been the better part of wisdom—at least judging from the experiences of the favorite sons this year. Massachusetts Gov. John Volpe lost his state's presidential primary to write-in candidate Nelson Rockefeller and Gov. Roger Branigin received a mere 31% of the Indiana primary vote in a three-way contest with Robert Kennedy and Eugene McCarthy.

The lesson seems to be that the parties' rank-and-file, when it is given a direct voice in delegate selection through the primaries, is no longer in a mood to put up with ersatz candidates. Even in the states where delegates are chosen by convention, the serious presidential candidates have considerable leverage over potential favorite sons.

Thus the presidential candidates who base

Mr. Hess is Deputy Assistant to President Nixon on Urban Affairs. This article appeared in *The Los Angeles Times,* July 24, 1968.

their strategy on the political clout of favorite sons are leaning for support on exceedingly thin reeds.

Second: The Myth of the Invincible Incumbent

Another truism of American politics is that an incumbent President can have renomination and probably re-election if he so desires. Just two 19th-century Presidents, Franklin Pierce and Chester Arthur, have been denied renomination, and, in this century, only those luckless Presidents William Howard Taft and Herbert Hoover have been rejected in the general elections.

President Johnson's decision not to seek another term, in itself, is not powerful proof that incumbent invincibility is a myth, but clearly his loss of popularity was a potent factor in his declination of candidacy.

However, there are other signs—on other levels of government—to support the conclusion that chief executives are in for increasingly harder times.

Examining the municipal elections of 1967, it is difficult to find a surviving incumbent. In Cleveland and Gary mayors were defeated in primaries; in Baltimore and Boston incumbents chose to retire in the face of near-certain defeat, although both were first-rate men.

The reason for this is not just demographic. It is also the result of the voters' sense of frustration brought on by the complexities of urban life at home and a long, grinding land war on the continent of Asia.

If the electorate continues to lash out at the "ins" (no matter how competent they may be), we are apt to be entering a period of one-term chief executives on all levels of government, including the highest.

(Parenthetically, although the reasons for this trend may be muddleheaded, the end result could be advantageous since the life cycle of multi-term administrations shows that they generally do their most creative work during the early years and are likely to exhibit signs of fatigue as the burdens of governing are extended.)

Third: The Myth of the Front-Runner as Sitting Duck

This myth is best stated by Prof. James W. Davis in his very good book about presidential primaries, *Springboard to the White House*. He writes:

"In American politics, when a presidential aspirant announces his candidacy, he becomes a conspicuous target for all of his opponents; and, if he participates in the presidential primaries, he runs the risk of being knocked out of the race or being badly mauled. The unannounced candidate, meanwhile, can sit on the sidelines, avoid the gruelling primary races, and hope that the front-runners become deadlocked or falter."

Yet in recent presidential nominations the prize has most often gone to the front-runner. After 1924, when the Democrats emerged from a 103-ballot deadlock to nominate John W. Davis, our major parties have only twice chosen late-bloomers (Willkie in 1940 and Stevenson in 1952). Generally the conventions have picked men who start early, organize thoroughly, and have the longest exposure to the electorate.

This does not mean that there are no longer any pitfalls in being a front-runner, but rather that the risks of being a shrinking violet are far greater—namely, that by the time a potential candidate's shyness wears off the nomination will be all locked up for someone else.

The reasons for this primarily have to do with the enormous breadth of the nominating process today. It simply takes a great deal of manpower and money to effectively run for President.

Which brings us to the next myth.

Fourth: The Myth That Only Rich Men Can Run for President

Will Rogers observed that politics has "got

so expensive it takes a lot of money even to get beat with."

It is estimated that Rockefeller and Goldwater each spent between $5 million and $6 million in their struggle for the 1964 Republican nomination, and, it seems likely Rockefeller and Nixon are spending in the same magnitude this year.

Great wealth, of course, gives a candidate considerable maneuverability. It is difficult to imagine that Rockefeller could have reentered the presidential race on April 30 after his public departure on March 21 without his having the ability to finance his own campaign.

Still, three of the four major party contenders today are men of relatively modest means and are all running well-heeled campaigns. Sen. McCarthy, so the newspapers report, raised $900,000 in 30 minutes at a New York City rally.

While the sums needed to win the presidency are truly phenomenal, so too is this nation's apparent willingness to pay the price. The old saying, "Whether rich or poor it's nice to have money," applies equally to politicians. But today any viable candidate (such as Nixon or Humphrey) or a major candidate with a unique ideological stance (such as McCarthy or Wallace) can raise enough money to adequately make his case.

The Goldwater nomination proved it was possible to raise sufficient funds without a Wall Street base; and Goldwater's general election campaign, from a fund-raising viewpoint, was an even greater departure. Harnessing modern TV and direct-mail techniques, his organization was able to fill its war chest with small contributions, and even ended the campaign with a surplus.

Considerable attention has been paid in recent years to ways of relieving the financial strain of running for President and high federal office. In my opinion, this is a very low priority item. The higher the office, the easier it is to raise money. If attention is needed in this area, it is in finding ways to help those who wish to run for the state legislature or municipal council—jobs of little glamor or visibility that usually take time and attention out of all proportion to the salaries or the ability to raise campaign funds.

Fifth: The Myth of the New Technology

In recent years a number of political writers, myself included, have reported on the wonders of the New Technology in American politics and of the changes that it will bring in our election system.

By New Technology we mean the increasing use and sophistication of public opinion polling; the employment of computers, not just in clerical operations, but also to stimulate campaign strategies; other advanced management techniques borrowed from the business world, such as the Critical Path Method, which can be used to schedule events or a candidate's time; and the rise and proliferation of the professional political management firms.

Yet how new is the New Technology?

For contrast, it may be instructive to examine the work of an Old Technician—Marcus Alonzo Hanna.

In 1896, when Mark Hanna managed the presidential campaign of William McKinley, he too used public opinion surveys, polling key states in the Middle West again and again to determine change in voter sentiment; he too instituted the most efficient systems of office management, such as competitive bidding, central purchasing, and strict audits; he too divided the electorate into voting blocs, just as a simulator does, setting up divisions within his Republican National Committee for women (although they only had the right to vote in Colorado, Wyoming, and Utah), Germans, Negroes, even travelling salesmen and bicyclists; he too carefully tailored his media campaign, turning out 200 million pieces of literature in 12 languages besides English (an average of 14 for each voter).

I think we have oversold ourselves on how

revolutionary is the so-called New Technology. Useful refinements, yes. Clever adaptations, yes. But I am now struck by the continuity rather than the radical changes in American campaign techniques.

Neither the tools nor the tempo leads me to believe that the future nature of politicking in the United States will be basically different from what our fathers and grandfathers knew.

Chapter 3

HUMAN BEHAVIOR

Every schoolboy has heard of the Industrial Revolution and knows at least that it changed the world from the slow-moving, rural-oriented, agricultural life of a thousand generations to today's city-oriented, jet-propelled society in which it is possible for a 10-year-old boy to know more about the world around him than Charlemagne or Richard the Lion Hearted ever knew in their own times. It has created an economic system that produces goods that have given the average U.S. citizen comfort greater than any enjoyed by kings in the past.

In this cocoon of affluence and comfort, one major factor has remained the same—man himself. He is still at war, but he now has more efficient weapons for killing than ever before. He is still dying of starvation in spite of his vast knowledge of agriculture and nutrition. He can still be excited by beauty, even while he is systematically destroying his environment. His knowledge is great enough for him to explore the oceans and travel to the moon, but he knows almost nothing about himself.

The suicide rate continues to climb. The divorce rate has shown a steady rise for years, and one out of every four marriages now ends in divorce. At least an equal number of unsatisfactory marriages endure for convenience or economic reasons. Each year the crime rate rises, the venereal disease rate continues to go up, and so does the number of illegitimate births. Judging from these developments, man seems to be profoundly dissatisfied with himself, his family, his community, and the world.

Our old attitudes do not always fit our new social environment. We must make new evaluations of our basic beliefs. Young people in particular have discovered that traditional religious and moral values do not always provide a satisfactory basis for their lives. In our churches, our government and our homes, there is sharp disagreement on what used to be called fundamental values. In the last third of this century we must come to terms with this human revolution.

In this chapter we have tried to touch upon the most controversial and explosive subjects. What is our national moral climate ("Anything Goes")? What about birth control? How necessary is it? Is there really a "population bomb" or has the Pill solved our population problem ("No More Population Explosion for the U.S.?")? What about marriage? Who should marry and why ("Growing Toll of America's Broken Homes")? How does religion view these problems ("Catholic Church and Birth Control")? What about science and its potential ability to control our heredity, our genes and our chromosomes ("Will Man Direct His Own Evolution?")? Is it something we really want? Is mankind facing these problems for the first time in his existence? How important are they? To conclude this chapter, we offer an interview with Margaret Mead, who has some striking observations on contemporary morals ("We Must Learn To See What's Really New").

Anything Goes: Taboos in Twilight Newsweek

The old taboos are dead or dying. A new, more permissive society is taking shape. Its outlines are etched most prominently in the arts–in the increasing nudity and frankness of today's films, in the blunt, often obscene language seemingly endemic in American novels and plays, in the candid lyrics of pop songs and the undress of the avant-garde ballet, in erotic art and television talk shows, in freer fashions and franker advertising. And, behind this expanding permissiveness in the arts stands a society in transition, a society that has lost its consensus on such crucial issues as premarital sex and clerical celibacy, marriage, birth control and sex education; a society that cannot agree on standards of conduct, language and manners, on what can be seen and heard.

While artists and writers hail this new candor as a release from an era of Victorian repression and hypocrisy, many Americans are bewildered and concerned about the swiftness with which all the old restraints are losing their force. Mores are changing so fast, in fact, that the biting, bitchy language of "Who's Afraid of Virginia Woolf?", which caused Hollywood to rewrite its Production Code only eighteen months ago, today sounds surprisingly tame. " 'Virginia Woolf' is vanilla compared to the film version of 'Ulysses'," says Jack Valenti, president of the Motion Picture Association of America, who has helped to modernize a Hollywood Production Code that is already obsolete. "Films can't live in a vacuum. They relate to the temper of the times, the postures of today."

These new postures alarm many citizens, psychologists and social thinkers who see in this rapid destruction of taboos a dangerous swing toward irresponsible hedonism and, ultimately, social decay. "It is the inevitable mark of decadence in our society," says British social commentator Malcolm Muggeridge. "As our vitality ebbs, people reach out for vicarious excitement, like the current sex mania in pop songs and the popular press. At the decline and fall of the Roman Empire, the works of Sappho, Catullus and Ovid were celebrated. There is an analogy in that for us."

There are others, however, who reject the notion that the new permissiveness is a sign of moral collapse. "We are just beginning to discover what morality is all about," says theater critic Kenneth Tynan. "It is concerned with how we behave toward each other, not how much of our bodies we happen to display. There will be no return to the horse and buggy or to full-length skirts."

Change. Indeed, the revolution in manners and morals that has produced a climate of candor is very real and unlikely to reverse

This article appeared in *Newsweek*, November 13, 1967. Condensed in the March, 1968, *Reader's Digest*.

itself. "We're going to have to live with a degree of freedom much greater than anything we've known in the past," says Father Walter J. Ong, the brilliant Jesuit theologian and author of "The Presence of the Word." "Man can't just say anything goes and hope to get by. We're going to have to employ our minds and morals in determining that some things go and other things don't. We're going to have to constantly reassess the situation because the situation will always be changing."

It has changed more dramatically in the past year than in the preceding 50. The teenage narrator of Norman Mailer's "Why Are We in Vietnam?" peppers the reader with a stream of profanity unparalleled in American letters. On stage in "The Beard," Billy the Kid and Jean Harlow assault each other with salvos of four-letter words, then end their sexual duel in an explicit act of oral intercourse. In "Scuba Duba," playwright Bruce Jay Friedman unleashes a bare-breasted floozie before sellout crowds. In "America Hurrah," giant dolls copulate onstage. And at Joseph Papp's exciting new theater, teenagers in a musical called "Hair" sing gutter profanity with the cherubic straightforwardness of choir boys.

Across the U.S., audiences pack art houses and neighborhood theaters to watch the multiple orgasms of a seldom-clothed young Swedish actress in "I, a Woman." Italian director Antonioni breaks the taboo against head-on, total nudity in "Blow-Up," and Hollywood, in important films like "In the Heat of the Night" and "Bonnie and Clyde," shows its starlets bare to the waist.

Glossily mounted films such as "The Born Losers" and "The Penthouse" use excellent acting and shock techniques to reflect the violence and sex fever of the front pages. Gentle, white-haired old Spencer Tracy, in his last movie, "Guess Who's Coming to Dinner?" dismisses bigots with a terse "screw all those people." Alec Guinness, in "The Comedians," asks Richard Burton about Elizabeth Taylor: "You mean she's a good lay?" "Portrait of Jason," a remarkable voyage into the twisted soul of a black male prostitute, compresses into less than two hours all the raw language and candid corners of life that today find free expression in almost every independent U.S. film. And, in "Barbarella," a film built around the endless seductions of a French comicstrip heroine, Jane Fonda hops from one nude scene to the next in celebration of the erotic life.

Best-selling literature, once reluctantly discreet, is open and explicit about everything in the sexual spectrum from incest to inversion. "Valley of the Dolls," "The Adventurers" and "The Exhibitionist" use language once reserved to green-jacketed books smuggled in from Paris. And these books—the works of Henry Miller and the Marquis de Sade, "My Secret Life," "The Traveller's Companion Series" and "Story of O"—today bring what used to be called hard-core pornography to the paperback rack at the corner drug store. Even the intellectual press in Britain and the U.S., including mass-circulation magazines like Playboy and Esquire, has been forced, in reporting the events of the day, to use language once only read on privy walls.

Off. In pop music, the Rolling Stones sing "Let's Spend the Night Together" while fans wear buttons reading "Let's Lock Loins." TV viewers have seen David Susskind talking frankly with homosexuals, as well as wine and shaving-cream commercials chanting: "Had any lately?" or "Take it off, take it all off." Dance companies from Africa and San Francisco perform naked in New York. Erotic-art shows draw enormous crowds. Skirts escalate past knees and thighs. Make-up is designed specifically to stay on in bed. "We're living in a Babylonian society perhaps more Babylonian than Babylon itself," says historian and columnist Max Lerner. "It's what's called a late sensate period. The emphasis in our society today is on the senses and the release of the sensual. All the old codes have been broken down."

This new freedom of expression is unlikely to reverse itself because the forces that have produced it are a permanent and irresistible part of modern life. The history of the arts itself has been a constant assault on forms and conventions to get at the essence of man and explore the deepest regions of his mind, spirit—and body. When James Joyce unlocked Molly Bloom's earthy, human, profane subconscious, he opened a Pandora's box that has become the common property of today's novelists and filmmakers, artists, potboilers and pornographers.

"What was once the realm of private knowledge has become public knowledge," says Father John M. Culkin, director of communications at Fordham and a disciple of media-master Marshall McLuhan. "Perhaps there's too much honesty but there's no doubt that these things have become part of the public domain." And this articulation of the inner self and man's own sexuality is not limited to artists alone. Today, the concepts and language pioneered by Freud are openly used in the discussion of sexual problems. "Freud showed us we were not alone," says Father Ong. "We feel so close to one another that nobody has any secrets any more."

This common admission of sexuality ultimately finds expression in franker sex-education courses in the Anaheim, Calif., and Evanston, Ill., school systems, in which grade-school children are encouraged to bring the whispered words of the playground into the classroom for open discussion. It permits the creation of special high schools for pregnant girls in San Francisco and New York. It enables both clerics and laymen within the Roman Catholic Church to challenge pastoral policy on celibacy and birth control. It even permits the manufacture of baby-boy dolls equipped with sex organs.

Appetites. The climate of candor in America today is not, however, simply a matter of art and expression pushing forward to the applause of an increasingly tolerant public. There have always been writers like Havelock Ellis and D. H. Lawrence willing to talk frankly and an audience willing to listen. But, until recently, agencies of moral order like the church, the government, the family and the community have dictated what can and cannot be expressed in public. Since World War II, in America, however, these institutions have simply been overrun by the demands of a mass society that wants to see and hear everything.

Nowhere has this process been more graphically dramatized than in the erosion of film censorship. In the 1930s fear of government regulation drove Hollywood to create its own Production Code, which forbade a husband and wife to be shown in the same bed and banned the word buzzard because it sounded too much like bastard. The Roman Catholic Church also controlled film content through its Legion of Decency, whose "C" or "condemned" rating could bar a movie from hundreds of theaters fearful of local boycott.

After the second world war, however, both code and church censorship started to crack. In 1946, Howard Hughes released "The Outlaw" in the face of a "C" rating and culled a fortune on the strength of Jane Russell's titanic cleavage. Seven years later, when both the Legion and Hollywood refused to sanction "The Moon Is Blue" because of the word "virgin," producer Otto Preminger released it anyway and was amply reimbursed by the public. Again, in 1956, Preminger defied the code and its taboo on dope addiction when he released "The Man With the Golden Arm."

Feeble. Since then, the code has been revised twice, and the Legion of Decency has changed its name to the National Catholic Office for Motion Pictures and has liberalized its judgments. But the power of both agencies is now feeble. Already this year five major films have ignored a "C" rating, among them "Blow-Up," "Reflections in a Golden Eye," and Preminger's "Hurry Sundown." "As far as I'm concerned the public makes up its own mind," says the 73-year-old chief executor of the Production Code, Geoffrey Shurlock. "America has in time grown up to accept sex. All the taboos are beginning to break down, which is probably the most healthy thing that could happen." Adds Fordham's Father Culkin: "Now the media goes directly to the public. The moralizers got so out of touch, they shouted for so long, that after a while nobody listened."

The courts, the last official restraining arm of society, have developed in recent cases such fluid guidelines for obscenity that local police agencies can seize and prosecute only those films and books that are "utterly without socially redeeming value." "Censorship of films and books has become simply a matter of taste," says veteran lawyer Ephraim London, an expert on censorship who has argued a number of key cases before the Supreme Court. "Today there's absolutely nothing you can't show or write about if it's done in good taste, absolutely nothing. If the courts judge something obscene, they are in effect making an aesthetic rather than a moral judgment. If the censorship rules of 1950 were in effect today, two out of every three films shown now would be banned." Even many of the tasteless hard-core paperbacks which could, under the law, be seized are more often than not ignored by district attorneys who feel no real pressure to do so from the community.

Not only has the mass society acquired the muscle, or perhaps more accurately, the money, to get what it wants, but what it wants has changed as well, under the pressure applied by a whole new generation of young people. As Keith Richard, 23-year-old guitarist with the Rolling Stones, proclaims: "We are not old men. We are not worried about petty morals." What the new generation wants is not simply bigger breasts and sexier scenes on wider screens. "They want to strip away all the sham and all the cant of their elders and to strive instead for truth and honesty," says TV impresario David Susskind. "This revolution has been made by young people and nothing will thwart it for the simple reason that truth will out. 'Tell it to me, baby. Tell it the way it really is.' These are the battle cries of the young."

Fashion designer Mary Quant, mother of the miniskirt, tells it as it is, or at least the way she sees it: "Am I the only woman who has ever wanted to go to bed with a man in the afternoon? Any law-abiding female, it used to be thought, waits until dark. Well, there are lots of girls who don't want to wait. Mini-clothes are symbolic of them. So are cosmetics that seem natural and stay on right into bed and out again, because that's the point. All this decoration is put on in order to seduce a man to bed, so what's the sense of taking it all off?"

Metaphor. The shattering of taboos on language, fashion and manners generally is part of a larger disintegration of moral consensus in America. Vast numbers of Americans distrust their government. Catholics in increasing numbers simply ignore the church ban on birth control. The family has changed from a breeding ground of common values into a battleground of generations. These dislocations have moved many writers to reach for the strongest language in their arsenal to capture the chaos of their time. "We're in a time that's divorced from the past," says novelist Norman Mailer. "There's utterly no tradition anymore. It's a time when our nervous systems are being remade. There's an extraordinary amount of obscenity around—and it's in my new book. I had to write it that way despite the fact that I hate to add to all that obscenity." But such language, insists Mailer, "is the only metaphor to express the situation that produces Vietnam."

Things have changed radically since Mailer, in "The Naked and the Dead," had to invent the word "fug" to evoke the raw language of the American soldier in World War II. Today Mailer, Hubert Selby, and a whole school of new young novelists use obscenity not merely as an imitation of street speech but as an antidote to their own outrage and frustration at what they feel is the increasing dehumanization of the high-technology industrial state. "The real choice we have is not between dirty and not dirty," says Mailer. "It is between the creative artist, with his more or less corrupt soul, explaining life with his instinctive and curious gift for language, and the scientist, with his more or less corrupt soul, explaining life with his lenses, galvanometers and probes."

Mammal. Obscenity and nudity and eroticism, then, have become prime weapons for the artist as humanizer. He uses them to remind man that, amidst his electrical appliances and armaments and credit cards and daily costumes, he remains Homo sapiens. "Why don't we stop pretending that we're not mammals and that we don't do the things mammals do?" asks poet-playwright Michael McClure, author of "The Beard." "There's nothing new about my play. It could have been done 2,000 years ago." Man as mammal, sexual, innocent, is the theme of today's erotic painters who use nudity to affirm life.

"The nudity in all these things is very pure," explains 39-year-old Wynn Chamberlain, who paints his friends in open, smiling, superhygienic nudity. "There's been a great confusion in the public mind between prurient art and nude art. I never thought of my art as prurient—rather as subversive, wanting to shake up the world, to get people to loosen up and relax." Adds Robert Rosinek, 31, who turns the sex act into an aesthetic matching of pure colors and forms: "I've taken sex back to the Garden of Eden. Sex shouldn't be this commercial, mechanical, jaded thing. I use the canvas as I use an empty bed. I try to create something beautiful in both."

Costume. In much the same spirit, the dancers of Ann Halprin's Dancers' Workshop in San Francisco create nude ballets designed to help liberate their emotions and conquer the audience's fear of the human body. "The human body is just another costume," says Mrs. Halprin. "Nudity is just part of a new way of being able to express feelings." This, in a sense, is the feeling of most artists, that nudity and sexuality must be faced and accepted by society as part of a general confrontation of life. Once the artist has created this mature audience, he can move on to more important matters. "You have to get to the point where people aren't shocked any more," says Ed Sanders, underground editor and lead singer with The Fugs, a scatological rock group. "It's not being jaded—it's when people know sex is not a threat to them and they accept it."

For Terry Southern, black-humorist, author of "Candy" and the screenwriter of "Barbarella," at least part of the battle is already over. "If you're writing about longshoremen," he says, "you can finally put down how they really talk and get it published. It's a nice thing to have over with, a kind of purging. Now a writer doesn't have to use those words again. He might, but he doesn't *have* to. As long as the old taboos existed, you felt you had to use them or you'd be selling out. It was all a big drag."

Inevitably, freedom of expression in an open society is as accessible to the smutmaster as to the serious artist. If the new candor has strengthened the writing of America's best novelists, it has merely polluted the pulp literature that sells to millions. Many best sellers simply pander perversions and profanity for profit. "These books aren't written, they're manufactured by formula," says Bennett Cerf, head of Random House and a pioneer in the publication of "Ulysses." "They set up a list of perversions and throw them in at 30-page intervals."

Gasp. The purveyors of this soft-core pornography legitimize their ventures with the same rationale used by serious artists: that they are breaking the bonds of puritan society and helping America to grow up. "Bernard Geis Associates is working toward a better, healthier, saner society," says Bernard Geis, publisher of "Valley of the Dolls," which chronicled the sexual aberrations of show-business figures, and "The Exhibitionist," just released, which salivates over the unhappy sex life of a Hollywood starlet. "We are working toward the last gasp. We will publish a book that will make the public gasp for the last time. When we do, we will have reached a more adult civilization." But, says David Slavitt, a poet and former *Newsweek* film critic who wrote "The Exhibitionist" under the nom de plume of Henry Sutton: "If pure pornography sold as well as the stuff I'm writing, Mr. Geis would sell pornography. After all, he's a businessman."

So is Radley Metzger, whose early career as a "serious" filmmaker left him broke until he formed Audubon Films, which makes and distributes "exploitation" movies all over the world. He has already grossed $1.5 million as the distributor of "I, a Woman," and will make more from his own "Carmen, Baby," a glossy but tawdry version of Mérimée in modern undress. Metzger's defense of the exploitation film is nothing if not logical: "If people think there is too much eroticism in motion pictures, what brought them there in the first place?" Metzger has found, as did Playboy publisher Hugh Hefner, that there is a vast and variegated audience waiting to be titillated. "Why are laughter, anger or pity legitimate reactions, but not sexual excitement?" asks Hefner.

Playboy is expected to reach the 5 million mark in circulation this year. Audubon is planning more expensive films aimed at a broader audience, and American International, in Hollywood, which has made its fortune on such variations on sex, violence, motorcycles and mayhem as "The Wild Angels," "Riot on Sunset Strip" and "How to Stuff a Wild Bikini," will launch its biggest production yet–$1.5 million–next spring. "These best sellers and films are vulgar," comments lawyer Ephraim London. "But they are no more vulgar than our architecture and neon strips and the pink flamingos on our lawns. Why should our best-selling films and books be any exception to a general vulgarity?"

Still, the force of this logic does not stop citizens like London himself from worrying about the impact of distorted images of sex upon children. In fact, the new candor in the arts does not horrify parents as much as it bewilders them, forcing them to reassess their role as moral arbiter for their family. Some parents simply put their faith in the good judgment of their children, like the mother of two teen-age girls in Atlanta who says: "If something is cheap, they can recognize it for the trash it is." But some parents are determined to stem the tide, like Ruth Vaulman, a Chicago housewife with five children who recently led a letter-writing and telephone campaign against a local showing of "I, a Woman." "Someone reminded me that Adam was nude. But Adam didn't go dancing across my neighborhood screen. Everything is just sex, sex, sex," says Mrs. Vaulman. "We mothers are concerned and don't know what to do."

Smut. They are not alone in their concern. Twenty-three separate bills on obscenity have already been introduced into the 90th Congress. One, which establishes a presidential commission on obscenity and pornography, passed this year after eight years of effort by South Dakota's Sen. Karl Mundt. The commission, to be composed of eighteen citizens appointed by the president, will spend up to $75 a day studying dirty books, working out a fresh definition of pornography and investigating the sale and distribution of smut with a view to proposing new legislation for its control. The commission has stirred very little enthusiasm in Washington. Most officials agree with the U.S. Post Office's general counsel Timothy May. "Sex is troubling for society, but government ought to stay out of it," he says, "unless there is widespread licentiousness which becomes harmful. The government is not here to enforce the Ten Commandments, and the wants of society are generally twenty years ahead of government."

Even the most powerful agent of moral restraint, the Catholic Church, has been struggling not to suppress the new candor but to develop a more flexible attitude itself in an effort to remain relevant within the permissive society. While conservative clerics in Rome, like Cardinal Alfredo Ottaviani, deplore the relaxation of mores in the West, more "progressive" prelates urge a liberalization of the traditional Catholic position on sex and sin. "A lot of religious people realize that the Carrie Nation approach to obscenity is no longer the style of our life," says Father John Reedy, editor of Ave Maria Magazine, one of a number of Catholic journals pressing for change. "Today's attitude is to appeal to the individual as an adult."

In fact, much of the new candor is coming from dissident Catholics themselves, among them the growing number of priests who are openly attacking the church policy on celibacy. One, James Kavanaugh, author of "A Modern Priest Looks at His Outdated Church," has left the church, but his attacks continue. "The church cannot subdivide the moral law into tiny absolutes," he says. "It cannot make God into a crotchety old lady with frayed nerves. The church's distorted image of man's weakness and inclination to sin prevents it from serving the people." "Religion has been used to cover up things," comments Lutheran theologian Martin L. Marty. "Some churchmen have simply said 'We are sick and tired of it.' They'll grab all kinds of instruments to change it–the most evocative tools at hand, both literary and linguistic."

Shape. In any case, no action, by either church or state, is likely to impede the advance of the permissive society. Already rumbles from other Western countries suggest the shape of things to come in America. Recently, in Holland, a nude girl appeared on Dutch national television with only a newspaper occasionally between her and the camera; there was no great public outcry. A new Swedish film, "I Am Curious," shows what one observer called "an animated Nordic version of the Kama Sutra," with four explicit scenes of lovemaking. In America, Terry Southern is at work on a novel that explores the possibility of producing "artistic" pornographic films for profit. And French director Roger Vadim in "Barbarella" presents not only his wife, Jane Fonda, in the nude, but a glimpse of the year 40,000 in which, as he explains it, "there are no taboos on sex, eroticism or nudity, no sin in nudity or the sex act."

Vadim's vision of the earth as a great pleasure dome is as speculative as anyone else's. But it does raise the crucial question of where the new permissiveness is leading, whether the breakdown of the old order is going to lead to some new moral system or whether it is simply going to lead to the progressive discarding of all social restraint. Some artists and critics feel it is not going to lead anywhere, that it is simply one more swing in the pendulum of history between Dionysian and Apollonian styles of behavior. "I would expect the pendulum to swing back," says British director Tony Richardson. "Another historical movement will occur, some major cataclysm, and society will need heroics, more codes, ideals. All victories are limited; they are never total. Just when you think you have advanced for all time, you find you are mistaken."

Architect and cosmic thinker Buckminster Fuller believes the pendulum is swinging back already–not the pendulum of history, but of evolution. As Fuller sees it, man's role as a procreator in an advanced society dimininishes as fewer and fewer offspring are needed to ensure the survival of the species.

"In the days of baby-making," he says, "the forbidden areas of the body were kept secret and promising in order to make us look forward to getting into bed. Once we start exposing ourselves as we're doing, sex gets to be a bore. The sexes themselves start to blur, and homosexuality increases, which also cuts down babies. Nature is putting on the brakes and man is unconsciously following. This is really an anti-erotic and anti-sexual trend."

Most social thinkers, however, are unwilling to accept the dictates either of history or evolution, believing that man still exerts a crucial control over the shape of his future. They see the tumbling of the old codes not as the beginning of a moral decline, but as the beginning of a search for new values. If society does collapse in a hedonistic frenzy, it will be because this search has failed. "I think it's good to have an expressive, free and imaginative society," says Max Lerner, "as long as you recognize some limits. These limits don't have to be puritanical. Without limits, our society can become as hedonistic as the world of the Marquis de Sade–going toward the most sadistic and primitive drives in the human being. It's not enough to break things down. Such a trend is not ultimately satisfying in itself. New values must be found and I believe young people are trying to find these values. That's where I place my hope."

Prudery. It is impossible to know, right now, what new values will rise from the rubble of the old dispensations. Obviously, the emergence from prudery and hypocrisy imposes new responsibilities as it opens up new possibilities. Surely the lesson has been learned a thousand times that freedom is what one makes of it. Father Ong is guardedly optimistic. "The new permissiveness," he says, "lends us access at last to areas that were so heavily guarded and repressed that they interfered with our understanding of one another. This can be a very humanizing thing."

The permissive society, then, is an inevitable stage in a time of transition, a collective experiment in which spring up cheek by jowl the honest movies and the trashy ones, the vulgar books and the serious, the tough-minded plays and the titillating–all tolerated with an implicit faith that the new freedom will ultimately humanize and improve rather than corrupt. The breakdown of the traditional consensus has broadened the options available to each individual as to how he conducts his life. What he does with this freedom is another matter, and so far confusion and anxiety have characterized the new moral atmosphere.

Pressure. In this situation, serious artists need all the freedom they can get to express the roots of disorder and the possibilities for order. And with that freedom goes a tremendous responsibility. "Individuals are going to have to stiffen their own moral principles," says Father Ong. "They're going to live under a great deal of pressure. They won't be able to reverse this permissive trend but they can point out rational limits. They are going to have to speak up in a pluralistic society."

Whether the new freedom produces good or ill depends on man himself. "Is man essentially a hedonistic, pleasure-loving, self-indulgent type?" asks theologian Martin Marty. "Or is he essentially a purposeful, work-oriented, self-denying creature? We simply don't know." What happens in the permissive society will go a long way toward telling us.

No More Population Explosion for the U. S.? U.S. News & World Report

Population explosion ahead for the U.S.? That has been the popular idea, fed by many predictions.

Not any more. Americans, it now is clear, are confounding the experts and forcing earlier predictions to be changed.

There is to be steady, rather moderate growth . . . not an explosion.

Maybe "the pill" is responsible. Or perhaps that is only a small part of the reason. A bigger part may be the simple conclusion among millions of married couples that big families no longer are the thing.

Once before, in the 1920s, married people came to that conclusion. Families simply stopped having so many children, long before there was a pill.

Back in 1910, for every 1,000 women of child-bearing age there were 126 births. By 1921, the rate of births had edged off to about 120 births for each 1,000 women of child-bearing age.

Then came the big slide. By the mid-1930's, the birth rate was down to about 76 per 1,000—a drop of more than one third.

That was the time when population experts predicted this country never would have more than 150 million people. Alarms were sounded that the people of greatest ability were not reproducing themselves. The outlook seemed gloomy.

Aftermath of War. American women then confounded the prophets. Birth rates began to zoom after World War II.

By 1957, for every 1,000 women of child-bearing age, there were 123 births. That was not up to the 1910 rate, but it was not far from it. So then the cry began to be widely heard: "population explosion." American women were pictured as being among the most prolific in the advanced countries of the world. Big families seemed to be the thing. Talk was of a half billion people in the U. S. someday—250 million before too long.

Now, once again, the experts have been crossed up.

The birth rate last year was below 93 for each 1,000 women. There is no real assurance that this decline of almost 25 per cent from the 1957 high is ended, let alone that it will be reversed any time soon.

There were 1.1 million fewer babies born in 1966 than would have been born if the birth rate of 1957 had continued. And in this short span, the U.S. population is 4 million lower than it would have been. People in the country now total about 198 million. Their number would have been 202 million had the birth rate in 1957 been continued. The 200-million mark still lies ahead, not behind. It will be reached late this year or early next year.

In years to come the slowing in population growth will become even more noticeable at present rates of birth. If these birth rates go on declining, the slowdown will be still more marked.

Pressures for Change. What has happened? The answer seems evident.

Today's younger people, moving into the marriageable age, usually have grown up in families considered large by standards of the 1920s and 1930s.

Memories of big-family problems are fresh. There was the crowding in dwellings with too-few bedrooms. There were the troubles about financing the skyrocketing bills for food and clothing. Then came the almost insurmountable problem of paying for college as youths left high school and home to get a higher education.

It appears that coming back into play is the old theory that children who grew up in large families tend to limit the size of their families.

Then, too, the idea of planning of family size is more widely accepted by groups in the population–farmers, lower-income families, Catholics, Negroes–than had been the case in the past. Birth control obviously has caught on, for whatever reason.

With what effect? With many effects beyond that of defusing the idea of a great and early population explosion in the United States.

Population pressures will be less intense, and will build up more slowly than had been imagined earlier. The overcrowding, apparent in many areas, will not spread as rapidly. There will be more time for communities to build new facilities and prepare in other ways for a more-gradual population growth.

Family size will remain low, on the average, not go on up from here. There were almost five persons in the average household of 1900. By 1930, after the declining birth rate in the 1920s, family size averaged about four persons. By 1950 it had fallen to 3.5 persons.

Now the American family averages 3.3 individuals. Only moderate change in family size is expected in the next decade.

All of this has broad meaning for every aspect of American life in days ahead.

The average residence will not necessarily need so many bedrooms. Children's play areas probably will not need to be so large. Those couples who postpone having children may prefer to live in apartments for a longer time, rather than buying homes.

As the birth rate goes down, more wives probably will be working at jobs outside the home, pointing to bigger incomes for new families.

Boom will not revive for those in lines of business related to babies.

Obstetricians are not likely to enjoy an upsurge in demand for their services. The same holds true for pediatricians. Maternity wards in many hospitals are being closed even now, for lack of patients.

Classroom Shifts. School boards will face change. Pressure already is easing at the kindergarten and first-grade level. It soon will be easing all through elementary school. Less building of new schools will be necessary. The wave of youngsters, however, is moving on to high school and college.

Even so, elementary schools will not be emptied. Once the birth rate stops going down, as it will at some point–and may be doing temporarily at the moment–the number of births will rise again. The current increase in number of women of child-bearing age assures that. However, the rise will be slower than in the days of worry about a real population explosion.

Instead of explosion in numbers of people, ahead lies an exploding shift in age distribution.

The baby boom is ended. Now comes the boom in young adults.

Over the years between now and 1980, young people aged 18 through 34 will account for two thirds of the expansion in total population. This group, now 22 per cent of the population, will rise to 28.5 per cent by 1980. In contrast, those under 18 will grow only slowly in numbers. They will decline in their share of the total. Those 35 through 64 years old will only hold their present relative share.

The Free Spenders. Impact of this shift will be great. Young adults account for most marriages, most births, most accumulation of household goods. People 20 through 44 years old account for more than 85 per cent of home purchases financed by the Federal Housing Administration.

People in this age bracket will show a percentage increase that is twice as large as that of the rest of the population in years ahead.

The prospect is that more than 1 million new households will be formed each year through the late 1960s. The number will rise even higher in later years of this century.

That isn't all.

Young families spend more freely, borrow more heavily. They spend, on an average, 101 percent of their income because they borrow more than they earn. Average for all families is 92 cents of spending out of each dollar of income.

Also, in young families with the husband under 25, the wife is working in 55 per cent of the cases. For all U.S. families, the figure is 39 per cent.

Young families tend to move frequently. More than 60 per cent change their address in any given year. Only 20 per cent of the population as a whole moves in any one year.

Young families tend to spend more than the average family spends on rent, home furnishings, meals away from home, automobiles and recreation. They spend less than the average of all families on home ownership, food consumed at home, clothing and medical care.

Businessmen will need to be aware of those facts.

Designs, styles, colors attractive to younger individuals will grow in importance. Demand will rise for apartments, travel, recreation, entertainment and services of all kinds, as well as for goods necessary in setting up a home.

Job competition will grow. Skills and education will become more than ever important. Pressure will increase for older people to retire earlier.

Catering to Youth. Politicians will need to offer an image and shape policies appealing to persons of younger voting age—21 through 34—if they want to ride the tide. This age group by 1962 had fallen to 28.9 per cent of the total voting-age population. It was more than 40 per cent in 1900. By 1980 the younger voters will grow again to 37 per cent of the total. Growth in their numbers from now on will run sharply ahead of the growth in those in the older voting ages.

Thus today's declining birth rate and the changing population "mix" will bring broad changes in many facets of U.S. life, and require changes in plans by businessmen, educators and many others.

The Growing Toll of America's "Broken Homes"

U.S. News & World Report

Nationwide concern is developing over the "broken home" and the role it plays in growing violence in the United States.

Homes disrupted by death, separation, divorce or desertion turn up in the early background of the men charged with killing President John F. Kennedy, Senator Robert F. Kennedy, and the Rev. Dr. Martin Luther King, Jr.

In city after city, juvenile authorities are finding much of their work has to do with fatherless youngsters running loose on the streets.

It is observed by family-counseling experts that most children in fatherless homes grow up to become stable and law-abiding citizens.

Even so, worry rises over the impact of the broken home as it becomes an established and accepted fact of life in modern-day America—far more than would have been thought possible a half century ago when divorce was still frowned upon by most people.

More Breakups. The divorce rate per 1,000 married women aged 15 years or older has been climbing steadily, with only two interruptions since 1958, when the rate reached a post-World War II low of 8.9 per 1,000.

Latest official rate, for 1965, was 10.6 per 1,000, and some authorities believe it may have gone up to 11 or more since then. The 1965 figure was then the highest rate for U.S. divorces since 1949.

In total numbers, too, the trend is upward.

Last year, 534,000 U.S. marriages were dissolved in the courts, more than in any other year in the nation's history except 1946, when an unusually high number of dissolutions was recorded from a backlog of cases that had accumulated during World War II.

Officials of the Department of Health, Education and Welfare say there is some evidence that remarriages are increasing, too—but not at the same pace as divorces in this country.

In that situation, the nation's army of divorced women continues to expand, coming to 2.2 million in 1966.

By that time, too, 2.9 million U.S. women were living apart from their husbands without divorce. Among whites, such women were about equal in number to those who had been divorced. Among nonwhites, separated or deserted women outnumbered divorcees 3 to 1.

Children without Fathers. What alarms welfare and law-enforcement officials are these facts:

About 3 out of 5 homes headed by women include children. Among nonwhites, the ratio is almost 4 out of 5.

Today 10 per cent of all households with children are headed by women, and among nonwhites the proportion rises to about 25 per cent. More than 7 million children under 18, or about 1 in 10, are being raised in fatherless homes. This total grows, year by year–with divorce cases alone involving more than 600,000 youngsters each year.

Illegitimate births, which passed the 300,000 figure in 1966, also are part of the nation's broken-home problem. Many babies born out of wedlock, especially among Negroes, are brought up without a father in the home.

Recently Dr. Murray Grant, public-health director for Washington, D.C., told Congressmen that 30.3 per cent of all births in the nation's capital were illegitimate–and for mothers under the age of 20, the figure was 60 per cent of all births. Nationwide, he said, 8.4 per cent of all births were illegitimate, and among nonwhites the proportion rose to 27.6 per cent.

Poverty compounds the situation.

Government records reveal that 3 out of 5 children being brought up in homes where the father is absent–for one reason or another–are in "poor" families. Among nonwhites, the ratio is 4 out of 5.

In addition to the 5.2 million American families headed by women, there are about 270,000 families headed by men with no wives present. Such families account for about 600,000 children.

This group, however, is seen as constituting far less of a problem–and not just in numbers.

Fathers, it is pointed out, can get better-paying work with which to support their children and often can call on a female relative to act as substitute mother for the family. Furthermore, remarriage rates for divorced fathers probably are higher than for women, welfare officials say–although full statistics on this are lacking.

Problem for Mothers. Among women trying to rear children alone, the job is different–and far bigger.

Sociologists and psychiatrists are quick to say that many women are rearing children successfully, despite absence of fathers. In many cases, it is said, the mental health of children has actually benefited when divorce ended their exposure to quarreling and tension between parents.

On the other hand, it is conceded that the everyday difficulties of raising children are magnified when mothers tackle the job alone. Factors such as these are enumerated:

- Working mothers find it hard to provide their children with adequate supervision during the day–and fatigue, coupled with anxiety, breed discord.

- Boys can suffer much emotional damage if there is no "male model" on which to pattern themselves.

- Often divorced mothers tend to smother their children, particularly boys, with affection as an emotional substitute for the missing husband–a frequent cause of later disturbance in the child.

Measuring the Effect. Not long ago Dr. John F. McDermott, Jr., associate professor of psychiatry at the University of Michigan medical school, told of a study of 16 boys and girls whose ages ranged from 3 to 6 at a time when their parents were separating and divorcing. Thirteen out of the 16 showed behavior changes that ranged from boredom to aggressiveness.

When the initial impact of parental separation is followed by tension and lack of supervision in the fatherless home, psychiatrists say, the child can suffer emotional ills or get into trouble with the law.

In 1950, Drs. Eleanor and Sheldon Glueck, in their noted study of 500 matched pairs of delinquents and normal children, found that 60.4 per cent of the troublemakers came from broken homes, while the same was true of only 34.2 per cent of the nondelinquents. Reported the Gluecks in their book, "Delinquents in the Making":

"More of the homes of the delinquents than of the nondelinquents were broken by desertion, separation, divorce or death of one or both parents, a large number of such breaches occurring during the early childhood of the boys; many more delinquents than nondelinquents had step- or foster parents; and more of them were shunted about from one household to another during their most formative years."

While many divorced or separated mothers manage to keep their youngsters in line, the broken home turns up with great frequency in the case reports on juveniles.

One study recently in Denver showed that only 25 per cent of Negro youths classed as delinquents lived with both parents. A two-parent home was the experience of only 39 per cent of Spanish-speaking delinquents and 41 per cent of "Anglo" or white delinquents.

"Symptom of Our Times." Said Juvenile Court Judge Ted Rubin:

"This is a symptom of our times. The rapid flow of American society brings a high divorce rate, so that young couples live several lifetimes in a few years."

The high cost of the broken home is being reflected, too, in the welfare payments to families with dependent children. This program now costs the nation between 2.5 and 3 billion dollars a year in aid going to families with 5.5 milion members, of whom 4.1 million are children.

If past experience is a guide, the nation may be paying further costs in the years ahead in emotional and mental illness—an element coming to the surface in the form of violence and lawlessness.

The Catholic Church and Birth Control

U.S. News & World Report

One of the most critical conflicts in the long history of the Roman Catholic Church appears to be developing among its half billion members over the question of birth control.

On July 29, Pope Paul VI issued his long-awaited encyclical "Of Human Life." That proclamation reaffirmed, in sweeping terms, the Church's historic stand against all "artificial" means of preventing childbirth.

Opening up within the Church, as a result, is a deep and dangerous rift.

Conservatives–including nearly all of the top hierarchy–are standing behind the Pope. But many priests and laymen are in open rebellion. Voiced is worry that defections will rise and that there will be a general weakening of the Church in times ahead. Repercussions reach far beyond the Church itself.

In recent years, the U.S. and other governments have been supporting growing programs of birth control. These drew guarded support from many Catholic voters and politicians at a time when the Church seemed to be relaxing its stand on birth control somewhat.

Doubts About Future. Now the latest word from the Church's highest authority is raising some doubt about the future of such programs.

This article appeared in *U.S. News & World Report,* August 12, 1968.

Pope Paul's encyclical, itself, was not issued as an infallible pronouncement. However, it is held to be "binding on the conscience" of all Catholics and other "men of good will."

Basically, the Pope restated and elaborated on the 1930 pronouncement of Pope Pius XI that all sexual intercourse "must remain open to the transmission of life."

Included in the ban is the oral contraceptive, a development in recent years which many thought might be the basis of a new approach by the Church to the subject of birth control.

Pope Paul, moreover, appealed to all governments to outlaw contraception, sterilization and abortion as means of preventing childbirth.

This appeal, and other elements in the papal statement, run counter to recent trends in the U.S. and elsewhere.

Laws Repealed. In America, one state after another has been repealing laws against the dissemination of birth-control information and devices. In 1965 the Supreme Court threw out a Connecticut statute outlawing the practice of birth control.

Catholic churchmen tended to go along with this trend. Richard Cardinal Cushing of Boston expressed the viewpoint of many when he said:

"Catholics do not need the support of civil law to be faithful to their religious convictions, and they do not seek to impose by law their moral views on other members of society."

At the same time, there was no massive opposition from Church leaders or from the 100 or more Catholic lawmakers in Congress as federal aid to birth-control programs got under way in 1965.

Today, an estimated 300,000 poor women in the U.S. are getting birth-control aid at clinics that are helped by federal funds—at a cost last year of about 28 million dollars.

Abroad, U.S. aid to birth-control clinics in poor nations has risen from 2.5 million dollars in 1965 to 35 million.

Problems in Latin America. Much of that outlay is going to Latin America, a heavily Catholic area plagued by a population "explosion" that is raising the threat of malnutrition, disease and civil strife on a big scale.

Some experts in Latin America are predicting that Pope Paul's ruling will bring only a temporary setback to birth-control programs. Said a family-planning official in Chile:

"I expect the bishops and priests will handle this matter with patience and tolerance. Some will just overlook the encyclical. Many women will at first obey the Vatican, then intentionally forget about it."

A point being made by observers not only in Latin America but elsewhere is that rising numbers of Catholic women of childbearing age have been resorting to the use of contraceptives as a matter of individual conscience —and the prevailing estimate is that few will change their habits now.

In the U.S., surveys reveal that more than half of such Catholic women are using contraceptives—usually "the pill"—and that many others approve its use.

European Attitudes. In France, a recent study showed about 56 per cent of practicing Catholics favored use of "the pill." And in Catholic Belgium, pharmacies report that the use of oral contraceptives is spreading over the entire country—despite the severity of penalties for any publicity given birth control.

Expectations are that some users will undergo a "conflict of conscience" because of the papal ruling. But conflict is seen as more likely to be felt among laymen directly involved in birth-control programs as a whole.

One instance would be Catholic physicians working with family-planning clinics. Another and more important group may be lawmakers.

In Belgium, Catholic legislators are described as no longer feeling free to support a bill permitting physicians and social workers to give advice on birth control. And in Washington, D.C., a well-known supporter of government aid to family planning said:

"I worry that some very influential Catholics in Congress who have been moving toward our viewpoint will now feel they have to obey the Pope and vote against us."

Clergy's Dilemma. It is within the Catholic clergy, however, that the experts now foresee the biggest "crisis of authority."

Pointed out is the fact that a priest's duty is to "proclaim and teach"—and furthermore, that Pope Paul specifically reminded priests of their duty to convey to their congregations and students the traditional views that he embodied in his encyclical.

A leading Catholic editor in New York said:

"Laymen, or most of them, undoubtedly are going on doing as they have before. If their own conscience is satisfied, they will see no reason to be moved by the encyclical.

"For the priest, it is different. He must make his choice. If he obeys, he may be teaching something that he feels to be against his conscience. If he disobeys, he will then invite suspension. I have no doubt that many will choose to disobey, and that we may be seeing many more Catholic clergy leaving the Church than before."

Just before Pope Paul's statement was issued, the Association of Washington, D.C., Priests wrote to Patrick Cardinal O'Boyle criticizing his conservative position on birth control.

They claimed to speak for 152 priests in the archdiocese.

A few days later, 172 Catholic theologians in the U.S. criticized the papal encyclical as "narrow," "insensitive" and unduly emphatic on sexual aspects of human love.

Pledges of support for the Pope's stand came from the National Conference of Catholic Bishops of the United States and from a reported majority of parish priests in the Washington diocese.

Beginning of a Schism? What many see developing is a wide rift between priesthood and hierarchy.

With some exceptions, such as the Netherlands' Bernadus Cardinal Alfrink, most top churchmen are backing the Pope. In Philadelphia, John Cardinal Krol warned that priests who find the Pope's ruling unacceptable "are mounting an insurrection against God."

Such divisions are seen adding to the burdens of a church already worried by signs of disaffection among laymen and defections among priests. Being voiced is the fear that papal authority itself will be weakened and perhaps destroyed.

As one measure of this concern, Pope Paul himself on July 31 made a fresh appeal to Catholic couples to understand and accept this ruling–which, he said, "caused us no small suffering."

On the other hand, a large body of conservative Catholics is known to feel that the Pope's statement will reinforce the Church against inroads allegedly caused by the wave of "updating" that began with changes wrought by the worldwide meetings of bishops in Rome between 1962 and 1965.

This much seems certain: Roman Catholicism's conflict over the issue of birth control is one of the most intense in the Church's long history–and it is a conflict of major importance to the world at large.

Will Man Direct His Own Evolution? Albert Rosenfeld

Not long ago a wealthy Southern shipowner, fatally injured in an accident, was rushed to the hospital. Though he was presumed dead on arrival, a team of doctors put forth heroic efforts to get his heart beating again. They succeeded, and kept it going, weakly and erratically, for some 40 minutes. When further efforts failed, they finally pronounced him dead. Meanwhile, during the same critical 40 minutes, a baby girl was born to the shipowner's only daughter. The daughter had married against her father's wishes. As a result, he had disowned her, though setting aside $100,000 for any grandchild who might be born before his death.

Was the new baby entitled to the inheritance? Was her grandfather dead when he got to the hospital, or was he alive?

Certainly, by all traditional standards, he was dead. Dead when he got to the hospital, dead when they got through with him. And yet doctors these days do frequently resuscitate patients who, not so long ago, would have been considered quite irrevocably dead. They labor mightily, restore the heartbeat, and by and by the corpse is up and smiling. If the shipowner had got up smiling, he would have been indisputably alive. This being so, could he really have been dead on arrival?

This particular case was settled out of court, so no judge or jury had to grapple with the questions. But consider another case that did get to court in New York State. A wife, separated from her husband, had already been awarded custody of the child. Now she was trying to deny her husband visiting privileges. He had no rights, she said, because the child had been conceived by artificial insemination, the semen having been obtained by the family physician from an anonymous donor. The husband protested vehemently; the insemination had taken place with his full knowledge and consent, and he had loved and nourished the child as his own. The New York court granted him visiting privileges. But when the mother moved to Oklahoma and reopened the case, the court ruled that her husband was not in any sense the child's real father.

If he was not the child's real father, who was? The anonymous stranger who donated the semen? If so, could he now claim the child as his? Could he demand visiting privileges? Conversely, could he be forced to support the child? Is the child his heir? Could the mother's husband, when the child was born, have had the right to disown the child and declare him illegitimate?

None of this is frivolous speculation. These are real questions arising from problems that trouble real people. Similar perplexities arise every time biology or medicine makes an important advance—such as learning to restart a stopped heart, or to inseminate a woman

"Will Man Direct His Own Evolution?" by Albert Rosenfeld, Life Magazine, October 1, 1965, © 1965 Time, Inc.

artificially. Once a scientific discovery is made, once it can be applied with reasonable safety, those who need it use it. But there is always a painful lag before the mechanisms and attitudes of society catch up with the new reality that science has wrought. As man's power to control life accelerates, this kind of lag will prove to be more than painful—it could be catastrophic.

The lag has been tolerable up till now only because the problems so far raised are childishly simple and straightforward compared to the brain-cracking complexities which are soon to be thrust upon us—legal, social, ethical, moral, esthetic, philosophical, religious. The lives of men will undergo transformations so drastic as to constitute a wholly new world, a world without precedent in human history.

Many articles appearing in *Life* during the past few years have shown the startling and audacious work that modern biologists are doing. In recognition of the power of biology, Dr. Jonas Salk founded an institute which, though primarily devoted to research, has committed itself to exploring the far-reaching implications of that research. "The time has come," he says, "when the public must be made aware of the great impact of biological thought and knowledge. Such awareness will lead to the further liberation of man and the flourishing of his great potential. But he will be called upon to avoid the new dangers that liberation brings. Here only his sense of values can be his guide. Meanwhile the managers of society should be given some advance notice of what may be in store."

The following account is not a comprehensive survey of present-day investigations in biology and medicine. Its intent is rather to give "some advance notice of what may be in store" as a consequence of current research, discovery and achievement in a number of different scientific fields—all of them related to man's new abilities to tamper with his body, and therefore with his psyche. Tampering after birth is nothing new. In fact, that is what the whole history of medicine and psychiatry is about. But the latest ways of tampering constitute radical departures from the ways we have known. They involve such procedures as the wholesale replacement of failing body parts with transplanted or artificial organs; the control of the body, brain and behavior through electronics, drugs and cybernetics; the freezing of "dead" bodies for possible earthly resurrection by the even more sophisticated science of the future.

Tampering before birth covers not only prenatal medicine—improving the health of the fetus while it is still in the womb. Far more than this, it covers the variety of new methods of conceiving and growing babies—inside or outside the womb, with or without sex. And it deals with the further possibility of modifying future generations through eugenics or through the actual molecular manipulation of the genes.

As scientists daily edge closer to the solution of some of nature's deepest mysteries, no idea seems too wild to contemplate. Would you like education by injection? A larger, more efficient brain? A cure for old age? Parentless babies? Body size and skin color to order? Name it, and somebody is seriously proposing it. Only two weeks ago in Atlantic City, the president of the American Chemical Society, Dr. Charles C. Price of the University of Pennsylvania, urged that the United States make creation of life in the laboratory a national goal. In sober scientific circles today there is hardly a subject more commonly discussed than man's control of his own heredity and evolution. And the discussions seldom leave much doubt that men will acquire this control. It is a matter of when, not if.

Scientists tend to agree that some of the most exciting future developments will come out of insights and discoveries yet to be made, with implications we cannot now foresee or imagine. So we live in an era where not only anything that we can imagine seems possible, but where the possibilities range beyond what we can imagine. In such an era it is hard to tell physics from metaphysics, to distinguish the mad scientists from the real ones, to judge what is a true possibility and what is sheer rot. But there is no resolving this kind of uncertainty. Even the scientists cannot give us sure guidance on what is really going to happen.

There are powerful institutions to give us guidance about what ought to happen—the most powerful, perhaps, being religion. Regardless of what science makes possible, moral approval or disapproval has, throughout man's history, influenced which advances he accepts instantly, which he accepts more slowly, and which he rejects altogether. In the new age, however, it is unlikely that any advance can be totally ignored. Scientific curiosity is one of the strongest motivating forces in the world today, and some scientists in some countries will pursue any line of research that fascinates them, regardless of prevailing moral attitudes. Some of the new discoveries will, at first, have only a limited impact on only small and restricted segments of the world's population. But the powers that can accrue to those who use them will be so overwhelming that the rest of the world will not long shut them out. And those who guide us, including the theologians, will not be able to guide us truly without taking them into account.

A sense of urgency is shared by many today. "These are not long-term problems," says Dr. Joshua Lederberg, Nobel Prize biologist at Stanford University. "They are upon us now." As man's knowledge takes on new dimensions, hardly any human concept or value will remain sacrosanct. Health and disease, youth and age, male and female, good and evil—all these will take on transformed meanings. Life and death will have to be redefined. Family relationships will be quite different. Even individual identity may be hard to ascertain. Nothing can be taken for granted.

The discoveries in the field of reproduction alone have already created real-life scenes that formerly would have had no plausibility outside the pages of science fiction.

Recently Dr. E. S. E. Hafez, an Egyptian-born experimental biologist at Washington State University, commissioned a scientist friend from Germany to bring him a hundred head of prize sheep. The entire herd is to be delivered to Dr. Hafez in a neat package he can carry in one hand. It will be a ventilated box and inside will be a female rabbit. Inside the rabbit will be 100 incipient rams and ewes, all of them embryos only a few days old, growing as if still in their natural mother. Then, following a procedure already well established in Europe, he will implant each embryo in a ewe where it will gestate and, in a few months, be born.

Dr. Hafez, whose research support includes over $160,000 supplied by the National Institutes of Health alone, sees no reason why his method would not work just as well with people.

He speculates that, only 10 or 15 years hence, it could be possible for a housewife to walk into a new kind of commissary, look down a row of packets not unlike flower-seed packages, and pick her baby by label. Each packet would contain a frozen one-day-old embryo, and the label would tell the shopper what color of hair and eyes to expect as well as the probable size and I.Q. of the child. It would also offer assurance of freedom from genetic defects. After making her selection, the lady could take the packet to her doctor and have the embryo implanted in herself, where it would grow for nine months, like any baby of her own.

Other research suggests she might even have alternatives to carrying the child herself. Five years ago, if you had looked in on the laboratory of Dr. Daniele Petrucci at No. 3

Via dei Ruini in Bologna, Italy, you would have seen him watching intently a nondescript, blubberlike blob under glass. The blob was, in fact, a tiny human embryo. According to Dr. Petrucci's account, he was responsible for its conception, and it was he who had devised the artificial glass womb in which the embryo now lived and grew.

He had begun with a female ovum removed surgically at just the right, ripe moment. He had then admitted male sperm, one of which had proceeded to fertilize the egg. Under his careful laboratory nursing, the egg had grown into this embryo.

The first press reports of Dr. Petrucci's work created a furor in Italy. Vatican sources as well as laymen roundly denounced Petrucci for manipulating human life in this fashion. An outraged citizen even demanded that the doctor be prosecuted for murder because he "terminated the experiment" at the end of 29 days. Another of his embryos lived for 59 days.

Petrucci, a Catholic, was overwhelmed by the outcry. He has since given up growing human embryos and gone on to less controversial experiments. Some scientists question Dr. Petrucci's claims despite the impeccability of his medical credentials. But the relevant point is that what he says he achieved seems feasible enough. Other scientists, including at least two Americans—Dr. John Rock at Harvard and Dr. Landrum B. Shettles at Columbia Presbyterian Hospital in New York—had already grown embryos "in vitro" (in glass) before him, though their embryos lived only a few days each. Still others, including Russians, continue to explore this area of research.

If none of the technical obstacles turn out to be insurmountable—a fair assumption—someone somewhere is going to bring forth an entirely grown-in-glass baby. No one can predict precisely how long it will take for the necessary technical breakthroughs to be made, but not too long after that first success—as was the case with artificial insemination—some people in special situations will start raising babies in this fashion. Apart from freeing the mother from the discomforts of pregnancy, the procedure would have advantages for the fetus, such as increased safety and ease of prenatal treatment for defects.

Acceptance of in vitro techniques would have profound effects at all levels of society. Yet, in vitro fertilization and development, thought it seems futuristic to us at this moment, may some day appear to have been a fairly crude way to grow human beings. More advanced techniques now in prospect altogether bypass the necessity for mating sperm with ovum.

Already it is commonplace to keep alive various kinds of human cells in tissue culture for extended periods of time, growing whole colonies from single cells again and again. It has been seriously suggested that it may be possible eventually to grow an entire organ, like a kidney or a liver, in tissue culture. Some years ago the eminent French biologist Jean Rostand even predicted that a man might one day be able to have a culture of his own cells—cells from almost anywhere in his body—stashed away somewhere so that a complete new replica of himself could be grown in case he met with an untimely accident.

Far-fetched? Certainly. Yet Cornell University's Dr. Frederick C. Steward has been achieving exactly this sort of asexual reproduction with the lowly carrot. It is, of course, a very long way from carrots to people, and Steward cautions that animal and human cells may behave differently. Here again, a series of breakthroughs are required to overcome the formidable technical barriers that still lie ahead before any definitive answers can be expected. Nevertheless, as a result of recent work, Dr. Rostand now believes more firmly than ever that tissue-culture techniques "would in theory enable us to create as many identical individuals as might be desired. A living creature would be printed in hundreds, in thousands of copies, all of them real twins. This would, in short, be human propagation by cuttings, capable of assuring the indefinite reproduction of the same individual—of a great man, for example!"

Would anyone like to name the man he would care to see duplicated by the hundreds, by the thousands—or even by the dozen?

Of all the variations that might be played upon the theme of human procreation, the ultimate—at least, the "ultimate" we can now project—will be the production of beings whose specifications can be drawn in advance. This could come about, scientists predict, through the manipulation of the genetic material itself, though the estimates of when this might come to pass vary considerably.

The basic genetic material, the stuff of which chromosomes are made, is deoxyribonucleic acid or DNA. In the coiled structure of the DNA molecule and the complex arrangement of its atoms lie the final secrets of heredity. DNA's genetic messages are written out in a four-letter code, each "letter" being a specific chemical substance. Scientists have begun to be able to read the genetic code—but only in a halting, incipient way, and it may take a long time before they become really fluent readers. But once we can read, we may then learn to "write"—i.e., to give genetic instructions—in the DNA code.

When that time comes, man's powers will be truly godlike. He may bring into being creatures never before seen or imagined in the universe. He may even choose to create new forms of humanity—beings that might be better adapted to survive on the surface of Jupiter, or on the bottom of the Atlantic Ocean.

Even without going that far, man presumably will be able to write out any set of specifications he might desire for his ideal human being. This is what many scientists mean when they talk about man controlling his own evolution. And who can find fault with that? Is there anyone not in favor of emphasizing man's good qualities and eliminating the bad ones? The rub, of course, is that "good" and "bad" are words that are easier to say than to apply.

There is at least one area of consensus as to what is good for man—the medical area. Most people would agree that it is good to reduce infant mortality, to make it possible for infertile parents to have children, to eradicate cancer and heart disease.

But consensus is not unanimity. Dissident voices are even now insisting that many of our so-called medical advances actually militate against human progress by aggravating the population problem, thus assuring an overcrowded planet where more people will die of war and starvation. Others warn of the deterioration of the human race because so many people with hereditary defects—people who formerly would have died at an early age—are often now being kept alive, to marry and pass on their defects. A majority undoubtedly would choose—at least for themselves and those they love—the benefits of health and longevity, and worry later about problems like overpopulation and the possible deterioration of the race.

Beyond getting rid of diseases and defects, there is the prospect that we can actually improve human beings—making them more intelligent, more talented, more virtuous—by manipulating genetic material. No one would argue that man couldn't stand some improvement, but having the actual power to do so presents some sticky choices. Who is it that we will appoint to play God for us? Which scientist, which statesman, artist, judge, poet, theologian, philosopher, educator—of which nation, race or creed—will you trust to write the specifications, to decide which characteristics are desirable and which not?

The manipulation of genes in this kind of precise detail—"genetic surgery," as it is often called—is a staggeringly complex task, and its realization may be several lifetimes of hard work away from us. Even so, it is not too soon to start grappling with the predicaments genetic surgery gives rise to, because exactly the same predicaments will arise with other developments we may expect to descend on us at any moment. In fact, our legal and social structures are too creakingly antiquated to come to grips with what is already here.

Take the relatively simple procedure of artificial insemination. In the U.S. alone many thousands of babies are born this way every year. Despite the commonness of the practice, its legal status remains questionable. The example of the custody case in New York has already been cited. Some judges have actually declared the practice adultery and ruled the children illegitimate. In such circumstances, does this brand the anonymous donor of the sperm an adulterer? Could a vindictive husband name him correspondent in divorce proceedings? On the other hand, since it is the doctor who directly administers the semen, should the doctor be named the adulterer? Again, these are serious questions being puzzled over by farsighted jurists.

Artificial insemination is today neither forbidden by the law nor condoned by it. The law simply has failed to deal with it at all. The public has had to muddle through as best it can. But with more radical biological advances in the offing, muddling through simply will not do.

In artificial insemination as practiced so far, the couple has nothing to say about the selection of the donor. The doctor ordinarily uses his own discretion.

To Dr. Hermann Muller, Nobel Prize geneticist, this seems a haphazard way of doing things. He proposes instead "germinal choice." A truly enlightened couple, in Muller's view, would forgo the purely egotistical satisfaction of imparting their own hereditary traits to their children, and instead choose —when it becomes available—from the sperm of "those whose lives had given evidence of outstanding gifts of mind, merits of disposition and character, or physical fitness" in order to endow their children with "the kind of hereditary constitution that came nearest to their own ideals."

Sperm banks have had the support of other scientists and for other reasons. Physicist Ralph E. Lapp, for instance, has urged that sperm be collected to insure an undamaged supply in the event of nuclear war or excessive fallout. Reliable techniques already exist for putting sperm in deepfreeze for periods of years without apparent damage or deterioration. In fact, at the State University of Iowa some years back, Doctors Raymond G. Bunge and Jerome K. Sherman conducted an extensive series of pioneering frozen-sperm experiments on animals. Satisfied on the method's safety and efficacy, they began using the technique on human mothers. Others elsewhere have since followed suit. Many healthy children today attest the validity of the method.

Dr. Muller's specific plan calls for a full dossier on each sperm donor. This is a most radical departure from the anonymity hitherto insisted upon and would certainly exaggerate all the legal and emotional risks involved.

Where the donor becomes known, could he be sued, in the absence of legal clarification, for child support? Could he have the terms of his will contested by descendants he never meant to be his heirs?

To minimize the problems, Muller suggests that when sperm banks are operating on a large scale, germinal choice should be made only from the sperm of donors no longer living and which had been stored for at least 20 years. To help couples make their choices more wisely, he would also provide professional counseling. Thus, across time and space, guided by experts, a mother could select as father of her child a Hindu philosopher, a Scandinavian athlete, a French poet. Some biologists warn that this kind of genetic selection is unpredictable, and that the children will not necessarily be like the fathers. But Muller insists that the chances of getting worthwhile children are better if you select a worthwhile parent, and, moreover, that germinal choice will result in the long-range improvement of the human race.

Genetic choice becomes considerably expanded, of course, when Dr. Hafez's egg-implantation techniques begin to be applied to human females. As a matter of fact, Dr. James L. Burks of the University of Chicago has recently succeeded in freezing, then unfreezing, rabbit ova, and fertilizing them in vitro, and now plans to do the same with human ova. With artificial inovulation as available as artificial insemination, with egg banks as well as sperm banks to draw from, either a genetic mother or a genetic father, or both, could be selected for the prospective child. Then both men and women could ignore heredity in their choice of mates. Women can be stimulated by hormones into producing a quantity of eggs a month instead of only one and thus could provide eggs for other women. A barren woman who could never hope otherwise to be pregnant could be afforded the fulfilling emotional satisfaction of having babies after all. If such inovulation were to become an accepted practice, it might also be acceptable for women to hire out as surrogate mothers just as they have traditionally hired out as wet nurses. A woman with serious heart trouble whose doctor feared to let her bear children might, by donating an egg, have her child carried by someone else.

We are, then, entering an era where children may be born of geographically separated or even long-dead parents, where virgin births may become relatively common, where women may give birth to other women's children, where romance and genetics may be separated, where some few favored men may father thousands of babies, where a permit may be required in order to have a baby. Can the traditional family—already a shaky institution—survive in the midst of all this? Do we want it to survive? If so, how will we insure its survival? If not, what will we substitute for it?

Not only the foundations of family life, but many of our laws, the themes of art and literature, and much of our ethics, morals and even politics, are based on a few simple premises which have been taken for granted from time immemorial: that any human being has two parents, one male, and one female; and that, in order to procreate, it is necessary for a male and a female to unite physically, the male's sperm fertilizing the female's egg, and the embryo then growing in the mother for its allotted time before being born into the world. Soon these premises may be shaken. Other basic premises will be too: that an individual has a quite definite identity which he retains throughout his lifetime, from birth to death; and that a person is either dead or alive, wtih no in-between nonsense.

Writers and artists already devote much articulate worry to the subject of how alienated they are, and psychiatrists' couches are full of people who say, in effect: Doctor, I don't know who I am. So, even before the new age of biology has set in, modern man has begun to face a crisis of identity.

If people today have such troubles, what of a child turned out "in vitro"? What is *his* status and identity as a human being? Will city hall record his existence? Who is his father, and who is his mother? Can he have any brothers or sisters? What are his citizenship and voting rights? Can the scientist who produced him simply keep him as an experimental animal?

Even you and I—in 1965, already here and beyond the reach of prenatal modification—could live to face curious and unfamiliar problems in identity as a result of man's increasing ability to control his own mortality after birth. As organ transplants and artificial body parts become even more available, it is not totally absurd to envision any one of us walking around one day with, say, a plastic cornea, a few metal bones and Dacron arteries; with donated glands, kidney and liver from some other person, from an animal, from an organ bank, or even from an assembly line; with an artificial heart, and computerized electronic devices to substitute for muscular, neural or metabolic functions that may have gone wrong. It has been suggested—though it will almost certainly not happen in our lifetime—that brains, too, might be replaceable, either by a brain transplanted from someone else, by a new one grown in tissue culture, or an electronic or mechanical one of some sort. "What," asks Dr. Lederberg, "is the moral, legal or psychiatric identity of an artificial chimera?"

Dr. Seymour Kety, an outstanding phychiatric authority now with the National Institutes of Health, points out that fairly radical personality changes already have been wrought by existing techniques like brainwashing, electroshock therapy and prefrontal lobotomy, without raising serious questions of identity. But would it be the same if alien parts and substances were substituted for the person's own, resulting in a new biochemistry and a new personality with new tastes, new talents, new political views—perhaps even a different memory of different experiences? Might such a man's wife decide she no longer recognized him as her husband and that he was, in fact, not? Or might he decide that his old home, job and family situation were not to his liking and feel free to chuck the whole setup that may have been quite congenial to the old person?

Not that acute problems of identity need await the day when wholesale replacement of vital organs is a reality. Very small changes in the brain could result in astounding metamorphoses. Scientists who specialize in the electrical probing of the brain have, in the past few years, been exploring a small segment of the brain's limbic system called the amygdala—and discovering that it is the seat of many of our basic passions and drives, including the drives that lead to uncontrollable sexual extremes such as satyriasis and nymphomania.

Suppose, at a time that may be surprisingly near at hand, the police were to trap Mr. X, a vicious rapist whose crimes had terrorized the women of a neighborhood for months. Instead of packing him off to jail, they send him in for brain surgery. The surgeon delicately readjusts the distorted amygdala, and the patient turns into a gentle soul with a sweet, loving disposition. He is clearly a stranger to the man who was wheeled into the operating room. Is he the same man, really? Is he responsible for the crimes that he—or that other person—committed? Can he be punished? Should he go free?

As time goes on, it may be necessary to declare, without the occurrence of death, that Mr. X has ceased to exist and that Mr. Y has begun to be. This would be a metaphorical kind of death and rebirth, but quite real psychologically—and thus, perhaps, legally.

But even death in the old sense, the physical death of the body, will be harder and harder to pin down with precision. There used to be an agreed-upon moment when the heart stopped, when the vital organs quit working, and the doctor could pronounce a man dead. But now that it has become commonplace to restore heartbeats and resuscitate the "dead," the final pronouncement is not so easily given. There is a case on record of a man who, after being worked over for hours in a Midwestern hospital, was finally given up as beyond retrieval. His wife, notified of his death by phone, collapsed and died of a heart attack. Meanwhile, the man on the table astounded everyone by starting to breathe again—and he finally recovered.

No wonder, then, that medical journals these days so frequently carry articles with titles like "When Is a Patient Officially Dead?" Doctors have lately been dividing death into several classifications. They differentiate, for example, between clinical death (from which a patient might now hope to be revived) and biological death, in which the cells and organs—and especially the brain—are irretrievably damaged. Dr. Hannibal Hamlin, a distinguished Boston physician, has been urging that death be defined as death of the brain, ascertainable by electroencephalograph readings. A brain-damaged victim with his circulation and respiration kept going artificially is, in Dr. Hamlin's view, merely a "heart-lung preparation." New medical definitions, if they can be agreed upon, would help clarify matters considerably. Meanwhile, the question will grow more pressing as new ways emerge to reverse damage done to vital organs and to bring people back from what used to be called death.

So likely do these further advances seem that there is a fast-growing movement afoot, spurred by Professor Robert C. W. Ettinger's book, "The Prospect of Immortality," urging that bodies of the dead be frozen instead of buried or cremated. Ettinger, who recently quit his job as professor of physics at Highland Park College in Michigan to devote full time to pushing his idea, proposes to quick-freeze the bodies with minimal damage and keep them in storage against the day when they can be revived and made whole again by the medical art and science of the future. Needless to say, Ettinger's proposals are highly controversial and most scientists refuse to take them seriously. Though research in whole-body freezing is being done, it seems a long way indeed from being achieved without considerable damage from the freezing process itself—a shortcoming Ettinger is the first to point out. The marvel is that Ettinger's proposals do have a valid basis and that they have struck such an instantaneous public nerve. There are already branches of the Life Extension Society and allied groups in 10 cities in the U.S. and abroad, dedicated to lobbying and evangelizing for the cause. They have been working hard, and not altogether fruitlessly, to get support for their "freezer program" from doctors, lawyers, educators, clergymen, politicians and the general public. Recently a man in Springfield, Ohio, almost succeeded in having his wife's body frozen, but medical authorities finally withheld the needed cooperation. Many people have already made provision in their wills to have themselves and their loved ones quick-frozen and stored as a long-shot gamble on future rescue from death. Before long, such a non-funeral is bound to take place.

Surgeons have been using parts from dead people to help save the living, and their long-range hope has been to establish storage banks for all kinds of organs and body parts that could be drawn on for implant in live patients who needed them. Some strongly advocate laws that would enable them to remove needed organs from cadavers without special permission. But if there existed a viable freezer program, cadavers could no longer be considered cadavers, and removing organs from them for research or for healing would be stealing parts they themselves might one day need.

Where, then, would the needed organs come from? Animals, perhaps. Ape kidneys, pig livers and a chimpanzee heart have already kept human patients alive for short periods of time. Dr. Lederberg suggests that animals might be especially bred to supply genetically reliable organs for people. Another hope is that organs could be raised in tissue culture, perhaps even from the patient's own cells. Or the practice of transplantation could conceivably be dropped altogether in favor of miniaturized implantable artificial parts. There is another, though more remote, hope—the possibility that the body might be taught to regenerate its own parts. Some animals, such as salamanders, normally regenerate limbs that have been amputated. At Western Reserve University, Dr. Marcus Singer has been able to induce frogs, which normally do not have this capacity, to regenerate severed limbs. "We cannot," says

Dr. Singer, "rule out the possibility that some day human beings might be able to regrow organs and tissues which they presently cannot."

In the freezer era, any mutilation of a corpse–its status as a corpse being after all only tentative–would be undesirable. Even standard autopsy procedures would be challenged, and the laws governing these procedures would have to be revised. This would be among the least of the challenges posed for legislators and jurists by the partial abolition of death–or, at least, its indefinite postponement.

When a man is put into the deep-freeze instead of into the grave, what happens to his estate? Are his heirs forever denied their inheritance? Is his property to be kept in trust for him, unusable by anyone else, perhaps for centuries? Can his widow or, rather, his wife–or his children collect his insurance? What about this man's retirement benefits, his veteran's pension? Do these go on being paid virtually in perpetuity, accumulating, with interest, in his account? And if overpopulation is already a worry, think of adding all those revivable corpses every generation.

If a corpse is someday revivable, could there be such a thing as murder? Or suicide? Would failure to freeze someone be considered murder? Might people who were bored or simply unhappy with the times have themselves frozen in the hope of coming back to life in a happier era? Might a criminal use the freezer as a means of escaping punishment? Certainly people with diseases now incurable might want to arrest the damage at the earliest possible moment to give themselves the best possible chance in the future.

Religion, no less than law, will have to help decide the right and wrong of all this, as well as other important questions. What, for example, of the soul? If a man has been dead for 30 minutes, then brought back to life, where was his soul in the interim? Did it leave the body and then return? Or was it there all the time? If it can be figured out where the soul dwelt for those 30 minutes, would the same answer serve just as well for a period of centuries? And what about a body that has been implanted with new organs on a wholesale scale, where even the heart and the brain have been replaced? Does the individual still retain the same soul? If not, where did the old one go, and whence came his new one?

The prospect of tissue-culture reproduction ties the riddle into further knots. If a new being is grown from the cell of a man still living, does it, too, have a soul? If he has none, is he human? Can he be saved? And suppose 100 people are grown from the cells of a dead man. Do they all have souls? Where were they meanwhile? Perhaps in the DNA of the cell nucleus? Could the present concept of the soul become barren of meaning, and would some other theological concept have to be substituted for it?

If scientists seem to be overemphasizing the confusions ahead, it is only, as Dr. Lederberg explains, because "we must try to anticipate the worst anomalies of biological powers. To anticipate them in good time is the first element of hope in developing institutional and technological antidotes."

Obviously, good things as well as evil can and do ensue from scientific advance. As just one example, a real breakthrough in understanding the specific molecular workings of the body's immunological systems would speed the conquest of diseases all the way from the common cold to cancer, would overcome the transplant barrier, and would give key insights into the nature of allergy and even the process of aging. This kind of breakthrough in understanding could come at any time, and if we ourselves were not the beneficiaries, our children would be.

Improved brain capacity is one innovation that appears likely. An actual physical enlargement of the brain might be brought about by genetic or prenatal manipulation. Even without that, we can do infinitely more with the gray matter we presently possess. A variety of experiments in hypnosis, drug therapy, electric brain stimulation and molecular biology point to the probability that specific memories–including all of experience and education–are stored at specific sites in the brain, and that they are stored electrochemically.

Several years ago Dr. Wilder Penfield, the eminent Canadian brain surgeon, discovered that when a certain spot in a patient's brain was electrically stimulated, it called up, in vivid detail, an incident the patient thought he had altogether forgotten. The stimulation of the same spot brought forth the same memory every time. Similar feats have been performed under hypnosis and under the influence of certain drugs. The long-range promise is that these powers of recall, instead of being sporadic and conditional, could be permanent and constant, and that our own conscious minds could replace the outside experimenter. Think what our intellects might be like if we could really remember everything, and have it all efficiently stored away for instant retrieval.

No one really knows what the capacity of the human brain might be, used to its limit. But this limit, whatever it is, may one day be overcome by hooking up the human brain to a computer. When this kind of brain-computer hookup is imagined, it is usually to envision the computer as remotely controlling and directing the brain–or a dozen brains, or a hundred. There is no reason why it could not work the other way around, as Dr. Simon Ramo suggests, with the computer serving as a vast storehouse of readily accessible information for the brain's use.

But we need not stop here. Some of the same experiments revealed that a man may be made to remember things that never happened to him at all. If memory does indeed consist of electrochemical changes in the structure of certain molecules in the brain cells, there is no theoretical reason why, when it becomes possible to alter these structures, experiences of any kind cannot be implanted at will. The brain thus influenced would never know the difference.

Dr. Holger Hydén in Sweden has performed experiments indicating that when mice are trained in certain skills, the training permanently changes the structure of nucleic-acid molecules in their brain cells. The learning seems to reside in these structural changes. Still-controversial experiments with flatworms suggest that "training" can be passed on simply by passing on the changed molecules themselves from one flatworm to another. This kind of research has bred speculation that subject matter of any sort might be taught merely by injecting the subject with what could in effect be an artificial virus containing nucleic acids of the appropriate molecular structure. A virus of the future, then, might give us algebra or French instead of the flu. In his recent book, "Profits of the Future," Arthur C. Clarke expresses his conviction that the famous "mechanical educator" of science fiction is no longer necessarily relegated to fiction. He believes information might be fed into the brain almost as sounds are recorded on a magnetic tape, to be stored there for playback on command.

If true information could be recorded and stored this way, why not false information? And if information is recordable as on a magnetic tape, might it not be erasable as well? Any knowledge no longer useful, any memory of an experience a man would rather forget, could be wiped out as if it had never been there at all. And artificial experiences could be supplied at will.

Not everyone would agree that these marvelous transformations are worth striving for. Their mere evocation will surely elicit as much dismay as delight. But research along these lines is bound to be intensively pursued. In fact, this must be done even to bring about the much more immediate and altogether noncontroversial medical benefits. The carrying out of the research itself cannot be anything but controversial—even within the ranks of the medical profession. Already being debated are the moral, ethical and legal dilemmas being posed by current research leading to the replacement of body parts.

Does anyone have the right to ask a man to give up his spare kidney and undergo major surgery such as kidney removal in order to give another man—even a close relative—a chance, and not always a good chance, to survive for a limited extra time? Transplant surgeons live in fear that they may lose a donor on the operating table—thus killing a healthy man on the gamble of saving a sick one. It is not even clear that a person has a legal right to volunteer one of his organs—especially if he is a minor—or to will his organs for use after death or to authorize the posthumous removal of an organ from a dying relative, though some states are trying, under medical prodding, to rectify these legal shortcomings.

At the moment, there is no way to guarantee absolute legal safety in these experimental areas. Recently a man who had been beaten to death was brought into a hospital. His wife gave doctors permission to remove one of his kidneys for transplant to another man. For 24 hours the doctors used a heart-lung machine to keep up an artificial circulation and heartbeat to be certain the kidney would remain undamaged. The victim's assailant, when he came to trial, insisted it was not he who had killed the man—that the man was, after all, still alive in the hospital, and it was the doctors who did him in by removing his kidney. (His arguments were not upheld by the court.) In more than one instance, a transplanted kidney, unbeknownst to the doctors, has brought active cancer cells with it. The transplant was a success, but the patient died of cancer.

All kinds of experimentation with human subjects, from the testing of drugs to the implanting of electrodes in the brain to the most complex new kind of restorative surgery, is coming under increased scrutiny and questioning by doctors and medical associations all over the world. Under what circumstances and under what controls should any patient be subjected to an unproven treatment? Should some people undergo unnecessary hazards to insure the later well-being of many other people they will never get to know?

Dr. J. B. S. Haldane, the late British biologist, always thought so. "I have often risked other peoples' lives in physiological experiments," he said at a London symposium in 1962, "and though none died, at least one was permanently injured. But they were all volunteers. . . . The exploration of the interior of the human brain will be as dangerous as that of the antarctic continent of the depths of the oceans, and far more rewarding. The 'officer in command' must be a man of proved personal courage, but not so softhearted as to leave his post of command because his orders have led to some deaths, mutilations or psychoses."

Few researchers would state this philosophy so bluntly. But at least one other who believes strongly in the necessity of human experimentation is Dr. Jack Kevorkian, of the Pontiac General Hospital in Pontiac, Mich. Kevorkian's pet scheme for furthering human medical research is bizarre. He would like some state that still permits capital punishment to offer the condemned man the choice of being placed under anesthesia—and never again to awaken. A skilled medical team would then use his body and brain for experimentation and study.

By using condemned criminals in this manner, Kevorkian believes, more medical knowledge would be acquired in a single year than is now gleaned in decades of worldwide efforts. Aware of how much his proposal smacks of the ghastly Nazi experiments of World War II, Kevorkian has written a book —printed at his own expense—spelling out the differences. He has talked to condemned prisoners, prison wardens, criminologists, medical researchers and state legislators about his plan, and still hopes he can convince someone to carry it through.

There are strong dissenters from this point of view. One of them is Dr. Irvine H. Page, himself an outstanding medical scientist, Director of Research at the Cleveland Clinic and editor of Modern Medicine. Dr. Page has grave moral misgivings about what he considers the cavalier attitude we have lately taken toward the human body, which he still looks upon as the sacred vessel of man's soul and spirit. We tend to meddle with it too lightly, Dr. Page feels, and a disregard for the human body can easily lead to a similar disregard for human life in general. He believes that, rather than push precipitately into experiments that entail unnecessary risks, research should go more slowly—and that the application of its results to human beings should go more slowly still.

It is fitting that doctors and scientists, who are most closely involved with the new developments, are the first to express their concern. But everyone will have to be concerned. It would be hard to exaggerate either the challenges or the opportunities for educators, for business leaders, for legislators and jurists, for artists and writers, for theologians and philosophers—and for you and me, personally.

One of the weightiest burdens is bound to fall on the statesmen and leaders of men at all levels of national and international life. They are, of course, already confronted with enormous probems brought on by science and technology. Nuclear weaponry, supplemented by chemical and biological warfare, threatens everyone regardless of race, color or creed. As space gets increasingly cluttered with hardware, including licensed communications satellites, a body of space law becomes imperative. Worldwide weather control, too, may be in the offing, and the accelerated exploitation of the oceans' resources. Now, with the biological bomb ready to explode, the need to face this complexity of problems takes on more acute, do-it-now urgency.

The most tempting solution is to let things ride and pay as little attention as possible to these mind-boggling developments. But a decision to ignore them is simply a decision to turn them over to any unscrupulous opportunist who chooses to employ them for his own ends. To appreciate the consequences, we need only imagine some totalitarian nation of the future, led by a man sure he knows what is best for everybody. He has at his command all the new means of controlling reproduction and the human brain and behavior. In addition to being able to raise entire populations in vitro or in tissue culture, he could implant electrodes or begin administering drugs to people at a very early age, maintaining his subjects in a constant state of hardworking subservience and at the same time in a constant state of euphoria by stimulating the pleasure centers of their brains. Practically no one in such a society would have any true choice in any area of life which we now consider important. But everybody would be "happy."

Who cares about the pursuit of happiness if everybody already has it? If everybody is happy, can anything be wrong?

If we think so, says Sir Julian Huxley, we must ascertain once again that we know what answers we would give to some basic questions: What are people for? What human values are we eager to hang onto? Without answers to such questions we remain helpless to use scientific advance as it should be used —as a tool to serve human values in a society that can still be called democratic.

The overriding political predicament, then, is this: how to plan and organize—intelligently, efficiently, flexibly—and at the same time safeguard the individual from intolerably restrictive state controls. Can there be real planning without real control? Some breakthroughs in political science, and in the other behavioral sciences, may be necessary to handle the problems created by breakthroughs in physics and biology. Obviously the professional political types, though they will ultimately be responsible for making the laws and administering them, cannot do it all themselves. They will need all the help they can get.

Artists and writers, for instance, can make a major contribution. There will be much more for them in the new age than new themes and new plots for plays, poems, novels and paintings. With a vast, opened-up universe of new possibilities and relationships to explore and portray, with unparalleled human powers and dimensions, they can help create an already badly needed new image of man.

Religion, though rooted in faith, is always affected by scientific advances. As these advances pick up speed and broaden in scope, they will inevitably raise profound theological questions. Apart from meeting these, theologians will bear a major responsibility to adapt codes of ethics and standards of value to an age where even the Eternal Verities are considered open to challenge.

Scientists themselves are, meanwhile, trying hard to build their own codes and standards out of logic and scientific knowledge. The growing movement is called Scientific Humanism, or sometimes Evolutionary Humanism. Influential on it have been such figures as the late French Jesuit scientist-philosopher, Pére Teilhard de Chardin, and Sir Julian Huxley, who has outlined his version of Scientific Humanism in a book called Religion without Revelation.

Many biologists are hopeful that the revelations of biology itself will give us new and profound insights into the true nature of man, allowing us to draw up laws and ethical systems that are consistent with that nature. The New Man science helps create may also be much better equipped to deal with problems that now look insoluble, and the new powers we get may give us answers we cannot now predict—or may even render some of the problems obsolete. So, even at a time when the daily newspapers are full of wars and riots and murders, and we despair that "human nature" can never be different, let us not give up hope yet. "Can the Ethiopian change his skin," asked Jeremiah, "or the leopard his spots? Then may ye also do good, that are accustomed to do evil." If it suddenly turns out that the Ethiopian and the leopard and you and I can change anything it pleases us to change, then it follows—does it not?—that even we may also do good.

It may be comforting to know that the statesmen and the theologians and the philosophers and the scientists are worrying about all these things, but we cannot let them do all the worrying for us, or make all the decisions for us. The time ahead is wild and uncharted. No one has been there, so there are no experts. Each of us, whose body and brain may be modified or whose descendants' characteristics may be predetermined, has a vast personal stake in the outcome. We can guarantee that good will be done only by looking to it ourselves.

We Must Learn To See What's Really New

Margaret Mead

For four decades America's pioneer anthropologist, Margaret Mead, has been studying man in his many environments, paying particular attention to marriage and family. Most Americans picture her in pith helmet pursuing primitive tribes in the jungles of the South Seas. But Dr. Mead's home base is Manhattan, where she is curator of ethnology at the American Museum of Natural History and teaches at Columbia. It is the problems of urban jungles and family patterns of sexually liberated modern man—and woman—that she and her fellow anthropologists are increasingly called upon to examine. Dr. Mead at 66 expresses opinions so original and provocative that they speak both to an alarmed older generation and to a restless youth. Asked to comment on these aspects of our society in conversations with Life *Reporter Irene Neves, Dr. Mead aired the following thoughts*:

• There is tremendous confusion today about change. This isn't surprising because people are living in a period of the fastest change the world has ever known. Young people have been confronted with the changes, but at the same time they have no sense of history and no one has been able to explain to them what has happened. We are always very poor at teaching the last 25 years of history. Adults have been shrieking about the fact that great newnesses are here but they are not talking about what the newnesses are.

• Young people have been dealing in utterly enormous amounts of despair. I think they feel adults have constructed a world in which they have very little chance to stay alive. They don't understand that while there are new dangers, there is also a new kind of responsibility and new hope. But all this discussion about having short skirts or long skirts, showing your breasts or not showing your breasts—dull. I'm not denigrating the crisis, but in order to cope with change you have to know what is new and what is old.

• We are having a tremendous revolution in the world of sex but most people are talking about promiscuity or four-letter words, and they are not the point. Swings between puritanism and license are as old as Methuselah. The present change is really a very different one—having recognized the population explosion, society will no longer have to make women's reproductivity of primary importance. Once we have realized this, we free women to be people, and whether we free them to copulate oftener or with more partners is less relevant. Without this change we would probably have had a swing back to a quite different sexual ethic and it would just

"We Must Learn To See What's Really New," by Margaret Mead and Irene Neves, Life Magazine, August 23, 1968,

be one more swing of the pendulum, but *with* it we are making an evolutionary change. This is just as important a change as the discovery of nuclear energy, and I think it is here to stay. But I wish people would realize what the change is. All this talk about who is sleeping with whom where is of relatively less importance.

• A great many of the kids now looking at the Vietnam war and having just confronted the reality of the bomb for the first time are acting the way English schoolboys behaved in the last days of World War I. The war was taking a terrific death toll then, and the boys who were just under military age all expected to be killed. There are quite a few young people who are doing that now, saying there is no use in going to class, we'll all get drafted and we'll all be killed. So you get this behavior of dancing on the eve of Waterloo except that now the young men are not dancing. This is not the gay fling before death–it's the saying that life is not worthwhile at all if it can do this to us, to some of us, to *any* of us.

• The major demand of the young today is for somebody to tell them they are good. They want the president of the college against which they are demonstrating to come out and march with them. They are saying, we don't want to use the back seat of a car anymore for sex. They want the college to say it is okay to use their dormitory rooms for lovemaking and they want their parents to let them use the playroom. At every point they are demanding a legitimization for what they are doing.

• There have always been young people who are questioning the system, rebelling against it and expressing it in their clothes and sex behavior, but it just wasn't blown up this way before. The mass media write prescriptions for youthful behavior like cookbooks and circulate them all over the country. The behavior of a few enterprising young rebels becomes a model to many young people who don't belong but get swept into it. This is the first generation who have been brought up by the mass media instead of by parents. We should really ask whether this is a good thing. We just might like partially to restore parents again.

• Leisure does not automatically develop the soul. And this is a real dilemma of Americans.

• Romantic love is not nearly as important as it was 20 years ago. It's much more important to get married than to be in love today. Most girls want to get married as soon as possible because they want to get away from their mothers. At one time in this country women grew up with other women in the home–grandmothers, aunts, servants, cousins. But the American pattern of family life now consists of a man, a woman and underage children. Women can no longer tolerate having another grown woman in the house.

• There are a large number of marriages of college graduates that break up between the ages of 25 and 35 and especially when they have married before going on to graduate or professional school together. We find there is a tremendous amount of breakups at the time the men get their professional degrees. Their wives have helped support them usually and they have pushed them to study and finish the same way parents do when they are supporting a child. The result is that the wife gets pigeonholed with the parents. These husbands don't feel any more guilty about leaving their wives than they do when they leave their parents. The alternative to this is that a lot of young wives had two or three children immediately so that their husbands couldn't leave. A man at 30 who has several children just cannot afford to support them and marry another wife and support the next batch.

• Different cultures and different periods have different styles of sex relationships. You have the typical European situation where a man had a lot of experience and the woman didn't, where the husband was supposed to initiate his wife. You have the American notion in which the boy and girl are supposed to be of the same age and equally ignorant and clumsy. We still have the situation where both are equally clumsy but they have read a book or seen a film. But this does not mean people have acquired any sophistication about sex whatsoever–they are still inexperienced children initiating each other and fumbling.

No one has the slightest proof that very many girls in the United States, age 16, are *enjoying* sex. Not the slightest proof. Why should they, with the partners they've got? Promiscuity has increased but I don't know at all that there has been an increase in variety of sex behavior. Maybe there has, but we've got to talk about what is happening in Omaha and Charleston and not just New York and Cambridge. We are at the mercy at present of an extraordinary propagation of ideas that are very quickly spread across the country. The current position is that young people are moving away from feeling guilty about sleeping with somebody to feeling guilty if they are *not* sleeping with someone.

• This recognition of the population explosion has opened the door to really responsible research on contraception. In the next 10 years we will have all kinds of contraception –the morning-after dose, the once-a-month dose, things for men, things for women–and we will be able to adjust contraception to culture and temperament. We have invented the Pill, but it in itself is not really a very satisfactory invention. We don't know what the biological effects are at all, and also the average inexperienced American girl doesn't want to take the Pill because she doesn't want to admit what she may be going to do. For girls like this, it is probably going to be desirable to have a morning-after pill.

• I would say the characteristic style of relationship in the United States, including marriage, is shortlived, intense relationships of which everything is demanded and which are broken off the minute they don't deliver everything. We ask too much too quickly of every single encounter. We also ask too much of marriage, and not getting it we despair too quickly and break it off.

• I have recommended that we have different kinds of marriages–an individual marriage in which young people who aren't ready to have children can legally live together. I don't think they should be ready for children until they have tried marriage for a couple of years first. Then, after a couple know they can get on together, there could be a second kind of marriage involving parental responsibility. I proposed it because the only alternative today seems to be getting married and getting divorced and getting remarried and getting divorced. But this idea doesn't find favor with the young. Young people want society's permission for every kind of premarital behavior. They would just like their parents to support them while they live together in the playroom, and so on the one hand they say, "Why get married?", and on the other hand they still want marriage presented as irrevocable. The ideal of young people in this country is still totally monogamous marriage for life. They want the ideal to be what it always has been, so that when they finally decide to get married they can believe it will be forever. It's a hopeless position, a ridiculous position and utterly untenable. But we live in this unreal world where people still assume in spite of the divorce rate that *their* marriage is going to be different.

• Pretending marriage is for life was fine when people died young and vigorous men could bury three wives and put nice gravestones over all of them. You also found the woman who, if she were vigorous, would bury three husbands. We had such a marriage style in an Indian tribe on the Northwest coast, where young men married middle-aged widows and that gave them a start in life. Then these widows died about the time men reached middle age, and they as middle-aged men married young girls. Then they died and left their wives as middle-aged widows who married young men. Everybody had fun. But you couldn't do this today because people stay alive so long. I think the longer people live and the more diverse their experience, the less likely it is that two people will stay married a lifetime. You see, if people get married at 20, they then have a reasonable expectation of being married for 50 years. The contemplation of 50 years together makes people less willing to tolerate an unsatisfactory marriage.

• We could, I believe, bring children up to accept the fact that this is a world in which divorce is a reality—a world in which people live a terribly long time, in which they change a great deal, in which they change their professions and their personalities and their interests. I think they should know it is a world where it is possible for a man to marry a woman who was marvelous and a good mother of his children but to whom he can no longer stay married after the children are grown.

• Most people today would say, I want my child to grow up in a household where there is a father. But there are all sorts of vicissitudes. Death used to be the worst vicissitude and today divorce is. We've the highest divorce rate you can find, but there are still only about as many homes broken by divorce today as by death 50 years ago. So, 50 years ago you couldn't guarantee a child that its mother or father wouldn't die; today you can't guarantee your child there won't be a divorce. But you can make a better start as parents.

• Women ought to prepare not to feel as abandoned as they do now if their marriage ends. Today when a woman has spent 20 years in a marriage and it ends, she feels very hurt. She has a poor chance of another marriage, her husband has every chance of another marriage. These are the facts and I think we ought to start preparing women for them. But we're not ready in any way. We haven't even accepted the fact of divorce. We still behave as if divorce were wicked or a failure. Why is it a failure any more than death is a failure? It's the death of a relationship. This is what the Anglican Commission in England has come up with. They said adultery ought not to be a cause for the end of marriage, that the only legitimate cause for divorce is the death of a marriage and it is dead if it is dead to one of the persons involved. But instead we have reached a point where we even have Roman Catholic mothers who are saying to their daughters: "Don't get married in the Church. Have a civil ceremony, because you don't know it's going to last."

• The family is the oldest institution of the human race. Other institutions have always depended on it and I think people will go right on doing this. But if we would take a look at the modern world we would realize that people today are taking extraordinary risks. Young people are marrying across wide expanses of the world, choosing partners of other classes, other religions, other races. And people who take these risks ought to realize that they are doing something different but that they take the risk because they feel it is worth it—because they care about differences, because they care about contrast, because they care about intensity. Such relationships do have greater intensity, but they are also more hazardous. If you are not going to marry the boy next door—and if you do you may die of boredom—then you have got to work much harder.

• I think it is dangerous when people become desperately despairing about marriage or race relations or the population explosion or cities or automation and feel we're going to live in a world of smog where we'll all be sealed up in little cells because we can't let in the air. Unless people believe the world is going to be better they won't make the effort to save it. All these present-day difficulties are desperately important, but they are not irreversible. We can do something about all of them but it will take the combined efforts of all *four* generations.

• The way Americans deal with anything that seems unmanageable is to run it into the ground by overuse. Take the case of the Mad Bomber. When he was loose he was terribly dangerous and might have panicked the whole city. But what did New Yorkers do? They made fake telephone calls and they made false bombs. They called the police and said there was a bomb under the dinosaurs in the Museum of Natural History, that there was a bomb here and a bomb there. The children all made bombs at school out of bicarbonate of soda and everybody turned it into a grand lark. The same thing happened with the individual bomb shelter. No one realized you would have to shoot anyone who came into your shelter. So the President announced that everybody had to have a shelter, and what did we do? We designed $15,000 shelters with wall-to-wall carpeting, TV, picture windows, a gun to shoot people with and plastic bags to put the bodies in. You got discussions on the radio as to whether you ought to shoot your neighbor and meetings in university towns about how they would kill the people who tried to come from nearby cities. Everybody was walking around saying, isn't this terrible? A lot of people started shelters but nobody finished them and we got rid of the idea. We exaggerate, we caricature, we overemphasize and then we eliminate.

Chapter 4
EDUCATION

The primary function of an education system is to transmit the knowledge, experience and wisdom acquired in the past. Education systems have always been able to produce scholars who discover new facts and develop concepts and theories. They have also produced, so far, a sufficient number of teachers to hand on the accumulated information to their students.

The process of becoming a teacher was once fairly simple. A reasonably intelligent person went to school and took a number of courses in history, literature, and other useful subjects in the academic field. In his last year or two of school he specialized in a particular field, such as English, math, or history. Then he went forth to teach others. Implicit in such a system of training was the assumption that the world and knowledge would not change very much during the teacher's lifetime—that the subject matter in the teacher's field of knowledge would remain relatively stable. In recent times, this has not been the case. The amount of knowledge in almost every field has increased so much that few teachers have been able to keep up with it—and too few have tried.

What education becomes by the end of this century is open to serious challenge—indeed, it has already been challenged on many campuses across the nation. To be prepared to improve the nation's educational system, we need to find out more about the students who will use it. Who are the high school students of today, and how do they look at their schools and at themselves ("On the Fringe of a Golden Era")? Are public school systems responsible for educating *all* of our citizens? Who steps in when the public school system fails ("Training the Unemployables")? Can private enterprise help this enormous public monopoly ("Company Adopts School and Things Happen")? Is our educational system so large already that it is not responsive to change ("Promise Turns to Disappointment")? Is it possible to obtain a superior education in a ghetto school ("P.S. 192, Central Harlem")? Are all college students today teen-age activist rebels? What *are* they interested in ("Convenient Myths About Today's Students")? How did our system get the way it is—and what hope for it is there ("The Humanistic Heartbeat Has Failed")?

"On the Fringe of a Golden Era" Time

"If Booth Tarkington were to write *Seventeen* today," says a Connecticut high school English teacher, "he'd have to call it *Twelve.*" Sociologist Reuel Denney notes with fascination the shopping list of a twelve-year-old suburban girl: "Water pistol, brassière, permanent." When a 16-year-old Louisville boy, as a practical joke, gravely announced at dinner that his girl friend was pregnant, the first reaction of the stunned family came from the boy's younger brother, 13. "My God," he said. "You'll lose your allowance."

Worldly, interesting, informed and even intellectual when barely out of childhood, young kids all over the U.S. are pulling down the entry age to teendom. Even as they do, the affluent society is pushing up the average age of school leaving. The lengthened span of teen-agery—what Johns Hopkins Sociologist James Coleman calls "the coming earlier to social maturity while having to spend a considerably longer period in a dependent role"—is further fattened by a growth rate of teen-age population that is four times as high as the U.S. average. The country now has 24 million people aged 13 to 19.

This one-eighth of the nation is chiefly formed and fashioned by the schools, where teen-agers spend half of their waking hours.

This article appeared in *Time* Magazine, January 29, 1965.

If Lyndon Johnson succeeds in getting "every child the best education the nation can provide," the schools' responsibility will grow ever greater. And by and large the pattern works: in the mid-1960s, smarter, subtler and more sophisticated kids are pouring into and out of more expert, exacting and experimental schools.

They Know More. Caltech President Lee DuBridge believes that "there is no question that today's teen-ager coming to one of the major colleges is better educated and more seriously motivated than ever before." Profiting by a vast improvement in teaching methods, curriculums and equipment, "our children know more about things than we did," says New World Foundation Consultant Frank G. Jennings. Ellsworth Tompkins, executive secretary of the National Education Association's 30,000 secondary school principals, holds that "over the past seven or eight years we have experienced in the schools the most important developments since the establishment of public education."

In no society of all history have more teen-agers gone to school and stayed there through such advanced ages. In 1900 only 13% of U.S. children of the ages 14 through 17 were students. By 1940 the ratio had risen to 73%. Now enrollment is close to 95% of the high-school-age population, and more than half the graduates will enter college. With 700 two-year colleges already enrolling nearly a million students, experienced trend watchers forecast than in 1980 the ordinary U.S. student will not leave the classroom until he is 20 or 21.

The burden of added numbers, rather than forcing down academic standards, has raised them. "The big drop in quality that many educators were predicting ten years ago just never took place," says Curriculum Planner A. Harry Passow of Columbia's Teachers College. Instead, the average peformance of junior and senior high school teen-agers on many tests has been gradually rising, reports E. F. Lindquist, president of the University of Iowa. Even though exams are tougher than a decade ago, and even though seven times as many students (1,500,000 this year) are taking them, scores on the formidable College Entrance Boards have stayed up—thus revealing how quickly excellence has attained depth. James B. Conant, whose "The American High School Today," published in 1959, became the bible of reform, is dumbfounded. Last week, addressing an N.E.A. convention of secondary school principals in Miami, he happily confessed that "writing about American education is almost as breathtaking as writing about international politics. Before a book is in print, parts of it are already out of date."

Tough Culture. Just as obsolete are most conventional notions about teen-agers, a word invented in the U.S. and popularized scarcely 25 years ago to supplant such earlier images as the carefree Huck Finn type, the early-to-work Horatio Alger model and the heavily psychological "adolescent" three decades back. It was the culmination of the process by which, as Sociologist Denney points out, the U.S. became the first nation to transform children from "a family asset as labor, to a family liability as student consumers." That liability is one that the U.S. seems willing to afford: it has created a flourishing sub-culture whose goals, heroes, styles and customs are, in the teen-age word of admiration, "tough."

The most startling part of the change may be the classic conflict between parents and children is letting up. The archetype of the James Dean-style cool youth is giving way to the likes of the teen-age hero of James Leigh's new novel, "What Can You Do?" "I've never been able to see the big rebellion scene in order to prove you're an individual," drawls Hero Phil Fuller. "Much less friction if you just go with it. That's elementary physics; the heat of friction is waste energy."

Parental Abdication. At the same time, adults who lived through a great depression, a shattering war, an anxious peace, and the whole onslaught of existentialism are less inclined than ever to proclaim what Margaret Mead calls "parental imperatives." Some of the slackening has been as silly as the difficent dad in Max Schulman's "I Was A Teen-age Dwarf," who takes his son on palsy walks. But much of the diminishing tension results from parental intent as well as parental abdication. Harvard Sociologist Talcott Parsons finds many young parents "committed to a policy of training serious independence in youth," to which children respond with seriousness—and an occasional wistful regret. "I don't get authority at home," sighs Dana Nye, 17, a student at Pacific Palisades High School in Los Angeles. "We're just a bunch of people who go about our business and live under one roof. One of these days I'd like to sit down and find out from my parents what they really believe in."

What a lot of parents believe, as one mother expresses it, is that "a parent who says to a child 'I don't know' is somehow better than one who says 'I know for sure.' " Inevitably many adolescents are left with few guidelines. "Their difficulty," says Harvard Historian Laurence Wylie, "lies not in living up to expectations, but in discovering what they really are." The result, according to

University of California Sociologist Edgar Z. Friedenberg, is the "vanishing adolescent"–made to mature earlier, yet in many ways still engagingly immature. And since "part of the American dream is to live long and be young," many adults ambivalently relish and resent the teen-ager's freedom and spontaneity. "Our whole culture believes less in authority," snaps one Detroit priest. "Yet the teen-ager is the only one criticized for not recognizing it."

"The very changes that society is undergoing have spawned something more than was bargained for," writes James Coleman in The Adolescent Society. "Adolescents today are cut off, probably more than ever before, from the adult society. They are dumped into a society of their peers, whose habitats are the halls and classrooms of their schools, the teen-age canteens, the corner drugstore and the automobile." That is where teen-agers get their tastes and values. They're in cahoots now," says Columbia Sociologist Arthur Jersild.

Noonday at "Pali." One anthropologically absorbing place to watch these characteristics in interplay is the wall-less roofed area for cafeteria tables at Pacific Palisades High School, bordering on Sunset Boulevard. "Pali," as the kids call it, is a new $7,000,000, red brick campus for 2,100 upper-middle-class students. "These are the students' cars," says English Teacher Jeanne Hernandez, pointing to a vast collection of "wheels" ranging up to Jags, "and there are the teachers' cars," pointing to a sedate group of compacts and the like. "It's so lush here that it's unreal," she says. "After a while you feel like a missionary in the tropics. If you don't get out, you go native."

The natives observe a rigid noonday ritual. The social elite–a breezy clique called the Palisades-Brentwood Singing and Drinking Association–hold court at cafeteria tables reserved by custom for them. Near by, like ladies in waiting, two plain girls snatch at conversational crumbs tossed by a pair of homecoming queens. At another table are the "social rejects"–girls on the fringes of the elite whose boy friends are now tired of them. "They are still allowed to go to parties," explains a guide, "but they aren't in on the really big decisions, like who the elite will back in student elections."

Toward the rear of the hall sit the service club members and the rah-rah crowd, "the squares who really believe in student government." Other tribes are the Saracens, who include a small motorcycling hood element; the clowns, a group of practical jokers who wear Mickey Mouse shirts to signify that all human existence is fraudulent; the intellectuals, who lounge on the steps of the administration building as the rest of the student body speculates over whether the long-haired girls among them are professional virgins or real swingers; and an amorphous crowd that defies classification by declaring unanimously: "I'm myself."

Parental pressure for grades at Pali is intense; students often retaliate at home by demanding cars, clothes, expensive vacations. "If you aren't aware of the underlying fraud," explains Senior Al Hunsaker, an A student, "then you become a grind. In a way, it's a massive put-on, faking out the community and the family without going through the suffering of a full-fledged revolt." "As long as we don't make waves," a classmate adds, "the administration is happy."

Dancing the Jerk. Drinking is common enough among Pali students, and the important thing is style. "It's all right to get blasted, if you can be witty or brave," says Larry Futterman, 17, "but if you get sloppy, you're way out." Glue-sniffing and marijauna are also out, because they bring on major trouble from the cops. Illicit sex is discussed more intensely than it is practiced, but even the talk is becoming boring since it involves a responsibility wary Pali teen-agers are not willing to accept. "We're not going to talk about sex, are we?" says a blond kid in horn-rims, yawning. The latest dance is the jerk: partners face each other three feet apart, then languorously sway their upper spine and arms while rhythmically punctuating the undulations with a savage pelvic thrust.

"You can't marry anyone important without going to college," says Candace McCoy, a Pali senior whose looks suggest the Mona Lisa melded with Gidget. "But there is more to it than that. I don't want to go through life uneducated." Her father, an aerospace engineer, "is always on my back about grades," but "mother just gave up on me about six years ago and decided I was destined to enjoy life, nothing more." Twice a week Candy dates basketball players, her way of steering between tribal obligations to the social elite and a "guilty" attraction for intellectuals ("They are so worthwhile"). The specific attraction is Jamie Kelso, 16, a skinny near genius who studies only those subjects that interest him, mostly political science and history.

"I enjoy three things," says Jamie. "Being in a bookstore with $10 in my pocket, a rainy day at the beach, and insight in terms of finding insight in myself." Like many Pali students, he does not especially enjoy his home life. "I'm kinda hoping to make a more meaningful person out of my mother, but it's hard work." Meaning is Jamie's favorite word. "What do good grades mean?" he asks. "And what if I go along, get married, have a good job and raise kids? Do we know what it is all about? Are the people around us really alive?" As for getting into college, he proposes a new kind of entrance exam: "The old eyeball test—the candidate and the admissions officer should look at each other until someone blinks." If the officer blinks first, he has to admit the kid.

Fashions in Fashions. Other schools, other mores—in fashions, music, buying, sex, goals and heroes.

Almost everywhere boys dress in madras shirts and chinos, or perhaps green Levi's—all tame and neat. The standard for girls is sweaters and skirts dyed to match, or shirtwaists and jumpers, plus blazers, Weejun loafers, and knee socks or stockings (required at Pali in even the hottest weather). There is a small vogue for black and white saddle shoes—cruelly called "polio boots" for their bulky appearance.

Sprayed, teased hair has mostly given way to the long, loose style. "You see some girls with big bouffs still, scratching their heads with pencils," sniffs Debbie Scott, a loose-haired Atlanta 15-year-old. Some girls even press their hair on ironing boards. If they carry lankness of hair to the Morticia stage, girls are also likely to put on textured or patterned stockings, pierce their ear lobes (with an ice cube to deaden the pain), and call themselves beat.

Behind every reasonably well-heeled teen-ager lurks a stereo set endlessly playing the Beatles, the tearful ballads of Joan Baez or the homogenized harmonies of Peter, Paul and Mary. Big in the older set: the twanging social protests of Folk Singer Bob Dylan. Thelonious Monk is generally classified with Guy Lombardo as "from another era."

Growing Down. In most such matters of fad, teen-agers are unwilling to give a moment's heed to adult criticism—for they know that grownups eventually get wise. Growing down to teen tastes, adults took over the twist, the Beatles, straight hair and tight pants, among dozens of other crazes. "Is nothing sacred any more?" moans one teen-ager.

Teen magazines thus urge their advertisers to pursue the consumer "not in the sweet by-and-by, but in the much sweeter now-and-now." Now-and-now statistics show that teen-agers spend $570 million on toiletries, $1.5 billion a year on entertainment, $3.6 billion on women's clothes—$12 billion all told. They account for 25% of the record industry, 35% of the movie audience. "Action, comedies with music," like *Beach Party, Bikini Beach, Beach Blanket Bingo* and *How to Stuff a Wild Bikini,* get made for only one sweet reason, explains Samuel Z. Arkoff of American International Pictures. "They're a kind of never-never land in modern undress." Teen-agers are not necessarily flattered by so much commercial attention. This month the student assembly at Lincoln High School in Portland, Ore., rebelled and condemned manufacturers who prey on "gullible teen-agers."

Sex at 16. "I didn't know what puberty was until I was almost past it," sings the fuddy-duddy father in *Bye Bye Birdie,* asking

Why can't they be like we were,
Perfect in every way?
What's the matter with kids today?

Kids today candidly talk about everything from puberty to homosexuality, but the actuality of free sex based on widespread use of contraceptives is nowhere near at hand. Some girls sleep with steady boy friends, circumspectly and not promiscuously. There are also the perennial pathetic girls who, as one boy explains it, "put out regularly, but they're either ugly or fat or, you know, kinda gross." Mostly, sex among teenagers is a joking game.

The crowd at San Francisco's Lowell High School, where students say there were three pregnancies last year, embarrasses a couple leaving a party to be alone by crying "Baaa" and jerking their elbows in a sideward motion, indicating that the couple intends to do more than make sheep's eyes. Interracial necking is acceptable, reports Clyde Leland, 15, "but usually they're the phonies trying so hard to be liberal." Denver's suburban Cherry Creek High is known for academic excellence and high-strung students, but it also has "woodsies"–dancing on the sand of a dry creek bed while beer cans pop and music from car radios blasts the night air. A current joke at Houston's Belaire High asks: "What's white and scares teen-agers?" Answer: the stork. Sherry Watson, 17, a popular member of the baton-twirling Bellaire Belles, is casual about boys. "Why, you've either dated them all once, or else they're like a brother to you and you wouldn't have them."

"Some couples who go steady are extremely idealistic," says Mrs. Sherrill Godwin, a counselor at Griffith High School just outside Winston-Salem. "That is why early marriages occur if she should get pregnant–from the idealism." Yet rural life is changing rapidly. Down on the farm, one time-honored way of learning about sex, watching the animals, is disappearing. "Today the animals are artificially inseminated," observes Mrs. Joseph Rademacher of Peotone, Ill. (pop. 3,300), mother of four sons, including teen-agers Bob, 16, and Bill, 14. "So I felt I should answer their questions rather than have some outsider tell them."

Goals and Heroes. Finding models and purpose is a major teen-age occupation. The traditional high school hero has been the star athlete. The serious young scholar who did not go out for a team was usually scorned as a "curve raiser" who made it tough on his classmates. The tradition may be changing. "I think the athletes are losing out," observes Daniel G. McMurtrie, 17, from Detroit's Denby High School. "It's In to be an individual and not to be afraid to bring up serious questions." Jimmy Fitzpatrick, a senior at Santa Monica High School, is in with the local surfing crowd. His hero is James Bond: "He's got everything. Everyone I know wants to be like him."

"The thing I like most is experience," says United States Teen Queen Luci Baines Johnson, 17. "I don't like to read about things, I want to do them." "Getting somewhere and proving yourself are the most important things," says Florence Jeffers, 16, a pert sophomore from Bridgeton, N.J., who is a class vice president ("Round up a posse and vote for Flossie"), a member of seven school clubs, and a prizewinning baker of chocolate chip cookies and chocolate cake. "I'd like to be a Jack-of-all-trades and a master of one." Carolyn Smith, 17, is taking seven periods of art at New Canaan (Conn.) High School, aims to be a professional painter, and is glad that, unlike most of her classmates, "I know what I'm going to do in life."

Jon Holdaway has been "bouncing around like a rubber ball. I'm immature, plenty," he admits cheerfully, "but I don't feel I'm mixed up." Holdaway, 18, is a track star at Seattle's Ingraham High School, a National Merit Scholarship semifinalist, and last summer was a tenor soloist in the first U.S. high school choir to tour Japan. He is torn between a career in political science or music, but in either case his goal is personal happiness. "That is the issue when you evaluate your life."

Sarah Greensfelder is firm on the subject of heroes: "It's not a very good concept, because you're always thinking of what you ought to be and not what you are." Sarah is 13 and an agnostic who nevertheless keeps a reproduction of the ceiling of the Sistine Chapel on the ceiling above her bed. She lives in a modest frame house in Mill Valley, near San Francisco, and licks stamps for Snick when she is not demonstrating for one cause or another. Zealously committed, she wanted to join the sit-ins at Berkeley, but her mother would not let her.

The Dung Heap. Negro teen-agers live in a world apart. "Culturally deprived, culturally deprived! That's all I hear," says Willie Armstead, 16, an A student at David Starr Jordan High School in the black ghetto of Los Angeles. "It's not so much that I mind being in an all-Negro school. What I care about is not being able to get together with white kids, or just kids with other backgrounds, and discussing ideas." Leslie Harris, 16, a talented musician and a student at Chicago's Wendell Phillips High School, has picketed the Chicago board of education to protest the skimpy treatment of Negro history in the standard public school curriculum.

Armstead and Harris are college-bound, but they are exceptions. For most slum kids, says Hunter College Sociologist Ernest Smith, "the American dream is not the American fact. These children cannot respond to what is being taught, and most educators resist changing the curriculums to aid these children." Kenneth B. Clark, New York psychologist and civil rights leader, holds that "the Negro kid who drops out of school is probably doing so to protect himself from a system designed to throw him in the dung heap of our society."

Already beyond the schools' help, for example is Harlem Dropout Harrison Campbell, 16, who quit Manhattan Vocational High School in the tenth grade last November. Campbell wanted to be a carpenter, "but I wasn't learning nothing no how," and no one urged him to stay on. Nowadays, he sleeps until noon, plays cards and records with his buddies unitl 3 p.m., then ambles over to a neighborhood school playground for a game of basketball or football. Campbell hopes to get a job soon, delivering telephone books at $11.80 a day. "That's good bread," he says.

The Transformation. "The youngster who has only muscle to sell is an obsolete man," observes William Levenson, education professor at Western Reserve. Whereas earlier generations believed that there were many ways to get ahead, today's teen-agers think that schooling is perhaps the only way to success. "The educational period which was once tentative and experimental," notes Anthropologist Mead, "is now quite as directly functional as the life of a weaver's apprentice during the Middle Ages." The resulting "college education syndrome" puts immense pressures on teen-agers. Some kids occasionally rise at 3 a.m. to study—one Washington mother has to forbid her girls to get up before 6. And so eager are kids to find colleges that when a wag at New Canaan High posted an invitation for interviews with the admissions officer of "Whasamatta College," five students signed up.

All pressure would go for nothing if the schools were failing. But they are not. The emerging truth is that the tentative innovations of the recent past—honors courses, team teaching, language labs, curriculum reform, "enrichment," comprehensive schools, independent study, advanced placement, nongraded classes, "new" this or that – have in the main worked toward a successful transformation of U.S. secondary education. Although the U.S. educational system is too varied, too unwieldly, too much subject to local control for the tide to be national, the direction is clear. Says J. Lloyd Trump, who pioneered the team-teaching method: "We're on the fringe of a golden era in education. It's going to come slowly, but we're heading there."

Discovery Method. The era was opened by such men as Harvard Psychologist Jerome Bruner, who perceived that "any subject can be taught effectively in some intellectually honest form to any child at any stage of development." The theory became practice at M.I.T., where a study group headed by Jerrold Zacharias devised a new high school physics course in 1956 based on the notion that it was more fun, and more instructive, to understand the principles of physics by performing experiments rather than by memorizing a mass of facts and rarely testing them in the lab. The system was called the "discovery method," and it quickly spread to the other sciences as university scholars joined with public school teachers to revise curriculums.

New math now reaches about 70% of the students in Grades 7 through 12. This year nearly half the high school students studying physics are learning by discovery; one-third of the chemistry students and one-fourth of the biology students are taking completely revamped courses. Along with the curriculum changes came a new technology—programmed instruction, audio-visual equipment, classroom television, computers—which freed schools from the idea that one teacher standing before a class of 30 children was the ideal form of instruction.

Combining the latest in technology and content, foreign-language study has grown and improved. Since 1958, when U.S. public schools conducted 46 language labs, the number has soared to 7,000. Instead of memorizing vocabulary lists and grammatical rules, the student teen-ager puts on headphones, listens to tapes, and get a result almost unheard of in earlier decades of high school instruction: he speaks and undertands the language.

Who Teaches Better? The discovery method has also improved courses in the humanities and the social sciences, with students increasingly asked to solve problems, not memorize answers. A "Power Reading" program in 23 Los Angeles high schools, for example, teaches students to define the author's purpose, analyze the logic, and compare the work to original sources. Having learned anew that writing equals thinking, schools are requiring more composition—and in the process they are finding that a widespread and sensible rebound from distorted permissiveness has permitted the rise of a generation of teen-agers who can spell. And the best of John Dewey's liberating progressive education, with its joy in learning, is a powerful precursor of the discovery method.

"There's no question," says Conant, "that the American public is now more in favor of tough, rough standards for those who can take it." Many high schools now require five courses a semester, not four. Hardly a high school exists without some sort of enriched academic program for gifted students. For super-nourishment, students can take advanced-placement exams, which may land them in the sophomore class at college and will at least eliminate the necessity of taking certain freshman courses. In 1955, when the College Entrance Examination Board introduced advanced-placement exams, 12,000 students from 104 U.S. high schools took them; last May 29,000 students from 2,000 high schools took them.

At Harvard, where early support for advanced placement helped the plan succeed nationally, almost half the freshman class arrived last fall having done some college-level work in high school, and 191 entered as sophomores. Those who enter advanced courses directly from high school do better than those who have taken the preliminary work as college freshmen. "One possible conclusion," jokes a Harvard official, "is that the high schools can teach better than we can."

That may well be the case at nearby Newton High School, guinea pig for most of the new curriculum changes. Four Harvard professors are teaching classes in social studies there, and students take advanced-placement exams in ten of the twelve available subjects. "I don't think we have a program here that was going ten years ago," says Principal Richard Mechem. The latest change: overhauling vocational training, which reflects a new—and overdue—concern of U.S. education.

Knights in Shining Chinos. The Great Society, or any society, needs manpower as well as brainpower. The scholastically brilliant will invent new computers, but the academically average must know how to run them. And although the U.S. has always provided an outstanding education to some, the wave of reform has given a better education to all. Says Carnegie Corporation President John Gardner, chairman of the presidential task force on educational goals: "Gifted and non-gifted students are being challenged to perform closer to the limit of their abilities."

Even an old-math mind can roughly multiply millions of teen-agers by the factor of better-trained intelligence and surmise that the next generations of Americans will look a lot smarter than the past. It will have to; a recent N.E.A. publication notes that "the first doubling of knowledge occurred in 1750, the second in 1900, the third in 1950, and the fourth only ten years later." The fifth and sixth, if the plot line holds its course, are close at hand. Teen-agers today do not think of themselves as "knights in shining chinos" riding forth on rockets to save the universe. But even the coolest of them know that their careers could be almost that fantastic.

Training the Unemployables U.S. News & World Report

Lockheed Aircraft Corporation, one of the first major companies to recruit and train workers among those formerly considered unemployable, is taking a hard look at results.

Its decision: Problems are many and solutions not easy to come by. But the unskilled, unschooled "hard core" can be trained to do a job that in most cases is as good as that done by a normally hired employe.

Lockheed regards its pilot programs in hard-core training as a success and is expanding them.

The company does not minimize the problems involved. Its officials do not feel that they have the total answer. But lessons learned at Lockheed could make the job easier for other members of the National Alliance of Businessmen, which, with Government encouragement, has pledged to find jobs for 100,000 unemployed by July, 1969, and 500,000 by July, 1971.

Lockheed has programs of varying degree in 10 of the 50 cities co-operating in the federal effort, but the company's first formal venture into hard-core training is at the subsidiary Lockheed-Georgia Company in Marietta, Ga., and the Lockheed Missiles & Space Company in Sunnyvale, near San Francisco.

Requirements in Reverse. Because it wants only the hardest of the hard core in the pilot programs, Lockheed has set up five negative standards and requires prospective trainees to meet four of them.

To qualify, a trainee has to be a school dropout, unemployed, with no consistent record of work of any kind and have an annual family income of $3,000 or below.

Among recruits, a "certain percentage" must have arrest records, and a heavy proportion are to be drawn from minorities. Most are Negro.

According to a Lockheed official: "We intended to make sure they were the hard core. Some men were weeded out at the start because they didn't meet the low standards. There were some who didn't get jobs because they were too well qualified."

At Lockheed-Georgia, 98 trainees entered the first 12-week program. They received $20 to $30 a week, plus $5 per dependent and an allowance to cover transportation.

Eighteen quit before training ended, and 10 were fired, in most cases because they failed to attend classes regularly or were habitually late. Of the 61 who finished training, Lockheed hired 43. Other companies hired most of the remainder. Of the 43 who stayed with Lockheed, only three were fired later for poor attendance.

According to Lockheed, most of the men who dropped out did so because they found they could not live on the small allowance that was paid them during training.

Allowance vs. Payroll. At the Sunnyvale plant, 108 trainees were enrolled in two programs. In one, they received a training allowance. In the other, they went directly on the company payroll at $2.40 to $2.80 an hour. Five quit, four were fired and one was arrested and convicted of a felony. None was fired for inability to do the work.

A Lockheed official says this: "A comparison study with a group of 50 new employes who met traditional hiring standards and entered the same occupations during the period indicated no difference between the hard-core and traditional trainees on rating of quality and quantity of work."

James D. Hodgson, Lockheed's vice president for industrial relations at corporate headquarters here in Burbank, originated the company's programs. He says:

"There are certain criteria. Has it hurt production? Has it increased employe turnover? The answer to both is no. Has it caused disaffection among other employes? Not to any significant extent.

"So we think from a company standpoint, it is a success. From the standpoint of the nation, people who have been thought unemployable have proved to be employable."

E. G. Mattison, corporate personnel director, agrees. He says:

"We used to wonder if the hard-core men could be trained. The answer is: They sure can. They can become as competent as regularly hired employes, some even better."

Lockheed-Georgia officials say they have had two job offers from other companies for every man trained in the program whom Lockheed cannot put on its own payroll.

Encouraged by results, Lockheed this year is doubling the size of the project at Sunnyvale and is enlarging the Georgia program.

Hiring from Minority Groups. Lockheed has hired minority workers as far back as World War II. It did not begin actively to recruit minority workers, however, until 1961, when it became the first company to adopt a Plan for Progress program in the Federal Government's drive for equal-opportunity employment.

Two years ago, nearly 1 in every 12 of Lockheed's 84,000 workers belonged to a minority. Today, with 92,000 workers on the payroll, the proportion is even greater.

Lockheed's president, A. Carl Kotchian, told company management in a special statement earlier this year:

"We know we must not let prejudice obscure a man or woman's worth. We know there are valuable human resources among the disadvantaged. And we know our own business, like all businesses, cannot flourish under conditions of national unrest."

Lockheed's interest in minority problems is not entirely unselfish. As a firm whose Government contracts totaled 10.6 billions between 1961 and 1967–88 per cent of all sales–Lockheed is acutely aware of Washington's interest in racial problems. There is an unspoken belief that a company could lose Government business if it does not co-operate in projects that provide employment for minorities.

The Elusive Recruit. The firm faced problems right from the start of the experiment in finding people to hire.

"These people aren't easy to locate in the community," says Mr. Hodgson. "We don't advertise because hard-core people don't respond." Most are located through the Urban League, the National Association for the Advancement of Colored People, various other minority organizations and state employment agencies.

Once recruits are found, one of the first tasks is that of bringing trainees up to what Lockheed officials describe as "proper standards of dress and decorum."

Getting the hard-core personnel to work on time or to show up at work at all can be a problem. For many, the training period marked the first time in their lives that they had to be at a certain place at a certain time.

Another Man's Shoes. At the Georgia plant, supervisors found many of the younger Negroes had trouble expressing themselves. To cure this, supervisors instituted "role playing," in which a trainee pretends to be a counselor, a worker who was having trouble or a successful worker.

"After a while," an official says, "men begin to open up in their attitudes, thus improving communications."

After an orientation period, trainees move into basic factory skills, such as riveting.

Then comes fabrication of parts, use of a drill press and blueprint reading. Next come specialized skills such as welding, sheet-metal assembly, electrical assembly and key-punch operation.

Throughout training, punctuality and care and maintenance of tools are emphasized.

Lockheed has found that an absolute necessity in training is close supervision and personal attention. The personal problems can be "unbelievable," officials say. Lockheed supervisors cite these instances:

- One man telephoned to report he couldn't get to work because his hog was stolen. This was considered a poor excuse, and he was about to be fired. Then it was remembered that "hog" was a slang expression for an automobile.

- Another man faced a short jail sentence for a minor offense committed before joining the program. His counselor persuaded the judge to allow him to serve time at night and on week-ends, and he was permitted to leave jail during the day to attend class.

- A country-raised applicant arrived at the plant in a taxi without a penny to pay a $4 fare. A counselor settled an argument between driver and worker by paying the $4 out of his own pocket.

- Another man missed work for two days because rowdies had broken the windshield of his car and he didn't have money for a new one. The police would not allow him to drive without a windshield. The supervisor personally advanced money to have the car repaired.

Problems and solutions are not always that personal. At Sunnyvale, a reduction in the work force made it impossible for Lockheed to hire a small number of men it had trained.

The company learned, however, that a plant in the neighborhood was hard-pressed for microwelders, a trade not taught at Lockheed. So it started a two-week course in microwelding, trained the men and then sent them on to the other firm for jobs.

Ready Adaptation. Difficulties arising from a worker's unfamiliarity with a modern industrial plant are rare.

According to Howard C. Lockwood, a minority-employment specialist:

"These problems are exaggerated. Our counselors find these people accommodate themselves to routine pretty well."

Quality of work is high, Mr. Lockwood says. "Their performance in some instances has been better than that of workers recruited in a normal fashion."

Mr. Hodgson says: "The stereotype is that many of the hard-core people don't want to work, that they would rather exist on welfare. But Lockheed's experience shows that most of the people are extremely motivated."

A major requirement in hard-core training, according to Mr. Lockwood, is to pay the worker a livable wage during training. Lockheed found the dropout rate much higher among those receiving a training stipend of $20 to $30 weekly than it was among those who went immediately on the company payroll at $2.40 an hour.

The Federal Government is picking up most of the cost of training the hard-core unemployed, but expense to a company still is great.

Under the program of the National Alliance of Businessmen, the Government will pay a company a maximum of $3,500 per man, an amount Mr. Hodgson says comes close to covering the actual outlay. There is no way of estimating other costs to the company, however, including the time of officers and administrative help for trainees.

After Training—. What happens when a hard-core employe takes over a regular job? Mr. Mattison, the personnel director, says:

"Many of the concepts we had about hard-cores being made members of the work force are inaccurate. They can be recruited, trained and hired to good effect. Our experience has been that some trainees almost immediately have been promoted once they start regular work."

On the basis of pilot programs, Lockheed finds that the "quit" rate is substantially lower than that of workers normally hired. The number fired is about the same.

Lockheed concedes that personal attention given the hard-core man can cause resentment among other employes.

"That's a problem you have to face with discretion and good taste to avoid reaction," says Mr. Hodgson. "If you give one person more training, another may feel he's disadvantaged. This has to be watched by any employer doing this kind of program."

The Trainees' View. What do trainees themselves think of the program?

One 21-year-old entered with the avowed purpose of "picking up some of that easy money"—the $20 weekly training allowance. After finishing the program, he told new trainees:

"I came here to play, but I soon found out it was a serious program. I want to tell you I'm 10 feet tall. I don't feel like a boy like I used to. I feel like a man."

One man—a Negro—applied for training with an other-than-honorable military discharge for spending 400 days in the guardhouse out of 700 days in the Army. He had six children but had never held a job for more than three months. Usually he had been fired for hitting his superior.

After completing the program, he told newcomers:

"This program has taught me how to listen. I've learned how to teach my children how to get ahead. And I feel better about life."

Mr. Hodgson has this advice to companies setting up similar programs: "One of the principal lessons we learned is humility. There are some real problems in this area, and they aren't easy.... The state of the art in dealing with people's problems is pretty low.

"The second thing we learned is the need to make changes. It's not as simple as just putting people on the payroll. You need special programs and accommodations. There must be a willingness to change, to learn, to solve new problems. When you hire hard-core, you set aside every traditional standard you normally use in hiring."

Company "Adopts" School and Things Happen

Jo Ann Levine

Adopted? Weaver High School?

Most people in Hartford [Connecticut] were surprised that anybody would want the increasingly troubled inner-city school.

So far, Weaver's adoption by Aetna Life & Casualty Insurance Co. on April 30 is a story of some fast sensitive moves by an enormous company with $8 billion in assets. It is a story of some instant moves that have helped the school in a small-scale, personal way—a way that is suggested by the term "adoption."

The adoption helped quell wild rumors coming out of Weaver High School—a school that has gone from 28 per cent Negro in 1962 to a present 70 per cent; a school with 1,500 students crammed into space for 900; a school quartered in a 44-year-old building; a school in a neighborhood where "those whites who wanted to stay and did are getting frightened."

It put a "valuable" sign on the high school and made people remember that Weaver High School has a higher percentage of seniors planning further education than the city's two other high schools.

Aetna's adoption policy is not to be a money sieve for the school. John D. Faunce, manager of special services in Aetna's public relations and advertising department, said, "We are not going to invest money as such; we are going to invest manpower." Why not money?

"For one thing," he said, "Aetna makes a substantial contribution in taxes to the schools."

Ezra Melrose, Weaver's principal, says, "No financial aid—fine. They will have less tendency to tell us what to do . . . although they are taking people away from their jobs, and that is money."

The only way Mr. Melrose would agree to the adoption is by making one policy firmly clear: Every single request goes from the school to Aetna. Said Mr. Melrose, "Nobody at Aetna, at this point, has the answer of how to run a city school.

"Nobody knows what the fallout is going to be," he continued.

The adoption has been a morale booster to the staff and has been greeted enthusiastically by parents and students. The superintendent of Hartford schools has gone so far as to practically put the other two Hartford high schools up for adoption.

Aetna's message to other businesses: "You may be a small business compared with us, but still you have some kind of expertise that you and you alone can do. . . . Just pumping in money isn't the answer."

This is the third high school adoption in the country. Michigan Bell Telephone started

This article appeared in *The Christian Science Monitor,* May 20, 1968. Reprinted by permission from *The Christian Science Monitor.*

it off with a high school in Detroit. Chrysler Corp. followed by adopting a second Detroit high school.

The Aetna people have met with parents, students, faculty. "So when they say they want to be involved, they have made a sincere effort," noted Mr. Melrose.

Added Mr. Faunce, "I don't think we have ever had a greater opportunity to show that we meant business, and we don't have to wait for Washington to get results."

On April 30 the adoption was announced. Said Mr. Faunce, "Wednesday I met with the students. Wednesday they asked for assistance with taking i.d. pictures for their new lounge."

Result? "Thursday morning at 9:30, the photographer from Aetna was there and in a matter of a few hours he had snapped 300 pictures.

Aetna asked that the students contribute 10 cents a picture to cover the cost. Mr. Melrose estimated that if Aetna had not volunteered to help, the pictures would have cost $90–money the school did not have.

The school newspaper's faculty adviser, an English teacher with no journalism training, said the paper needed help. Result? Two men from Aetna met with the paper's staff. One was Charles Dixon, a former newspaperman now in Aetna's public-relations department.

He noted: "One of the newspaper's problems is symptomatic of Weaver High School's problems–the paper is run largely by white students, although Negroes comprise 70 per cent of the school population. The staff is making a strenuous effort to overcome this and to recruit Negro reporters to their staff."

Noted Mr. Faunce, "These are just two of our people with special talents. I can see that this is a small involvement and only a beginning."

Some 40 supervisors of 35 Weaver High School students already involved in a work-training program at Aetna had little first-hand knowledge of the school the students attended.

Result? They visited the high school.

"They came back changed people," said Mr. Faunce. "They went to Weaver, had lunch in the cafeteria with their students, went to class with them."

Weaver had no place for a group of students to take some special three hour exams without being interrupted.

Result? Aetna was able to provide space in their office building (which contains some 6,500 employes) and a nearby apartment of an Aetna employe under supervision.

More "fallout," reports the school's principal:

"We have two 1969 graduates going into an engineering program. They have finished all the math programs here and need courses in descriptive geometry and advanced engineering drawing."

Said Mr. Faunce," I asked if we could be of assistance. I didn't know how. I approached our engineering department and found there a man most anxious to assist. 'Let me see the book,' he said."

Result? Next year a man from Aetna will go over to Weaver High School early in the morning to teach two boys special courses–courses the school could not afford.

Besides Weaver's much-broadcast problems, it has some important positives: It leads the city's three high schools in the percentage of seniors planning further education. And, Mr. Faunce points out, "the school has great spirit."

Aetna is well known in Hartford for being civic minded and for pioneering in training programs.

Promise Turns to Disappointment Jack McCurdy

For reform-minded educators like Dr. John Goodlad, the last decade has been a period of extreme promise and disillusionment.

"It began with fond hopes," he recalled, and a ferment of planning to change radically the face of education in America.

When this movement gathered momentum in the late 1950s, the intent was to educate teachers so they would be properly prepared to handle the new ideas, curriculum and materials which were destined for schools across the country.

"But somewhere it fell apart," Goodlad, dean of the UCLA graduate school of education, said. "It became just new content with old teaching techniques."

The result has been that the effect of the millions spent on innovative programs in recent years "has been blunted on the classroom door," he said.

"We have learned that the new curriculum in the old mold just won't work. The curriculum projects haven't had the impact we had hoped for because we haven't focused on the teacher and the organization of the school."

Then came an effort, he said, to "put the old curriculum in a new school structure," such as using the same content in new teaching situations like ungraded classes. It was just as big a failure.

This article appeared in *The Los Angeles Times*, July 23, 1968. Reprinted by permission.

"What we have had is a glaring lack of models of all new schools to show how the new ideas can be put together in new school settings," he said. "Because of this deficiency a formidable gap between ideas and practice has developed in education."

Goodlad, author of numerous books and articles on school reform, made his remarks at a recent research roundup in individualized instruction and educational change at UCLA.

Here, he said, are some very fundamental things that would be happening in education if the last decade had been fruitful:

1–School boards, schools and teachers would be working with clear educational objectives.

2–The instructional emphasis would be on "learning how to learn," on basic principles and concepts, not on "bits and pieces" of facts which may well be superseded tomorrow.

3–"Multi-media" learning packages would be in use in classrooms, including recordings, films and computerized mechanisms.

4–Extensive instructional recognition of individual differences in children would be reflected in classroom practices.

5–Use of the basic principles of group dynamics and human interaction would be widespread in schools.

6–The fundamental tenets of educational psychology would be in evidence, including motivation, reinforcement and transfer of learning as teaching techniques.

7–Less attention would be paid to the age and grade as criteria for what a child is taught. ("Surely we know by now that age has little to do with what children are capable of learning.")

8–Flexible use of human resources would be in effect, tapping the expertise of many leaders in society, such as musicians and artists, for classroom models.

9–There would be clear evidence that education had arrived "in the golden age of instructional materials" with a wide variety of books, teaching aids and other items.

On a recent tour of classrooms across the country, Goodlad said he and his staff found none of these things to any degree.

"There was almost a complete absence of deliberate goal-setting and evaluation," he said. "There was little use of the basic principles of learning. The instructional process was still the 'teacher-talk-to-child' technique.

"There was little use of differential techniques to accommodate individual differences in children. This defies everything we know about human beings, yet schools are still trying to bring children up to some fictitious norm.

"Books still dominate the classroom as the medium of instruction. Everything was graded with little team teaching. And so on. I was shocked."

What they did find, he said, was the reason why this is true.

"The educational setting just isn't conducive to change," he said. "Principals and teachers are hungry to sit down and discuss new ideas. They wanted to talk to us and to each other. But there is something about the schools themselves that won't let them."

For one thing, "there just is no place for teachers to sit down and talk," Goodlad said.

Most schools provide teachers with no place and no time to relax, talk and hold serious discussions about their profession.

Teachers cannot be expected to spend a full day in school, five days a week, with 30 to 35 children and then "grasp new ideas and materials," he argued.

"Less than 40% of the schools we visited hold regular faculty meetings. And most of these meetings deal with inconsequential things, not with educational issues."

But the biggest obstacle to change emerged in the form of school bureaucracy and "its care and feeding."

"Bureaucracy itself is not a bad thing," Goodlad said. "It takes away the routine, time-consuming tasks which get in the way of teaching and other productive acts."

The problem is that in too many school systems the emphasis has shifted from the bureaucracy existing to save time to becoming an end in itself and a way of doing everything–including teaching.

"The question is: do we reward people in education for getting things done or for keeping the bureaucracy running?" he asked.

"In the big city system especially, we tend to promote people who keep the machinery running. Then one who wants to do something different, upsets the machinery and is forced to be the same as everyone else."

Goodlad said, "It is not likely that people are going to be rewarded who turn their back on the system. If they grow up in and learn that system, their own security and job depends on maintaining that system."

In this kind of situation, he said, "it takes a powerful, devious person to rock the boat, and there are very few really creative people in any field."

Thus, "the major part of the problem in education is not a lack of new ideas but in creating the conditions for change, in which change becomes the norm rather than stability and status quo being the norm."

Unfortunately, he said, in many school districts "we talk about creativity on the one hand and on the other we suppress it. If we encourage stability throughout the system and reward people accordingly, we are creating the same kind of classroom climate."

Goodlad strongly urges "recognizing deviant behavior (in schools) rather than conformity. People who over-value order and conformity are the big threat."

Major external pressure for change can be exerted by "countervailing structures which are large enough and with enough prestige to be effective."

An example is the Institute for the Development of Educational Activities, of which Goodlad is research and development chief. IDEA has organized a group of schools in Southern California and made them the showcase for innovative programs.

Goodlad recognizes that change is extremely threatening to the security of people.

"Change is going to mean an enormous state of disequilibrium that will be very threatening to many in education. The goal is to change the norms of bureaucracy in order to make that disequilibrium desirable behavior," he said.

"Viva disequilibrium!"

P.S. 192, Central Harlem–Kids Learn Here Richard Bumstead

On the last day of school this year, as mothers came to gather their children from the classrooms of P.S. 192, a fortress-like elementary school on the western fringes of Harlem, a youngster walked home alone, pushing a red fire truck that he had brought to his first-grade class for "show and tell."

We met him in the black-topped schoolyard.

"Do you go to that school?"

"Yes."

"Do you know who the principal of that school is?"

"Yes, it's Dr. Gang."

"Does Dr. Gang know your name?"

"Yes," he said with a toothless grin, "It's N-A-T."

Dr. Gang may not actually know Nat, one small black face among 1,400 students in grades K-6, but Nat believes he does, and that counts a good deal for a boy making his way in a hostile slum environment.

And if Nat ever falls behind in learning how to read–a fact Dr. Gang can easily detect by a glance at the reading progress chart that covers two walls of his office–he will make it a point to meet him, his teacher, possibly his parents, and anyone else who can help Nat master that crucial skill.

"I expect every child to be reading on grade level," Dr. Gang tells his faculty. "And if he is not, I want to know why. I won't accept an answer like the fact that a child has an emotional problem. If he does, I want to know what we are doing about it."

When he became principal in 1962, Dr. Gang found the normal pattern of reading retardation that was associated with "special service" schools, an official euphemism for schools located in "disadvantaged areas." The pupils at P.S. 192 were reading, on the average, two to four years below their grade level.

The school population at that time was split about equally between Negroes and Puerto Ricans. Now, Negro, Puerto Rican, and children from other Caribbean countries, notably the Dominican Republic, each constitute about one-third of the school population, with a smattering of white and Chinese students.

In six years, Dr. Gang and his faculty have succeeded in raising reading comprehension scores to the point where about 70 percent of the pupils are functioning at grade level or better, and the rest are not much more than a year behind.

In other ghetto areas, however, pupils are reading two or more years behind grade level, and as they grow older, their scores get worse.

This state of affairs, long suspected by parents and civil rights leaders, was confirmed when the Board of Education released,

Reprinted with permission from the September, 1968, issue of *Educate,* © MCMLXVIII Gellert Publ. Corp.

and the *N.Y. Times* published, the results of the 1966 Metropolitan Achievement Tests in reading, *by school*. For the first time, the public could compare how well each school was teaching its students how to read.

The results from P.S. 192 bore out the public praise given the school by Dr. Kenneth Clark, Roy Wilkins, and other civil rights leaders, not only for the reading program, but also for the general tone of the school. The obvious question was raised the city over by irate parents waving the *N.Y. Times* under the nose of their children's principal: "If Dr. Gang can do it, why can't you?"

Dr. Bernard Donovan, NYC superintendent, attributed the difference between P.S. 192 and other schools to the "creative leadership of the principal."

The NYC Elementary School Principals Association, on the other hand, published their analysis of the reading scores at P.S. 192 and concluded, "Far from producing a miracle of miracles, this over-estimated over-praised school has accomplished merely ordinary results in reading."

In a rebuttal the Association refused to print (Dr. Gang resigned in protest), he argued that they erred in reporting the median scores for grades 3 and 4, and neglected to say that the fifth-graders, whose scores fell below the grade level, had never been enrolled in the intensive reading program.

The controversy over reading scores and what they meant tended to obscure the fact that Dr. Gang had splashed a bright color on the rather bleak canvas of the public school's record in the ghetto. And he did this with the same resources available to any of the other special service school principals. The innovation—if one can stretch the word—comes from a creative mix of materials at hand and the infusion of nothing more startling (nor more demanding) than some ethical principles derived from basic Judeo-Christian beliefs.

P.S. 192 was Dr. Gang's first principalship in a career in education, always centered in New York City where he grew up, that started after World War II when his former fifth-grade teacher, then a principal, persuaded him to take over a class for six months upon his graduation from CCNY. Dr. Gang soon cancelled plans to go into law. "That's how I got into it, the best way possible, by trying it out and liking it."

Years of teaching in an elementary school on the fringes of a ghetto area, seven years as an assistant principal, during which time he earned a doctorate in human relations from NYU, put him in position to take the opening at P.S. 192, which had been operating under the direction of an acting principal for 10 years.

He found a typical rate of reading retardation at school, apathetic and defeated children, a neighborhood that had severed connections with the school (no parents association, little communication either way), and a staff that would tolerate one of its members saying (though many did not believe it), "These children can't learn."

At first, he played it "by the book," which says a new principal should spend a year following through on his predecessor's policies and learning the terrain before striking out on his own. But in two months, compelled by what he saw, he stuffed the book in a file drawer, called the faculty together, and started changing things without seeking permission from the next highest level for every step he took.

"I don't feel it's the role of a principal to sit back and wait until he is told what to do, or to check with headquarters of the district superintendent before he does something."

For example, the school's reading program —the key to the school's success—evolved from the now officially discredited program of "Higher Horizons," whose purpose was to show slum-bound youngsters the heights to which they could aspire. Three teachers were assigned to P.S. 192, one of the 90 schools selected for the program, to arrange the out-of-school activities.

Dr. Gang didn't agree with the philosophy

of the program as it would apply to P.S. 192. "I couldn't see where you could tell a Negro or Spanish-speaking child that he could be President–which is what "Higher Horizons" is all about–and yet not teach him to read or do his numbers," Dr. Gang said. "In fact, it is a greater crime to suggest he could under these circumstances."

So he assigned these three teachers to instruct first graders in reading. Each one took groups of six to nine children and worked with them for an hour a day, five days a week. Between the classroom teachers and these three, every child in the first grade received this intensive, almost individualized instruction, which was supplemented by their regular classroom work in reading.

This concentration of effort on the first grade upset other teachers who had to struggle along with non-readers in their classes, and Dr. Gang himself realized that he was sacrificing classes to make an effective start. He explained to the faculty that he wanted to wipe out the term "remedial" from the school's lexicon. Remediation, he said, was not to be used as a technique, dubious at best, to overcome early reading failures. He favored preventing reading problems in the first place, hence the emphasis on the first grade.

The next year, the original class (now second-graders) continued the program, while the new first-graders started the same schedule their predecessors had worked through. By imaginative juggling of staff positions, Dr. Gang has put together a staff of nine teachers to hold these small reading classes. Thus, the children entering junior high school in the fall of 1968 are the first class to have received six years of the intensive reading instruction. All other students are now enrolled.

(Dr. Gang converted storage space into nine reading classrooms, although "teaching closets" might be a more accurate term, so that children would not be distracted by another group working in the same room. These hardly conform to the official guidelines on classroom space, but they serve the purpose.)

The classroom teacher is held accountable for the reading progress of each child, as she is for his performance in other areas, but the difference here is that accountability is operationally defined. Dr. Gang expects pupils to be reading on grade level, a precise concept in the reporting of reading scores. About four times a year, each teacher posts the reading scores of her pupils on the chart in Dr. Gang's office, so that one can see the progress–or lack of it–from the child's original point at the beginning of the year to the minimum objective, the lowest level of next year's reading range. Any large white space is sure to trigger a conference with Dr. Gang.

How much the public display of the reading progress chart affects a teacher's motivation is difficult to determine–there's a steady stream of people in and out of Dr. Gang's office–but one might suspect a reluctance to be singled out as a teacher whose class is not up to par. Dr. Gang says he simply prefers a visual reporting system to the job of digging around in file drawers for the information.

Although Dr. Gang puts the pressure on his teachers, he holds himself accountable for the entire reading program. "In our business, we say the kids failed. It's like a doctor saying it's the patient's fault if he dies. But it's not the kids who have failed, it is we who have failed the kids. If a kid is three years retarded in reading, we have failed that kid by three years."

Dr. Gang promised the parents that if the pattern of reading retardation were not reversed and if a considerable number of children were not reading at grade level in spite of the intensive reading program, he would resign. For the tests given in April, 1968, the mean reading scores for the second and fifth grades at P.S. 192–the two grades whose scores the *N.Y. Times* publishes–are 3.4 and 6.0 respectively. These exceed the national norms of 2.7 and 5.7.

(These scores are the mean average for the reading comprehension part of the Metropolitan Achievement Test, and the *N.Y. Times* publishes this average for selected grades in each city school on advice of the Board of Education that it is the most significant.)

In terms of reading on grade level, 62 percent of the second grade class is reading above grade, 28 percent at grade level, and 10 percent below. In the fifth grade, 49 percent of the students are reading at or above grade level, 41 percent are reading one year below grade level (4.0 to 4.9), and 10 percent fall two or more years below.

Again, this is the score of a golfer playing against par, not against opponents. By the community's response to Dr. Gang's efforts, he is doing a good job, but interestingly enough, a couple of observers said, "only what he is expected to do."

Underlying the mechanics of the reading program, Dr. Gang fashioned a kind of spirit in the school that would draw out a child and give him a tolerance for the inevitable, though temporary, failures associated with learning how to read. Ghetto children are said to be peculiarly sensitive about extending themselves, having been slapped down most of their lives.

The first step was to ban any reference to the "disadvantaged."

"I don't want the kids to get the idea they are poor creatures, different from the rest of the world," Dr. Gang explained.

Early in his tenure, headquarters sent a film crew to the school to shoot a scene depicting the deplorable conditions that an impending bond issue would clear up if it passed. The director wanted to rip the window shade and pack a classroom with more students than normal. Dr. Gang threw them out. As far as he was concerned, his students were not going to see themselves displayed on TV as examples of the poor, disadvantaged kids in the ghetto schools.

Once the sense of difference is done away with, then the children can be accepted on their own terms, not as victims of poverty. Among the assumptions of the school are the statements that "there must be a real respect for and a devotion to the integrity of each child," and "the atmosphere of the school must be one that engenders mutual love and concern among all those who live there."

These are educational cliches unless demonstrated by example. Dr. Gang set out to do it with the children and the staff through whom, he believes, these qualities of respect, integrity, and dignity are transmitted to the children. The qualities are not, in other words, teachable.

How can one show love and concern for a child to which he can respond? You hug them, squeeze them, tweak their cheeks, lift them, lay your hands on their head—Dr. Gang does this constantly as he wanders through the school, to the delight of the children and, one might add, their parents if they happen to be looking on. It's the old-time politician's baby-kissing style, yet it is doubtful that Dr. Gang could maintain this intensity of contact, day in and day out, solely for the purpose of impressing parents, teachers, or members of the press—the man is too accessible, too warm and expansive, to be insincere.

On another level, the value Dr. Gang attaches to the concepts of dignity and integrity led him to ignore the stated policy of integrating Spanish-speaking children into school. Almost 60 per cent of the school population at P.S. 192 comes from a Spanish background, half of these from the Dominican Republic. Spanish is the only language for many of these children.

According to Board policy, these children should spend 12 weeks in an orientation class, then be assigned to a regular class where they, theoretically, would learn the language by living it.

This approach was not working in P.S. 192 (nor in the rest of the city; the Board is considering changing it). Instead of becoming fluent in English, the children would sit quietly, missing most of what was being said, though they were not stupid, simply out of touch.

"This was a violation of dignity as far as I was concerned," Dr. Gang said. "Here these kids come from a rich culture, yet the city school system says to ignore it."

He organized a Spanish-speaking class, using a bilingual teacher, and the students were taught to read Spanish and to relate to their environment in Spanish. English was taught as a second language, and only when the child attained fluency was he transferred to a regular class.

"We've been doing this quietly for about five years," Dr. Gang said, "and it's worked beautifully, even though we haven't been on speaking terms with the gal at headquarters who is in charge of the other program."

Relating to children, constantly devising or reassessing curriculum, plugging away at reading every day knowing that one's efforts are public knowledge—this requires a certain kind of teacher, and Dr. Gang has been building his staff for the past seven years.

About 25 percent of the 65 teachers, the number varies, are holdovers from the pre-Gang days. Otherwise, the staff is rather young, about half of them with less than 5 years experience, although more than 90 percent are classified as regular teachers. About 20 of them are Negro or Puerto Rican. There are 10 male teachers.

Nobody is appointed unless Dr. Gang asks for them, and he has had ten persons to choose from for each vacancy in recent years, although in the beginning, he and the assistant principals covered classes themselves rather than hire teachers who could not measure up. Prospective teachers now serve a kind of informal probationary period, working on a per diem basis so that Dr. Gang and the rest of the faculty can observe their style.

Although he never fired any teacher with tenure, some of those he inherited retired or transferred when they found the new system not to their liking. Some left because their own colleagues made it quite evident that they could not tolerate their incompetency. The result is a young staff, dedicated, com-

DR. GANG'S 14-POINT PROGRAM FOR P.S. 192

1. *Each child will succeed.*
2. *Each child is expected to be functioning on or above the grade in which he is.*
3. *The need for remediation is to be prevented; it is not a technique to be relied upon to overcome failure.*
4. *Reading achievement is basic to success.*
5. *The development of the child's personality is essential to his success in school.*
6. *There must be a real respect for and devotion to the integrity of each child.*
7. *The atmosphere of the school must be one that engenders mutual love and concern among all those who live there.*
8. *The administration of the school must give to every teacher the respect for her professional status and human dignity.*
9. *Teachers must be given the freedom and opportunity for professional growth.*
10. *Our children are entitled to no less than the wealthiest private schools can give to its children.*
11. *A school in which there is failure is a failing school. There can be no built-in excuses for the failure of a child. If the child fails, then the school has failed to meet his needs.*
12. *We know of no bounds that set limits to the potential of each child.*
13. *Every human being in the school must feel the pride in being part of a successful venture in living and learning.*
14. *Practice in the profession of education commits one to be responsible and accountable for the molding of human lives. The profession cannot tolerate inferiority or even mediocrity. A commitment to excellence is the only measure.*

petent, willing to experiment, but leavened by a scattering of experienced teachers who are able to temper youthful enthusiasms.

In line with his philosophy that the objective of educational leadership is to "unlock" people, Dr. Gang gives them the widest latitude in which to operate–as long as they produce. In reading, for example, he doesn't care what method a teacher uses, but the kids better damn well be reading up to the next grade level at the end of the year.

Arlene Winters, a sixth-grade teacher and the UFT chapter chairman, confirmed that Dr. Gang "recognizes creativity and leaves a great deal of freedom in the classroom" on the basis of her own experience with a delicate subject–sex education. Her students came across a discussion of the subject one day while reading the newspaper in the social studies period, and they asked her for some kind of guidance. Knowing that the current city policy was to avoid the subject, yet realizing that her students did need this kind of instruction, she asked Dr. Gang for permission to put together a unit, and he readily agreed.

She approached her students' parents to help her work out a set of objectives, and they became so involved that she ended up teaching the unit on a weekday evening to both parents and children. The unit has since been given by other teachers at P.S. 192, and Miss Winters is invited to speak to curriculum experts as the city system gropes toward an acceptable way of presenting the subject.

Last year, the faculty worked on a new program for the fourth, fifth and sixth grades. The students at this level will be organized, as their younger brothers and sisters are now, on a non-graded basis–in other words, assigned by criteria other than chronological age: reading score, interest level or social maturity.

Studies will be grouped around a core curriculum: one, combining reading and social studies; the other, math with science. Newspapers will serve as the basic text in social studies, allowing the teacher to range from events in the news to historical antecedents–relating the Columbia University riots, for example, to the Bill of Rights, or the conviction of Dr. Benjamin Spock to the freedom of the press trial of John Peter Zenger in 1735, a bit of New York State history.

Dr. Gang believes that the basal readers for fourth, fifth and sixth grades reveal little differences among them, and if the teacher wants to develop reading comprehension she must work from interesting materials. Miss Winters put it less politely, "We are searching all over for books that aren't about some stupid 'Dick and Jane' but about something you can build a life on."

Having smashed the traditional structure of subjects and grade levels, how can Dr. Gang measure results against intentions other than by the reading chart in his office or the scores from city-wide tests? "I don't know yet," he said. "It's one of those things we are working on. But the important thing to remember is that we, as a faculty, are involved in the process of setting our own objectives, methods, and standards. Nobody is handing a program down to us and when we figure out how to judge results, the system will work, because it is ours."

Just as he involved the faculty in building a curriculum, Dr. Gang brought the community into school affairs. He invited parents to Kaffee Klatches in the school cafeteria in the morning and set up a number of parent workshops. He issued library cards to interested parents so they can check out books, most of which were donated to the school. When people discovered he habitually stayed at the school until early evening, they would come over and chat with him. The teachers, too, carried the school to the neighborhood by walking each of their children home after school and spending a few minutes with the family over a cup of tea. Gradually, the neighborhood came to realize, as a result of this outreach, that P.S. 192 was an open school, and that their concerns were listened to.

One of the most notable instances of school-community cooperation has been the school trips that are paid for by funds the community raised. Having contained reading retardation within acceptable limits, Dr. Gang re-instituted his version of the "Higher Horizons" program. During the last two weeks of school this year (New York City dismisses children at the end of June), one grade went to Montreal, some third-graders took a two-day bus tour of New York State, 60 fourth-graders flew to Jamaica to study the Island's culture. One group visited Washington, D.C., and were received by President Johnson prior to a meeting of the Cabinet. In all, 600 children went traveling, all who wanted to and had their parent's permission. The cost of the trips was budgeted for $20,000.

To raise this kind of money, Sidney Poitier and Harry Belafonte, in appreciation of the work being done at P.S. 192 as reported by various civil rights leaders, organized and appeared in a show that was staged in the auditorium of the nearby Music and Art High School. This year, the PTA sponsored a Fiesta Day–games, food, dancing–on a Sunday.

It would be a mistake, however, to give the impression that everything falls into place at P.S. 192. Miss Winters said that, in spite of the intensive reading program, "we haven't reached all children and there's all that potential being wasted."

Dr. Gang himself argues that what P.S. 192 has accomplished should be the normal state of affairs, and that the publicity the school has received can be explained only in the degree that P.S. 192 exceeds the results of other special service schools.

And it worries him that visitors–the school has had hundreds of them over the last few years–don't really grasp the totality of what has happened at P.S. 192. "I sometimes sit back and watch people copy my reading charts to the minutest detail. Great! At least they will be talking about accountability, but do they really understand the meanings of these things? Maybe, maybe not. It's not something you can teach, you must live it."

Yet, as much as Dr. Gang argues for accountability, it's questionable that he could have functioned as he has done in a system that jealously guards authority and frequently monitors the programs at the school level. On paper, the New York City system appears to be this kind, and the flood of policy papers emanating from 110 Livingstone Street does create a "check-it-with-headquarters" psychology.

Dr. Gang, far from sending up trial balloons before making a move, goes right ahead, sometimes knowing that a new program would be frowned upon, if not squelched entirely if it came to light before he could point to results.

"Whatever I am responsible for, I have the authority to do," Dr. Gang maintains. "If I exceed my authority, then fire me."

And he has exercised that concept of authority in a school building that houses the district superintendent who could not have been blind to either the unauthorized programs or to the constituency Dr. Gang was building among civil rights groups and the community. Success is Dr. Gang's shield against the educational establishment, a basis for judging his administration that is perfectly all right with him. (He argues that principals should be hired by a contract which is renewable every three years at the pleasure of the governing body.)

As a member of the school staff, and therefore in the position to weigh his successes against the lapses, Miss Winters said, "Dr. Gang is fine, but he has an awful lot of faults. I think the tragedy is that there is no other principal that I know of who is half as good–a tragedy because we still have a hell of a long way to go."

Convenient Myths About Today's Students

Alex Sherriffs

Youth is always of interest to society—it is the next generation. However, these days adults are interested in youth to a degree approaching fascination.

There are even myths abroad about youth, and of two kinds: (1) Some describe youth only as bad and point to riots, vandalism, stompings, and drugs. (2) Some describe youth only in glowing terms, seeing them as more responsible, compassionate, involved, unselfish and idealistic than ever before. This myth has been so often stated that mere repetition has given it credibility.

However, there are a number of serious in-depth studies on today's youth, and their data are clear in their meaning. And these data are as available to those who promote myths as they are to me.

Compared to earlier findings about the young, youth are found these days to be better trained intellectually; to be more lonely; to have friendships that are shorter in duration and more shallow in nature, more like acquaintances in our experience; to have trouble with authority. As Nevitt Sanford says, how could it be otherwise when they have had so little experience with it? They are prone to silence and withdrawal, to be less able to postpone gratifications, to be less able to tolerate probabilities and compromise, they demand absolutes (of which there are few in life). Anything less than absolute is considered to be hypocrisy. And youth are found to be afraid of risk, of error.

Mr. Sheriffs is Education Advisor to Governor Reagan of California. This speech was delivered at the Commonwealth Club of California, San Francisco, May 19, 1967. Reprinted with permission.

As Dana Farnsworth of Harvard says, they are intellectually better prepared, but socially and emotionally less mature than in earlier days.

These findings describe enough members of the "generation" to set its climate. There are, of course, individual differences.

The "Silent Generation" of the 1950's has continued on much as it was, only now the labels are different, and we now have the myths.

"Apathy," a self-description of the silent generation, has been replaced by speaking of being "uninvolved." Instead of the status posture of the 1950's, "being casual," we now find youth "keeping its cool." "Non-commitment" has become "alienation." And "pluralistic ignorance" increases. A word about pluralistic ignorance: Because of extremely limited communication between the members of the group, it can happen that though no one believes something, everyone may believe that everyone else believes it. And with a powerful drive to conformity, youth sometimes continues to behave in response to an average that doesn't exist.

An example of pluralistic ignorance may help clarify the term: One Saturday afternoon a rooting section crowd became a mob and behaved in ways far beyond the acceptable.

On the following Monday I asked my class of 400 to educate me, as a psychologist whose specialization is youth. I asked them to indicate by show of hands, was the rooting section great? Could it stand a teeny bit of improvement? Or was it poor?

I gave the choice "great" first. Some hands went up in the back of the room, some here and there. The other class members were looking around as would the audience at a tennis match during a fast volley. "What was in?" was their question. Soon, with hands going up around hands that were up (the "ripple effect"), 83% were voting "great."

I then asked for more information, in an anonymous paper, telling me how it was great, and how it might be greater. To my amazement all but eight students turned in papers (for anonymous also meant voluntary). I don't get this good a response on midterms.

In the secrecy and privacy of those papers, 86% stated that the rooting section should be abolished. And over 50% stated, "But what's the use of my feeling this way, when I'm the only one?"

I could give all too many examples of this kind of behavior—"in" voting before the group, contrary to personal and private belief.

Let me note here that youth is not without our societal values, but it is all too often blocked in expressing them.

The mythologists fail to acknowledge the normal growth pains of adolescence. By failing to acknowledge them they lead adolescents to incorrect and harmful interpretations of their own necessary and normal behaviors.

I refer to the need of the adolescent to find his identity. This is part of what adolescence is—finding where one begins and where parents leave off, standing away from home base with some support of one's own age companions, trying on for size both rebellion and adult values—and then, when comfortable, returning to the family with the apparent insight that "Pop has mellowed and matured."

One cannot go directly from a child to an adult role. If we believe some mythologists there must be powerful magic during the summer vacation between high school and college, for in June we graduate boys and girls, and in September we greet men and women. This is the great American puberty rite. What do they do during those three months?

And adolescents have to learn what mature adults know, that dependence and independence are both human needs. To the young it is as though they must choose one or the other. An adult knows that independence to establish individuality is essential, and that dependence on friends, spouses, children to make life worthwhile is equally essential.

And there is that normal search for sex-role definition. In our society with its rapid change in this area, with women recently given the vote, and "the pill," with father having left home during the late 19th century to go to factory, mill or mine (the industrial revolution), and now returning by way of the barbecue pit, and the husband-and-wife PTA, it is complicated.

My grandparents knew something quite different than did my parents, than do my wife and I, and now than do our children.

Defining one's own sex role is complicated, and I sometimes have said when speaking to high school audiences, as I look around at all the long hair on straight bodies, "I assume that some of you are postponing the decision."

Anyway, our children are human beings growing up, not simply political animals. They need some warmth and support. A number of intellectuals seem to have forgotten this.

Consider the myth of great participation and activity by students these days, and try to square with this myth the following facts: A new chancellor arrived on the Berkeley campus, where students are presumbed to be terribly involved in matters of rules, due process and freedom (or perhaps license). The students were invited, 26,800 strong, to meet with the chancellor to hear his views on the University and the students' role. Where to hold such a meeting? The stadium? It was decided to settle for 900-seat Wheeler Auditorium. Just as well, for the chancellor found only 13 students in those 900 seats.

Consider a half-day's program devoted to rules, due process and judicial reforms on the campus. It was highly advertised, and involved student government, faculty and administration. A total of 19 appeared—six to visit friends on the program committee.

Consider Winter Quarter Orientation for 900 students, with invitation by letter. The chancellor, a vice chancellor, a faculty representative, the dean of students, a student body vice president, and the Glee Club essentially overwhelmed the 27 students who came.

Consider an incident on the grounds of a California middle-class high school. A big kid challenged a little kid to a fight. The small one tried to avoid it. Two hundred classmates gathered around. The bully suddenly kneed his target in the groin and then, while the youngster was writhing on the ground, used his toe to remove the eyeball. It took minutes to achieve this.

The point is that not one of 200 said "stop," or went for a teacher. They watched as though it were a television screen.

A clergyman was horrified, not by the sick bully, but by the fact that in a democratic society not one of 200 functioned in relation to societal values. He interviewed the 200. Their responses were, "I'm not my brother's keeper. It was not my fight. I did not want to get involved." But many did say, "I felt sick inside."

Consider one of the longest episodes of interference with the exercise of due process of law by an organized group in the history of the United States: 250 to 400 persons on the Berkeley campus, some of them students, who captured a police car and the persons within it and held it for 32 hours. You should be concerned. But are you also concerned by the fact that 26,000 other students took no active interest? Did not behave as though they knew whether this was right or wrong?

Our real questions in each of these examples are two: (1) Where were all those others who had a duty to be involved? (2) Why have the mythologists pretended that a minority was the majority?

As to the first question: A number of factors have operated together to produce a majority of youth who are so immobilized in relation to their own feelings, so oriented to what is "in" for the group, so incapable of dealing with the minority who now dominate the stage—political and social—that they, the majority, have simply deserted.

I will mention three such factors: These youngsters are the first children raised by parents who were unsure of their role as parents—even of their rights as parents, the first parents in history who instead of depending on their common sense and human traditions and personal feelings, had to look it up in a book like Spock or Gesell.

This came about, of course, because of a breakthrough in knowledge about human behavior, the insights of Sigmund Freud. These insights have led to much good, but they have been very costly, too, while the layman tried to digest them.

The mental hygiene movement, made up of laymen at first (except for Freud, who was the beginning), often carried distorted notions to educators and to parents: notions of child-centeredness, of the problems that grow out of frustration, of the significance of rejection, of stages of development, and much more.

As we know, some progressive education

went astray. Most educators have corrected many of their errors, but not before the idea of "don't frustrate Johnny" had been tried. Would he really flower? He surely did, but into a monster.

(Note that Freud actually said that the way to maturity was dealing with, not avoiding, frustrations.)

Parents have had a tougher time, and are still very much caught. They have lost their confidence and turn to so-called experts.

Who before Freud went into anxiety states over having to bottle-feed a baby? The possibilities that the child would feel rejected were not considered, nor were they generally real.

I can sum it up with an illustration: I gave an anonymous questionnaire to almost 1,000 sophomores. Two of the questions asked were: Do you love your parents? Do you respect your parents?

Ninety-three percent checked "yes" to the first question. Only 51% checked "yes" to the second question.

I called in every eighth student to ask, "Can you help me to understand this difference between 93% and 51%?"

One girl's response covers most of their answers: "Sure, I love my parents. They mean well. But respect . . .? When I was in a social club at Berkeley Hi, I came home one day and told my mother that our club was going to have its overnight party at our house. Mother turned pale. I told her that chaperones were no longer 'in' and she turned paler.

"I hoped she would say, 'No, you aren't,' and get me out of it, because I didn't have the courage to say no to the others. But no, she called the parents of the other girls and asked them what she should do.

"Listening, I could hear that they wanted us girls to be popular, they didn't want to seem 'kooks' to others. They decided, 'Let's say yes, this time.'

"In short, my mother discovered her values —and mine—by a telephone poll."

And whole communities have even been negotiating codes of ethics between parents and youngsters of junior-high and high school age. My students first called this to my attention. In one such community code, the first topic is "Moral Standards," with sections on "Parents' rights," "Youth's rights,"—essentially a labor-management contract for the year. Orinda, Moraga, Piedmont, Fairfield, and Daly City are some communities which have traveled this path. The parents do mean well and they know they have a problem. However, youth can only believe that societal values are quite negotiable.

Youngsters need adults to model after, to respect, to copy. They need a point of view. They need adults who believe in themselves and in something. The young can decide what to be like, and what not to be like, only by observing adults.

They can learn little from observing jello.

In fact, too often adults imitate the young rather than the reverse. They develop a language, they develop the twist, they adopt a costume, they find heroes. Before long, the parents adopt the language, learn the twist, mothers dress like daughters, and even the Beatles become adult favorites.

Fifteen years ago adults shook their heads at the normal antics of youth; now they say by their actions, "You've got it made." This is unnerving to the young. To become adult is almost to lose position and status.

A graduate student was telling me of her brother who stated that he would not become an adult. If he did, he would only lose what he had. She told him he would have to become an adult, for he would become older. "I won't!" he insisted. I asked, how old is your brother? "Twenty-four."

And, outside the family, other adult models, many teachers, clergymen, school and college administrators, and deans of students, behave in the same ways—and they are representatives of our society and of its institutions.

Too many of them prefer peace and popularity over respect, too many think that the normal expression of authority is a burden and a trial, though delegated to them by a democratic society.

Face it: They are either insecure or naive.

So much for the impact of mistaken psychology. Now for the second factor we should note also the impact of what we have called "progress."

At the turn of the century, most youngsters in growing up had experience with real responsibility and real challenge in relation to the family's work. Most families were engaged in agriculture. Their children had experience with a variety of adult models doing real work in a real world.

Today only 7% of families produce all of our food and fiber.

At the turn of the century there was also ample opportunity for youth in commerce or industry, for real work with real purpose. It was even necessary to pass child labor laws to keep them in school or at home. Today, if all students wanted such experience, we would have a shambles, for we scarcely have jobs for all heads of household.

In 1900, only 9% of 17-year-olds were in school, now there are well over 90%.

Today, for many, responsibility and challenge are found only in relationship to grade-point average. And for many, work is only for one's selfish pleasures: a transistor radio, a record player, a sports car.

The third factor is that we have prosperity. Middle-class youngsters generally are given what they want, for the parents can't think of a reason to deny them.

We must not forget that it is more satisfying to build, to grow, and to participate than simply to be spectators as others create.

In view of all these things, it should not be surprising that we have confusion of freedom with license, confusion of democracy with anarchy, and spoiled children and spoiled adults who take the law into their own hands, sometimes in erratic outbursts of undisciplined or even violent behavior.

In my opinion, then, the fables are fables, the myths are myths. They are convenient myths for some, some of the time.

They are convenient for the parent who finds an excuse for his failings.

They are convenient for that administrator and for that official who finds an excuse for his passive, fence-straddling posture, at a time when society craves and sorely needs simple statements of belief and faith.

They are convenient for some youngsters who find temporary satisfactions in an incredible amount of attention and in a distorted sense of importance–as they put it, "in being rather than in becoming."

They are convenient myths, but they are potentially as costly as any myths have ever been to a democratic society.

We, here, all understand that man without shared values, attitudes, codes and restraints becomes merely his animal self, and might makes right.

We all understand that we are fortunate to have a democratic society, where we can make our own laws and change them, where we can choose our own leaders and remove them, where we can determine our own goals and change them, too–a condition experienced in history by only a small fraction of 1 percent of those who have lived on this earth.

We all understand that our challenge is the proper balance between freedom for the individual and freedom for other individuals.

We all understand that democracy is fragile. By its very nature, it depends on the active participation of the majority. Plato was pessimistic. He feared that postwar letdown and prosperity would lead to the withdrawal of too many from responsibility and public affairs. After democracy, Plato saw despotism.

And we all understand that the Left and

the Right are probably better organized and more effective than ever before. We understand that they pretend to attack one another, yet their real attack is against you and me and our institutions. How could they attack one another, when they are so much alike: arrogant, rigid, intolerant, hostile, and without faith in the majority? They need one another now. Their quarrel with each other may come later, to see who gets the spoils.

If we "Let George do it," George will. And George will do it for his own good rather than for ours.

We all understand these things.

Fifty percent of our population is 25 years of age or less. Does youth understand these things? And are we helping them do so?

Edmund Burke remarked, you know, "All that is necessary for the triumph of evil is for good men to do nothing."

Am I pessimistic? Not necessarily. Am I worried? Yes. But certainly improvement is possible.

For one thing, as I have noted, youth is still made up of a majority with positive values and with the desire to live meaningful lives. They do not lack values, but they are blocked in expressing them.

And there are things we can be doing:

1. School personnel, and all of us, have a responsibility to communicate the excitement of the democratic experiment. I am not speaking of sloganism or superpatriotism, nor am I suggesting more attention to symbols of our society. I am speaking, rather, about the very essence of that society.

Even the very young can become excited about the idealism of democracy. Even the very young can understand that in anarchy we have the law of the jungle, the weak fall to the strong, that in the jungle there are no civil liberties and no civil rights.

2. We all have a responsibility to communicate to youth the traditional values of this society, the concept of progress within law—for example, that enforcement of laws, transmission and perpetuation of values, are largely the responsibility of each citizen functioning in his own way; that a mother should be able to allow her child to walk to school, not because there is a policeman on every corner, but because she can count on her neighbors to support the social order that protects her child.

3. Society's representatives must maintain the integrity of their age and position. Being "one of the boys" is a kindness to neither youth nor adults. School personnel particularly must accept their roles as models of adulthood. They can't escape it. They must not, like permissive parents, fold before each ambiguity. And to hide behind the mask of "public relations" is costly in the long run.

4. Adults should be freed to be themselves, without need for psychological gimmicks as substitutes for the real relationships of adults with youngsters.

5. Our institutions, or their representatives, should not negotiate that which is not negotiable by them—the role that society has assigned to an institution, the rule of law, or other basic values of the society.

6. Those in positions to do so should encourage the development of self-expression and communication between people. We must reduce the silencing factors in a silent generation.

The cheapest route to status is that taken by the destructive cynic and critic. "Cutting low" and "putting down" are two devices of ridicule employed to raise self-esteem at the expense of others. The young have developed these techniques to an exquisite art. And they are directed against those with enthusiasm, who try to stand up to be counted, who present ideas that are not "in." Similarly, sarcasm by insecure teachers discourages participation by members of the group. We must allow for trial and error, and not demand utter conformity or perfection.

7. Our society has frontiers these days as exciting and challenging as any in the past.

Today's frontiers are more ideological than physical, so they are more the frontiers of the educated.

If a youngster can see no purpose in life, it is only because our representatives fail to point out that for the sake of man and society we must learn how to live as free people in spite of the dilemmas of population explosion, knowledge explosion, the pressures of other societies and cultures, big government, conservation, to say nothing of the silent generation and LSD.

8. We must understand that the high value we place on mind and intellect is legitimate, but has become almost an obsession. This has shaken the confidence of many in their own feelings, emotions and values. We must consider carefully the value we give the intellectual, for intellect untempered by compassion and values is of limited benefit, just as feelings and emotions unchecked by evidence and reason become of problematic virtue.

9. And, as we look at our condition today, is it too much to suggest that those of moderate persuasion have perhaps the most to become passionate about? We should compete a bit with George, who is doing more with the stage we have left him than we had anticipated.

The Humanistic Heartbeat Has Failed James H. Billington

The American version of the international student upheaval demands not just a new structure, as in Paris, and new politics, as in Prague, but new substance in higher education itself. Our collegiate discontent arises largely among well-fed students in the humanities and the social sciences and is the consequence of a spiritual poverty in academia that, in some ways, is as explosive as the material poverty in the ghetto. Rebels in the cities have kept "soul" alive; the modern American university seems to have lost its soul amidst unprecedented material growth. The university, as the center of rational criticism in our civilization, has an obligation to become its own most searching critic. It should not leave the job by default to the demagogic anti-intellectualism of either reactionary politicians or revolutionary students.

"If you don't know where you are, you're in the right place," read the hand-painted sign at Columbia University, the last of 20 university campuses I recently visited. It was the first day of classes after 10 days of upheaval; and I was given a flood of word pictures of the university in turmoil: "New York's newest form of zoo" (my disgusted cab driver); "a battlefield rather than a university" (a young teaching assistant in politics); "a beautiful happening that has drawn us all way out in left field" (a leader of the student strike rushing off to a "liberation class").

James H. Billington is professor of history at Princeton University. This article appeared in *Life* Magazine, September 20, 1968. Reprinted with permission.

It was not the chaos at Columbia that depressed me but the lack of constructive ideas for the future. It corresponded with the poverty of educational thinking that I found almost everywhere. Universities which presume to analyze everything else in our society have failed to take serious stock of themselves.

The blunt fact is that liberal education is largely dead. Its humanistic heartbeat has failed, and rigor mortis is setting in throughout the giant higher educational system. The humanistic ideal of involving the whole man in the quest for order and beauty through the ennobling exposure to other men's accomplishments has been mostly replaced by the training of task-oriented technicians.

The trouble begins in the large universities, on which American higher education principally depends for leadership and ideas. They have been called multiversities, megaversities and a good deal else. But the false impression has been created that there is some kind of enriching variety built into all this gigantomania. The sad fact is that each is just another branch factory of a nationwide knowledge industry. Faculty and administration shuffle from one branch to another—interchangeable parts in a highly mobile market. Students are a standardized, subsidiary by-product of an assembly line whose main product is publications. Thus, after mastering the three "r's" in elementary school, young America must now face the three "c's" of higher education: commercialization, competition and compartmentalization.

In its relentless search for money, the modern university has let concern for "image" replace aspiration for an ideal. Public relations with the outside world has often become more important than human relations within the university itself. Plato deliberately left the marketplace of ancient Athens to set up his academy; modern America has thrust its academicians back into the commercial arena. Marketability–not truth–has become the criterion of intellectual value. Almost no one in the status-conscious education industry has seriously challenged Clark Kerr's view (*The Uses of the University,* 1963) that the "really modern university" is simply "a mechanism . . . held together by administrative rules and powered by money"; that academic subjects will ultimately survive only if they earn their own money, and that "it only pays to produce knowledge if through production it can be put into use better and faster."

Competitiveness is the corrosive consequence of commercialization. "Admission to Amherst College is competitive," begins a typical college catalogue, and the elbowing continues all the way up the Byzantine staircase that leads to the ivory tower.

Instead of sharing knowledge, graduate students often seek to hoard it. When I once accidentally came across a dozen books in English literature oddly placed in the Baltic periodicals section of Widener Library, a Harvard graduate student explained that I had stumbled on someone's "secret stockpile of reserve ammunition" designed to "shoot down the opposition and impress the professor in one of those dog-eat-dog first-year graduate seminars."

Competitiveness gets worse as the young scholar moves into the academic "job market." Since modern college administrators more easily recognize market values than intellectual ones, "making it" in the race for advancement almost invariably involves blackmailing administrators by threatening to take outside offers. Thus, university presidents are repeatedly in the position of systematically rewarding *dis*loyalty to their own institutions.

Compartmentalization further cuts down the possibilities of human communication–let alone human community–in the modern university. Departments, which largely control the higher educational process, have only an incidental interest in the intellectual lives of any students not fully apprenticed to their narrow guild. There is a lack of dialogue not only among students, faculty and administration but also within faculties, and even within the different sections of individual departments. The faculty meeting of Columbia during the recent student unrest was the first in living memory to bring together in one place all faculties located in the Morningside Heights area.

We are producing a generation of scholars who prefer to provide definitive answers to small questions rather than tentative answers to important ones. In the process, the undergraduate, hemmed in everywhere by narrow compartments, feels fragmented and frustrated. "We were all divided up into punches on an IBM card," a Berkeley student told me. "We decided to punch back in the riots of 1964, but the *real* revolution around here will come when we decide to burn computer cards as well as draft cards."

"We have just not been given any passionate sense of the excitement of intellectual life around here," said the editor of the Columbia *Spectator.*

A student columnist in the Michigan *Daily* wrote, "This institution has dismally failed to inculcate, in most of its undergraduates at least, anything approaching an intellectual appetite." He spoke of the drift "towards something worse than mediocrity—and that is absolute indifference. An indifference towards perhaps even life itself."

This truly is a "sickness unto death"; for humanistic education is nothing if not a continuing celebration of life. Both the subject and object of humanistic study are the whole man—where mind and passion meet, where creativity and criticism interact. Humanistic studies—history and philosophy, arts and letters—directly involve men in the anguish, achievements and aspirations of other people, and in enduring human questions of artistic form, moral value and personal belief. These questions, dealing with the quality of life, are relevant to everyone—and not merely to departmental specialists.

Since the "output" of the humanities is the enrichment of individual lives rather than the corporate economy, their study languishes in the "marketversity." "We have more information and less understanding than at any time in history," warns Robert Hutchins. But the "great books" and "great ideas" around which he built a humanistic curriculum at the University of Chicago a generation ago have been largely replaced by narrow monographs and methodologies even at Chicago.

"At least we feel badly about it," one Chicago student wistfully said. Only occasionally does someone publicly protest in the manner of the Dartmouth student at the end of a "Great Issues" conference a few years ago: "In the course of all these meetings," he said, "I have never heard anyone mention the word God. Isn't *that* a great issue?"

In the monetary language which the marketversity best understands, one should perhaps divide the blame for the present bankruptcy among the stockholders (alumni), the management (administration), the professional staff (faculty) and the consumers (students).

The alumni have helped kill off humanistic education in America by not insisting that it be kept alive. This was, after all, the only kind of education most college students received in the essentially prescientific era prior to World War II. But rather than concern themselves with the *educational* life of their alma maters, these old graduates are inclined to confine their criticisms to the political views of the faculty and the sexual views of the students.

The alumni are perhaps easiest to forgive, since they do support higher education, financially at least, and are legitimately preoccupied with other things. But it does seem ironic that self-styled "defenders of hallowed custom" will go to battle for just about every college tradition except the one which brought colleges into being in the first place: the ideal of a liberal education.

The administrators bear special guilt—not for their apparently inescapable preoccupation with fund-raising and coordinating, but for their lack of intellectual acumen and moral passion in diagnosing the ills of their own institutions.

"We are hedged in by prima donna professors, feudal departments that do the hiring and a professional union that won't let me fire anyone on tenure," one college president complained. But his tone of weary resignation provided another reminder that university presidents with the stature and authority of a Woodrow Wilson or a Nicholas Murray Butler are a thing of the past.

Constantly preoccupied with short-term crises and outside economic pressures, the typical college administrator has an almost neurotic need to reassure himself with familiar platitudes. Thus, there has come into being a kind of "rhetoric gap" between the oratory and the reality of higher education. On the commencement platform, the university spokesman celebrates the values of liberal education; but back at the office he has no time to discuss the essence of it with those most intimately involved: students and faculty. The report of a committee to investigate student life at Columbia was not made public by the president until one week before the recent upheaval, when the students themselves threatened to release it—eight months after it had been submitted, two years and four months after the committee had been formed.

The university administrator senses that the humanities are in trouble, but he consoles himself with the thought that the English department is "as big as ever," as a western college administrator told me. "We do better than most with the humanities," a Harvard professor said, "but attention here is focused on a $50 million college fund drive exclusively for the sciences."

The faculty bears a deep responsibility for the death of the humanities. It is not simply a case of scholarship at the expense of teaching, but a neglect of both in favor of committee rituals, cocktail parties and a subtle corruption of humanistic scholarship. A variety of faculty foibles and failings have contributed.

There are, first of all, the pipe-puffing Platonists, who identify the humanities inextricably with the ideal of a natural and remote aristocracy. At its best, this tradition was rich and liberating—in the famous Harvard philosophy department of James and Santayana; at Princeton in Whitney Oates' pioneering cross-departmental Special Program in the Humanities; or in the humane study of literature at Yale under figures like the still-active Maynard Mack.

But if the humanists previously were too isolated in Platonic academies, they now seem too anxious at times to imitate Aristotle as counselor to Alexander the Great. This new cult of perpetual political involvement has created a breed within the academies who are variously known as "action intellectuals," "in-and-outers" and "voyeurs of power." Honest criticism and honorable consultation are the obligations of citizenship, but there is real danger today that the humanist, exploited for his articulateness, may become little more than a make-up man tidying up some public figure's image or activist's program for public presentation.

The heaviest death blow to the humanities, however, has come from the sycophants of science. They have spread within the traditional humanities a crippling inferiority complex that has led to a loss of confidence in dealing with qualitative problems of value, taste and belief. The advent of the computer has often encouraged the trivialization of scholarship and the belief that the things that count are those that can be counted. The largest of the humanistic guilds, the mammoth 25,000-member Modern Language Association, has computers in its headquarters but few readable articles in its publications.

"Not only are there no real men *teaching* history," one Ivy League undergraduate complained, "but there is a resentment against those real men who *made* history. The lecturer in our course on modern European history discussed every social class and psychological complex known—but never even mentioned the name of Napoleon."

The problem is emphatically not a simple case of the "two cultures"—scientific and humanistic—warring against each other. Scientists such as J. Robert Oppenheimer, the late director of the Institute for Advanced Study, have often been the most passionate patrons of pure humanistic scholarship. Moreover, humanistic interest in the sciences has produced some stimulating new intellectual activity in the history of science, linguistics, anthropology, etc.

The most important problem arises within the humanities themselves, and among the more aggressive promoters of new methodologies in the neighboring social sciences.

Accepting a naive, positivist view of science which is largely rejected by modern scientists themselves, the behaviorists have largely taken over the academic study of politics. One no longer reads the works of great political theorists in "professional" political science, any more than one reads noncontemporary philosophers in "professional" philosophy.

"As intellect and reason become increasingly identified only with science," warns Sheldon Wolin of the Berkeley political science department, "too many people feel driven either to private irrational withdrawal or to purposeless, irrational violence." Anxious to keep alive an awareness of past political thinkers, Wolin has sought (unsuccessfully so far) to set up a separate Department of Political and Social Thought at Berkeley and has collaborated with other theorists in founding a new learned society to overcome their feeling of isolation within the primarily behaviorist American Political Science Association.

A paltry one out of every thousand dollars of government funds given for basic research in 1966 went to the humanities. The much smaller amount given by private foundations to support research and teaching was some 23 times greater in the sciences than in the humanities. The federal government has recently shown an indifference bordering on contempt for humanistic scholarship: first in the original Selective Service recommendation that humanistic but not scientific graduate students were to lose draft deferments; second, in the decision of the House to cut sharply the already small authorization of the National Foundation on the Arts and Humanities to about one fifth the amount recommended by congressional committees.

Princeton originated an interdepartmental Council on the Humanities 15 years ago and sponsored publication of 11 volumes surveying the state of the humanities in America which pointed to many critical needs. However, Princeton's new $92 million academic development campaign is devoted exclusively to five "key interdepartmental areas" of "critical national importance"–none of which (except, in part, the library) are in the humanities.

The continued acceptance of giant scientific grants tends to cannibalize other university funds rather than "free them for those subjects that don't pay their own way," as one college dean put it. Another Ivy League university which has accepted much government money for the sciences in recent years but is also strong in the humanities will spend this year $38.50 of its own funds to support scientific research for every dollar spent in support of humanistic research.

What difference does the death of the humanities really make? It means, first of all, that we are feeding our best young people what former Secretary of Health, Education and Welfare John Gardner has called the "anti-leadership vaccine." By learning to "factor" every human problem into technological sub-problems, the student may never be encouraged to see the big picture in perspective.

"As a civilization, we no longer know how to do anything," comments Jacques Barzun, former provost at Columbia. "We can meet no situation, pursue no purpose, without stopping work and studying." The situation might be described as paralysis through overanalysis; and, as Barzun puts it, "Turning the academic experts loose on the so-called problems of society tends toward the general paralysis."

Consider, for instance, the two greatest practical problems America faces today: Southeast Asia and our cities: It is tragic for us all that–with pitifully few exceptions–academic discussion has been uninformed by any deep historical perspective based on first-hand human knowledge of the life and culture of either Vietnam or the ghetto.

"Where are our Vietnamese experts?" plaintively asked John Fairbank, president of the American Historical Association, at a congress of Orientalists last year. Although the United States has been deeply involved in Vietnam for nearly 15 years now, we still have no one in a high policy-making position with any deep knowledge of Vietnamese culture. Instead, we have the optimistic faith in scientific predictability and cultural uniformity voiced by Presidential Assistant (and former M.I.T. professor) Walt Rostow that "all peoples of the globe . . . sail the same voyage, are bound to the same destination."

Nor has the behaviorist establishment equipped us very well to anticipate the great problems of the cities. The ghetto riots and breakdowns of confidence in recent years call into legitimate question the optimistic assumption of the fashionable "community power studies" that conflicts would be resolved through democratic processes. The archetvpe of this genre, a study of New Haven by Robert Dahl of Yale in 1961, conveyed little sense of the uniqueness of the Negroes' plight in the cities.

We seem able fully to grasp national and racial feelings only when they translate themselves into violent movements with an "output" of destruction that can be recorded on our sociological seismographs. Had we seriously encountered earlier, through literature and history, the moral issues and human passions involved, bloodshed might have been prevented—and at least some imaginative resources stored up for creative rather than repressive responses to crises.

Can the humanities be revived to play a role in healing some of the ills of our civilization? There is a glimmer of hope.

The current student ferment is in many ways a cry for the renewal of humanistic education in America. To be sure, it is sometimes hard to see anything more than symptoms of a declining civilization in a student generation that enjoys unprecedented subsidies and liberties yet often seeks to demean, if not destroy, the universities that shelter them. Some have turned their backs altogether on the great tradition of rational discourse within an atmosphere of mutual trust which, after all, is the lifeblood of any university. Some are loudly proclaiming (with characteristic disregard for rational argument) that it is already 1984 and they are Che Guevara or Ho Chi Minh. But many of the most sensitive students simply feel spiritually starved; they protest against the failure of the arid classroom to provide the humanizing education that the college catalogue had promised. In their often clumsy way, they are trying to bridge the rhetoric gap—but they see no hands extended from the other side.

Thus, the tuned-out student generation has joined (or merely identified with) the two heavily publicized young peoples' revolts of the mid-sixties: the hippies, with their passionate belief in instant esthetics and salvation-through-hallucination; and the New Left, with its equally passionate commitment to instant morality and salvation-through-confrontation. Both groups are purer than their detractors contend. They generate an authentic feeling of human community; and they are trying to put esthetic and moral questions back onto the intellectual agenda of the Machine Age.

But while the hippies and the New Left are raising many of the classic questions, they offer few real answers. Their undisciplined emotionalism and blind totalism would prevent them from working within almost any conceivable academic framework. Intellectual activity itself could hardly thrive, and might not even survive, the total mystical withdrawal or the total revolutionary upheaval which appear to be the ultimate ideals of the hippies and the New Left, respectively.

On balance, however, both groups represent a deserved rebuke to the modern university. For behind the affront to tradition lies the reprimand which one of their culture heroes delivered more than a century ago to Emerson, who was boasting that Harvard now taught all branches of human learning. "Yes," said Thoreau, "all the branches, but none of the roots."

Only if we admit that the humanities really are very nearly dead is there much chance of pruning away old branches to make room for new growth. Even at the University of Chicago, where there are many cross-departmental programs, a semi-secret recent study by a faculty member concluded that a *real* regeneration of the humanities would require the liquidation of almost all the traditional departments. The future may lie with those who are less encumbered by inherited structures and vanities: the unified humanities department at M.I.T., which has devised a new set of courses for its scientific elite; the effort to define a new core curriculum at Upsala College in New Jersey; or the proposal of Daniel Bell of Columbia that undergraduate specialization be completed before a final senior year of broad general education.

Whatever the redefined curriculum, meaningful humanistic education will have to be conducted in smaller, less impersonal human communities. Hopeful models are the cluster colleges of California–privately supported at Claremont and publicly supported at Santa Cruz–which combine the overall curricular diversity and resources of a large university with the living and working scale of the college. Smaller colleges in the Midwest are gaining outreach by following the lead of Antioch and Beloit in regularly sending students out for work or community service in a totally different environment before bringing them back for their final years of study. There is a growing realization that the small college has a humanizing role to play educationally if it can survive economically; that there is much stimulus in experimental colleges within larger universities (such as those at Fordham, Chicago, Michigan State); and that new structures for shared "living-learning" experience can enrich even relatively small collegiate communities (Wesleyan, Bowdoin).

There is a danger, however, with experimental programs of producing conscience-salving tokenism rather than opening a continuing process of radical innovation. The option introduced at Princeton, of taking some courses with no grade except Pass or Fail, seems still in the realm of such tokenism. Though the "pass-fail" program has encouraged many students to venture outside their specialty, it usually serves to intensify the amount of neurotic student concentration on the "real" courses from which the all-important grades and class ratings are derived. Far more effective would be a program that devoted an entire term or year to pass-fail courses–or one that liberated the last two years from courses and grades altogether for tutorial, seminar and independent work with one continuing supervisor.

Our universities will best meet the over-all need for renewal of society if they begin with their own self-renewal. People at all levels in Swarthmore told me that the atmosphere on that campus was never better–in both intellectual and human terms–than during the week last fall when all classes were called off and the entire community engaged in systematic small-group discussion devoted to a long critique of the college by a commission appointed by President Courtney Smith. An institution that was more entitled than most to self-congratulation was dipping into the more rewarding realm of self-renewal.

The gradual disappearance of teachers dedicated to making humane learning relevant to students in all fields has led many to look beyond the faculty for gurus. Maharishi Mahesh Yogi last winter filled Harvard's Sanders Theatre in a way no professor could have done. Yale's William Coffin evoked an unprecedented and sustained student ovation in a packed Princeton chapel after a recent speech on radical Christian protest against current American policies; the most popular adult at Stanford seems to be Dean of the Chapel, B. Davie Napier, who regularly attracts capacity crowds to "Mem Chu" (Memorial Church) to hear his unorthodox sermons often based on texts from folk songs.

It may even be that just as the original humanists in the Renaissance formed an alliance with science against a dogmatic, scholastic theology, so now humanists may have to form links with a liberalized religion in order to combat the intolerant scientism of the modern marketversity. President Frank Haig of small, Jesuit Wheeling College in

West Virginia points out that theology—wherever it has ceased being taught exclusively by priests out of rote duty—has tended to become one of the most lively and popular subjects in Catholic colleges. Comparative religion is a rapidly growing field in larger universities and Oriental religions in "free universities."

"The rich but empty educational establishment may even have to reexamine its condescending attitude toward the denominational college," observed a Protestant minister who graduated from one in the Midwest. Certainly many in this student generation are anxious to be confronted with living traditions of value and belief, along with the intellectual techniques of analysis and expression.

For the larger university the hope is that one can re-create for the good of our entire civilization what the marketversity is not producing: the free, unselfish and joyful pursuit of wisdom within an atmosphere of mutual respect and ideological diversity. We will need to give authority to men with ideas—administrators willing to hire teachers outside regular departments and even outside the academic profession. We will need leaders to help overcome by example rather than rhetoric what the student-faculty report at Berkeley has called the "lack of intellectual fellowship"—the sterile opposition between the "passionless mind" of the formal curriculum and the "mindless passion" of student rebellion. One can hail the work of Clark Kerr in diversifying and enriching the state system of education at California, yet still question his image of the college president as a man "in the control tower helping the real pilots make their landings without crashes even in the fog." A new generation of students wants to know where and why the pilots are flying, what the purpose is of using a foggy airfield, and what the plane is carrying.

These restless students have begun the needed work of regenerating the American university by confronting it with the need for more commitment, not just more committees. The university is committed only to scholarship, people and the free and ennobling interaction between the two. If it is to survive, the university cannot accept the extremists' commitment to hallucinogenic drugs or hallucinatory politics. But if it is to revive, it must find radically new approaches that will in their own way expand the consciousness of a complacent America and lift its imagination beyond the supermarket pushcart. There may be a groping for greater sense of community even in the bizarre courses listed by the "Mid-Peninsula Free University" near San Francisco on "advanced group loving" and "people heaps"; a call for a richer, more diversified creative arts curriculum in the flowering of creative crafts at Penland, North Carolina, or even of such experimental art forms as the "guerrilla theater" and nude body-painting sessions in Southern California.

Student turmoil in America offers no inevitabilities and has produced too many pretentious prophecies. The "handwriting on the wall" is mostly adolescent graffiti. My only message is that humanistic scholarship is fun. Joy in posing and solving questions for oneself may help one create fewer problems for others. Indeed, the real argument for reviving the humanities may well be that they provide useful occupational therapy for a disturbed humanity that has been showing some suicidal tendencies.

Within and beyond our academies, we still have a chance to create a civilization that could surpass all others—even the Greeks, for theirs was built on slavery. We now have machines to do the work—unless they in turn have enslaved us. But our relatively young, sometimes arrogant civilization desperately needs a deeper sense of both the grandeur and the evil in humanity. Man is a fallen angel as well as a naked ape.

Chapter 5

THE BLACK AMERICAN

Newcomers to the great American cities have always had a hard time getting established. People who were "foreign"–people whose dress, manners, and language were different from those of the white, Anglo-Saxon, Protestant majority–were often treated with suspicion and contempt. The Irish were the first large group of immigrants to get that treatment, and then the Poles, the Czechs, and, last, the Italians. Last, that is, until the most recent migrant began to arrive in the cities. This last migrant was the most "different" of all. He came from within the United States and his skin was black. He came from the rural South beginning at the time of World War I. His destination was the manufacturing cities of the North, where he hoped to find work in the factories.

Like the European migrants before him, he moved into the poorest section of town where the rents were low. And, like the earlier migrants, he sent back home for his relatives and friends. From the time of World War I, the Negro population of the Northern cities–and later the Western cities–increased steadily. Some of these black migrants found the better life in the cities that they were looking for. More of them did not. The basic problems that the black man encountered when he first arrived in the cities still exist today: jobs and housing.

Two very important things have happened since the Negro migration began. First, the children of the man who moved from the South are grown now. They were born in the city and grew up there. They demand all the rights and privileges accorded to everyone else who lives in the city. Second, the United States government has begun to help the black man in his struggle to obtain equality. The first major step was the Supreme Court's decision in 1954, *Brown* vs. *Board of Education of Topeka,* which ordered an end to racial segregation in public schools.

Have these efforts been sufficient? Judging by the rebellions in the large cities in recent years, we can say they have not. The reluctance of the Southern school systems to bring about complete integration and the existence of schools in the Northern cities that are virtually segregated because of neighborhood housing patterns can be viewed as evidence of white America's reluctance to treat the black man as an equal. Most telling of all is the unemployment rate—nearly twice as high for Negroes as it is for whites. The cost of maintaining a segregated society is high. Not only is it measured in dollars, but in lives and property damage as well.

We begin this chapter with a speech by the late Senator Robert F. Kennedy ("Now We Must Learn To Speak to Each Other"). The cruel subtleties of racism are hard to ignore, even by a black man with a well-developed sense of humor ("Racism Is a Sick Joke"), as we learn from Bob Teague. What is life in the ghetto like ("The Ghetto")? How do those who live there look at themselves and the world ("The View from Watts Two Years After the Riots")? Finally, how has the racial situation in our cities come about and where is it heading? Unless our nation makes a significant effort to solve the racial problem, what can we look forward to? These subjects are examined in "Roots of Riot," an article based on the report of the National Commission on Civil Disorder, better known as the Kerner Report.

Now We Must Learn To Speak to Each Other Robert F. Kennedy

Through the eyes of the white majority, the man of decent impulse and moral purpose, the Negro world is one of steady and continuous progress. In a few years, he has seen the entire structure of discriminatory legislation torn down. He has heard Presidents become spokesmen for racial justice, while Negro Americans enter the Cabinet and the Supreme Court. The white American has paid taxes for poverty and education programs, and watched his children risk their lives to register voters in Alabama. Seeing this, he asks, what cause can there be for violent insurrection, or dissatisfaction with present progress? But if we try to look through the eyes of the young slum-dweller—the Negro, and the Puerto Rican, and the Mexican-American—the world is a dark and hopeless place indeed. The chances are that he was born into a family without a father—often as a result of welfare laws which require a broken home as a condition of help; a Negro's chance to live to 20 is the same as a white man has of living to 40. I have seen, in my State of New York, these children crowded into one or two rooms, with eight or ten relatives, without plumbing or heat for the cold Eastern winter, each night trying to defend against marauding rats.

The growing child goes to a school which teaches little that helps him in an alien world. The chances are 7 out of 10 that he will not graduate from high school—and if he does, he has an even chance of acquiring as much as the equivalent of an eighth-grade education. A young college graduate who taught in a ghetto school sums it up this way: "The books are junk, the paint peels, the cellar stinks, the teachers call you nigger, the window falls in on your head."

For the rest of life also there are statistics: 43% of ghetto housing substandard and overcrowded; 14,000 people treated for rat bites every year; a quarter of a million Puerto Rican schoolchildren in New York City, of whom only 37 went on to college last year; infant mortality at twice the normal rate; and, because of inadequate diets and medical care, mental retardation at seven times the community average.

In Oakland, there was a "Job Fair." Fifteen thousand people came to ask for work. Jobs were found for two hundred and fifty. And the other fourteen thousand, who wanted to work, but for whom there was none—where are they tonight?

Many of them are in fact not even recorded in our statistics. The Census Bureau, the Labor Department, the draft boards—the whole apparatus of government cannot even find from one-fifth to one-third of the adult men we know live in the ghetto. They drift about the cities, separated from society, as if they were of no greater concern to us than so many sparrows or spent matches. Twenty thousand or more in Los Angeles, perhaps twice that in my own city of New York—where are they and what are they doing, these legions of the damned and forgotten? When—and how—will they next remind us of their existence?

And let us be clear that all this is true despite the laws, despite the programs, despite all the speeches and promises of the last seven years. It must be for us a cruel and humbling fact—but it is a fact nonetheless—that our efforts have not even maintained the problem as it was: economic and social conditions in these areas, says the Department of Labor, "economic and social conditions are growing worse, not better."

But this is not all that the young man of the ghetto—the Negro, the Puerto Rican, the Mexican-American—this is not all he sees. Every day, as the years pass, and he becomes aware that there is nothing at the end of the road, he watches the rest of us go from peak to new peak of comfort.

He is told that Negroes are making progress. But what can that mean to him? He cannot experience the progress of others, nor should we seriously expect him to feel grateful because he is no longer a slave, or because he can vote, or eat at some lunch counters. He sees only the misery of his present and the darkening years ahead.

Thus he is denied the most fundamental of human needs: the need for identity, for recognition as a citizen and as a man.

Here, and not in the pitiful charade of revolutionary oratory, is the breeding ground of black nationalism and "reverse racism," and of aimless hostility and violence. The violent youth of the ghetto is not simply protesting his condition, but making a destructive and self-defeating attempt to assert his worth and dignity as a human being—to tell us that though we may scorn his contribution, we must still respect his power.

How fortunate we are that so few Negroes have taken this course. No people has borne centuries of oppression with greater fortitude and patience. Even now most Negroes miraculously retain the faith that justice will come through the orderly operation of the democratic process.

Does all this give us direction for the future? I think it does. For the fact is that Americans are not cruel or unjust or indifferent to suffering. The whole chronicle of our nation records the ultimate triumph of compassion and the spread of opportunity. Those are, and they remain, the basic instincts of the American people. What we must do is to build new bridges of trust and cooperation in a mutual commitment to justice. We can begin with a dialogue between the two Americas, which in turn will require that we look into ourselves. We have spent hundreds of millions of dollars trying to learn to speak to other peoples. Now we must learn to speak to each other. If the churches will affirm their involvement with the least among us, by working in the ghetto, and carrying the moral imperative into every suburban pulpit; if labor, with the fervor and drive of the '30's, will organize and fight for those who still languish in depression; if political parties see these problems as a chance, not to seize office, but to serve the nation; if we do these things, then we can engage in a dialogue between black and white which will reveal the misery of the one and liberate the fundamental decency of the other.

Racism Is a Sick Joke Bob Teague

If you look at the racial problem from a black man's point of view, you can see the jokes as well as the injustices. Which is to say that you can then understand this: The underlying syndrome that must be attacked is much more subtle than a white policeman's nightstick. It's more like a topsy-turvy vaudeville routine in which all the funny lines come from the straight men.

A favorite comic theme among the "concerned and enlightened" elements of white society is "Let's Stamp Out Racial Hatred." Hoo boy! Hatred has very little to do with the central problem, Charlie. What is done to and withheld from black folk day by day in this country is based on neither hate nor horror. On the contrary. It is coldly impersonal. Like the brains of precocious computers.

Simply put, it seems to me that white folk are convinced, deep in their bones, that the way they run this melting pot—with black folk unmelted at the bottom—is nothing more than the natural order of things.

What happens quite naturally, for example, is that a black *bon vivant* who shows up in a clean shirt at a posh restaurant is approached by white customers who beg him to get them a good table, please. There is nothing malicious about it. They simply think of black men in clean shirts as waiters.

Similarly, a black man caught on foot near a public parking lot is likely to be buttonholed by a pale proud patrician who wants his limousine fetched in a hurry.

And even the most militant white egalitarians are prone to compliment one another by saying, "That's real white of you, Edgar." Obviously, the notion that anything white is inherently superior to its black counterpart is built into the white American idiom, and thus into the white American mind.

Do you think it's accidental that the bad guys in Western movies are the ones in black sombreros?

This is not to suggest that white folk don't feel a respectable amount of guilt now and then, here and there. What the hell. They're human, too. In fact, I personally witnessed a veritable orgy of private and public breast-beating among whites early this year—that is, after they had recovered from the initial shock of learning from the President's Commission on Civil Disorders that "the main cause of black violence in the ghettos last summer was white racism."

Although I had reached a similar conclusion by the time I was 10 years black, I nevertheless judged the President's commission to be somewhat crude. You shouldn't spring a thing like that on 180 million unsuspecting

Mr. Teague was formerly a reporter for *The New York Times*. He is now a newscaster for a New York City television station. This article appeared in *The New York Times Magazine*, September 15, 1968.

suspects without warning. They didn't even have time to consult their lawyers.

Fortunately for the white masses, however—before their breasts had been pounded into lily-white pulp—a nationally famous Washington ventriloquist intervened. Through a captive puppet, he delivered a one-line joke that helped to bring white America back to normal. "It would be a mistake," the straight man said, "to condemn a whole society."

The implication was clear: Perhaps only a small minority of misguided whites were the culprits.

The collective sigh of relief was still in the air when a black civic leader, a former city councilman, died in East St. Louis. Naturally, since the natural order had been restored, the Valhalla Cemetery refused the corpse—on the ground that "everybody else buried in Valhalla is white." Who said the people who run cemeteries have no sense of humor?

A popular variation of the Valhalla skit was played this summer in the Republican political arena. Bold headlines stirred up a fuss around the two leading contenders for the G.O.P. Presidential nomination because each belonged to a private club, in different states, that bars black folk from membership—as if nearly all white folk don't belong to a Society of, a Committee to, a Council for or a Convention on that maintains the same standards of purity.

I am exposed to the same basic joke almost every time I walk into an all-white apartment building to keep an appointment with a friend. I see panic in the eyes of the pale residents coming out as I go in—trying to recall whether they locked their doors. And the doorman himself seems to be trying to remember the standard procedure for What to Do Until the Cops Come.

Although it has taken me many years to reach this point of view—perhaps because I managed a getaway of sorts from the ghetto—I understand now that neither the Valhalla Cemetery nor the doorman and the rest of white America are motivated by hate. To their way of thinking, the business of keeping black folk at a comfortable distance is not a matter of racism, not a choice between right and wrong. It's like fearing the bomb, saluting the flag and sending a card on Mother's Day. It's an automatic reflex action. In other words, no emotion of any kind is necessarily involved.

Consider, for example, those magazine and newspaper advertisements for "flesh-colored" bandages. The color they mean blandly ignores the color of most flesh on this planet. Mine in particular. But the top bananas who dreamed up that bit would be sorely aggrieved if someone called them racists. Some of those chaps are probably card-carrying fellow-travelers in the N.A.A.C.P., and their wives probably sent food to the poor people's shantytown in Washington. Their "flesh-colored" bandages are merely a profitable manifestation of a common assumption among white folk: White skin is what human flesh is *supposed* to look like. Anything else—black skin certainly—is irrelevant. Sort of a whimsical goof by Mother Nature.

How else can a black man explain those ubiquitous cosmetic ads showing a pale proud beauty using the facial lotion that promises to give her "the natural look"? The joke here is that this same beauty, and those who swear by "flesh-colored" bandages spend as much time in the sun as possible to darken their natural looks. They even buy chemical tans in bottles. And did you ever hear a commercial Goldilocks say, "Goodness gracious, my tan is much too dark"?

A spin-off joke from that particular farce is the honest pretense among whites that only their backward brothers—way down yonder in Mississippi—are hypersensitive to color. The white liberal party line says in effect that truly civilized whites regard black skin as a rather flamboyant costume for humankind, but nonetheless legitimate.

This is self-deception, of course. My experience has been that most white folk are so caught up in the seductive *mystique* of White Power that their brains are rarely brushed by the notion that the "natural order" in this country is in any way forced and unnatural.

Only last week one of my white friends—to be known here as Charlie—called my attention to one of those "flesh-colored" ads. Although Charlie is well past 35 and literate and had read similar ads over the years, he was seeing it clearly for the first time.

"Man, look at this," he said, wearing an embarrased grin. "They even insult you in the ads, don't they?"

Charlie's insight is not yet complete, however. If it ever is, he'll say "we" instead of "they."

How could good old Charlie have missed the point of that joke for so many years and thus become an accessory to the largely unconscious white conspiracy? It was easy. Just as it is for white gossip columnists to report regularly that the sexy movie queen who appears to be nude on the screen is actually hiding the goodies in a "flesh-colored" bra. They wouldn't dream of explaining such illusions in terms of "a bra that virtually matched her skin." Those gossip columnists, by God, know "flesh color" when they see it.

All of which is to say that white folk are immersed in such a totally racist climate that —like fish born in the ocean—they have no reason to suspect for a moment that they might be all wet. Wherever they look in this society, there are white institutions, habits, signs, symbols, myths and realties that reinforce their notion that black folk rank somewhere between King Kong and Frankenstein's monster on the scale of lower forms of life.

I recently read a best-selling novel which was not about the race problem. Yet the hero and his adversaries made the point again and again in passing that the busty blond heroine was clearly depraved and lost beyond recall since, between sexual acrobatics with the good guys, she allowed a "boogey" into her boudoir. That novel has sold more than 900,000 copies in the hard-cover editions, and more than two million more in paperback. I am not saying that its success is based in any way on its casual racial insults. The point is, it's a typical visual aid in the process of white indoctrination.

Television is even more effective in that respect. Here again, of course, white folk control both the medium and the message.

If a superintelligent visitor from another planet were to deduce, strictly from television, the nature of the 22 million black pariahs who exist in the crevices of this society, he undoubtedly would get an impression that was 99 44/100 per cent pure nonsense. From the electronic evidence of omission, projected around the clock, the visitor might gather that black women are rather dull and sexless creatures. Apparently nothing known to science or Madison Avenue can help black girls to develop "the skin you love to touch." With scarcely a blond hair to call their own, they obviously are not the kind of broads who "have more fun." And without one toothbrush among them, they have no interest in the leading toothpaste that "gives your mouth sex appeal."

Black men are equally irrelevant among the fauna of the natural TV order. It is tacitly suggested, for instance, that they are socially backward—black Square Johns, so to speak. Otherwise they would be seen driving "the low-priced luxury car" to seduce more swinging chicks.

It's true that black satellites are sometimes seen in TV dramatic series, but usually as cardboard characters with virtually no lives of their own. They are perpetually in orbit around the full-blooded white supermen who perform brain surgery, fall in love, bounce children on their knees and worry about middle-aged spread.

My impression is that many white folk

would like to portray black people in a more sophisticated manner. But, alas, they cannot forget all those Tarzan movies of their youth. These made it official that black folk are natural-born spear carriers, dangerous savages and beasts of the white man's burdens.

Then, too, there are all those cannibal cartoons in the slick magazines put out by and for white folks. Who wouldn't be somewhat repelled by a black gourment whose favorite entree is fricassee of Charlie?

Such examples of how black folk are systematically misrepresented or shut out from the stuff that the American Dream is made of are virtually endless. The smiling faces on greeting cards are never black faces. Department-store manikins don't resemble anyone you are likely to meet in the ghetto. And all plastic angels who symbolize the Christmas spirit are pink.

The net effect of these deceptions is that each tailor-made reality buttresses the other in the minds of whites. This explains in large measure why so many white folk are genuinely baffled by the grumbling and violence in the ghettos. Which is the basis for the popular white joke that ends with the punch line: "What do you people want?"

When black folk bother to spell out the answer to that riddle—with expectations that can only be described as naive—the consistent white responses add up to rather predictable pranks: another study of black frustration; another conference on brotherhood; another million-dollar crash program to tear down an old ghetto and replace it with a new ghetto.

As one of the best buffoons in the Federal Government observed after the riots last summer: "The very existence of the ghetto is un-American." But that line was much too oblique for most of white America to comprehend.

I am not suggesting that white folk don't even try. On the contrary. They conscientiously integrate a school here and there—even if it means doing something silly, like busing half the youngsters from A to Z and the other half vice versa. At the same time, however, they automatically prevent black families from buying or renting homes near the school in question. And they bar black folk from the jobs that pay the kind of money that would enable them to afford such a pristine neighborhood.

But getting back to how hard white people try, I witnessed one of their truly valiant efforts against insuperable odds this year. The occasion was the hint dropped by the President's Commission on Civil Disorders that the "ghetto is created by whites, maintained by white institutions and condoned by white society."

Most white folk were truly sorry about that. They rushed from their enclaves of affluence to the nearest ghetto to make amends. However, once in the wilds of Harlem and its scattered subdivisions, they simply could not resist telling corny jokes. Like the one Hitler told as he toured a concentration camp: "Jews stink."

What the Führer was smelling, of course, was Nazism. And in America the heady aroma of racism is equally confusing to the thin straight noses of the master race. Otherwise it would not be possible for those deadpan middle-class comedians to come up with such boffos as: "Why can't the black man pull himself up by his bootstraps like the other minorities have done?" While guarding the boots with bulldog tenacity day and night.

Admittedly, that is a rather large generalization. I have no doubt that some white skeptics will challenge me to prove it. My answer is this: Regard me as sort of a black J. Edgar Hoover. You didn't ask him to prove his public generalization that "Martin Luther King is one of the most notorious liars in the country."

Furthermore, I am prepared to generalize again. From my experience with white storekeepers over the years, I judge that many white merchants make a special hard-sell effort when a black customer shows up—to unload whatever raunchy merchandise they have in stock.

Example: One of my soul sisters overheard a white housewife chewing out a white butcher for putting rotten meat on display. "Can't you see it's not fit to eat?" she demanded.

"Lady, this is not for you," the butcher said matter-of-factly. "It's for them. Believe me, they don't know any better. They're like pigs."

Although black folk are reluctant to admit it in this age of militant reassessment of their position, they do feel a certain amount of pity for white folk now and then. Like Sam Bowers, who resigned this year as Grand Dragon of the United Ku Klux Klans in Georgia. Sam said he wanted "to work for a united America where black men and white men can stand shoulder to shoulder."

When I broadcast that item last spring, I couldn't help thinking: What grievous tortures poor old Sam must have suffered upon discovering the joke of white supremacy.

Another public confession was made recently at the opposite end of the spectrum by a self-declared white liberal—a Northern youth who had risked his life as a field worker in the civil-rights movement in Mississippi. Out of curiosity, he said, he took a trip on the LSD express. And the jig was up. Under the influence of the so-called mind-expanding drug, he realized for the first time that, in the Deep South of his soul, he honestly believed that black people were not now, never had been and never could be as deserving as whites. The immediate result of his insight was a nervous breakdown.

That young man was neither the first nor the last of his breed. The mass media these days are overpopulated with white liberals who portray themselves as "champions of the inarticulate masses." The sick joke here is that the masses—especially the black masses—are not at all inarticulate. They tell it like it is and like it ought to be—with precision, persistence and profanity.

But white society can't grasp the meaning of all that yammering—being too busy washing brains, their victims' and their own. They therefore have no real difficulty in maintaining their cool and the status quo in the face of massive protest and violence.

Being highly inventive jesters, white folk entertain themselves with a monologue that says, in effect, black folk are too stupid to realize that something phony is going on here. It goes like this: "It's the Communist agitators and Communist dupes who are behind all this violence."

One-liners like that are probably what killed vaudeville.

If black folk don't laugh out loud at such routines, it is because their funny bones are dulled from the same old stale material. Real comedy depends on surprises. So why should a black man chuckle over the annual Congressional Follies built around civil-rights legislation, for example? He knows in advance that the new Civil Rights Act is going to wind up like the so-called Open Housing Act of 1866—unenforced and soon forgotten.

Enforcement, he is told, would "infringe on the rights" of the white minority. That's a good one, too. But it is as familiar as, "Why does a fireman wear red suspenders?"

As for the sight gags in white society's repertoire, these too have worn thin from overexposure. How many times can an individual black man be amused by the blind-cab-driver routine? After the 37th time, it no longer strikes him as suitable material for a laff-in.

Did I say "individual black man"? Actually, there is scarcely any such animal as far as white eyes can see. They recognize "the first Negro who" and "the only Negro to," but not as individuals—instead, as freaks or symbols. Which is to say that white folks have a habit of arbitrarily assigning a rather standard personality to a black man. His real self is like an iceberg, deeply submerged in a sea of white assumptions.

One of my soul brothers was recently promoted to an executive position with a giant corporation in New York City. He had earned it by bringing in more sales orders over the last five years than anyone else in his department. You can imagine how chagrined he was when several of his white colleagues dismissed his personal achievement with humorless jokes like this: "It pays to be black these days. Man, you've got it made."

Such an attitude is not founded primarily on jealousy, as it might appear on the surface. White folks are simply incapable of seeing a black man as anything beyond his blackness.

At least twice a year, for instance, I am approached for an interview by one national magazine or another. My experience as a newspaper reporter and television news broadcaster has provided me with a wealth of interesting material from face-to-face encounters with four presidents, a half-dozen princesses, scores of prizefighters, hundreds of politicians, assorted pimps, paragons and pin-up queens. But not one white interviewer ever shows the slightest interest in anything except my blackness.

"What is the role of the black newsman?" they want to know.

"The role of a black man," I tell them off the record, "is or ought to be the same as it is for everybody else in his profession; in this case, to gather the facts and report them with as much integrity, clarity and objectivity as he can muster." End of interview.

I am also rather weary of getting letters from white television fans that read like this one:

"When you first began broadcasting the news on television, I watched you every night, but I realize now, years later, that I was so conscious of the fact that you were black that I didn't hear a word you said about the news. Now, I am happy to say, I still watch you every night, but only because you are a damn good newscaster. . . ."

What I'm getting at here is that white folks are generally flabbergasted by a black man who can fly a plane, mix a martini, speak unbroken English or shoot a round of golf. Such a black man is something like the celebrated dog that could walk on its hind legs unassisted.

About the only realm of this society which seems to be perhaps one-third of the way toward the verge of catching the spirit of this thing called the free democratic society is professional sports. Even here a string of qualifying exceptions must be taken into account. To mention just a few: Boxing is obsessed by the search for a "white hope"; football is convinced that a black quarterback could not lead his team to the goal line; and baseball, like all the others, shuts out black men from the managerial and decision-making level. And besides all that, there is a great deal of friction and apartheid on the so-called integrated teams.

But baseball still deserves a better grade than white Americans generally. In the first place, black players are no longer required to be supermen like Jackie Robinson. If you watch baseball these days, you see black men fumbling routine grounders, dropping flies, striking out with the bases loaded and winding up the season with microscopic batting averages. Just like whites. And no one suggests that such derelictions are peculiar to one race or another.

Furthermore, if a white interviewer shows up in the locker room, he is full of questions about the spitball or the squeeze play that didn't quite work in the ninth. After all, why should a third baseman, even a black one, be limited to discussing racial jokes?

So how long is it going to take the rest of this country to evolve even as little as baseball? In my judgment, another 100 years at the very least, if this society manages to survive that long.

Why so much time? Well, it seems to me that while one side of those split personalities called white Americans is striving with all its might to open their minds and their society, the other side is being pulled in the opposite direction by what white Americans accept and automatically maintain as the natural order. As you can see for yourself, it is something of an unequal race.

The Ghetto: A National Problem Nation's Cities

Racial segregation is not a local problem; it is a national problem. In origin it is not an urban problem, but it has been dumped on our cities to solve, with nearly 95 percent of all Negroes outside the South urbanized. It is now many cities' No. 1 problem, and one city governments cannot cure without many kinds of help, including all-out cooperation from state and national governments. It is a problem nobody can solve until millions of people, both white and nonwhite, understand it better and pitch in to play their own large or small part in the solution.

And unless somebody solves it, many great cities like Washington, Philadelphia, Detroit, Baltimore and Chicago may find themselves deserted by the white middle-class and abandoned (except for small enclaves of luxury housing for the rich) to the nonwhite poor, trapped in the slums by their poverty, and the nonwhite middle-class, trapped on the border of the slums by segregation and the lily-white suburbs' refusal to let them in. Already Washington has become 63 percent nonwhite, Detroit 39 percent, St. Louis 37 percent, Philadelphia 30 percent, Chicago 30 percent. Between 1950 and 1960, as everyone knows, Washington offset a growth of 181,000 Negroes with a loss of 226,000 whites; Chicago, a growth of 321,000 Negroes with a loss of 399,000 whites; New York, a growth of some 700,000 Negroes and Puerto Ricans with a loss of some 800,000 other whites.

Racial segregation is not a single problem but the sum of many different ones—a different community problem for almost every city and neighborhood, a different personal problem for every segregated nonwhite. Different as all these are, they are all parts of two basic problems—one almost new and seething with new bitterness, the other old and deep rooted in old prejudices.

One problem is the plight of the 5 million-odd urban nonwhites who are almost desperately poor—the plight of the 45 percent of all Negroes the 1960 census found living in "deteriorating" or "delapidated" housing.

The other problem is the frustration of the other 5 million-odd nonwhites who are no longer poor—5 million-odd urban nonwhites who, against great handicaps, have earned their way up to family incomes over $6,000 (up from 4.74 million indicated by census in 1963). These million nonwhites have adjusted their lives to middle-class aspirations but still find themselves denied middle-class acceptance and status.

These two very different problems call for equally different housing solutions, money solutions, opportunity solutions, timing solutions—and nothing but more confusion can result from confusing the two.

It is just plain nonsense to think all non-

This article appeared in *Nation's Cities*, April, 1967. Reprinted by permission.

whites are alike and to act as though their problems could be solved in the same way. The fact is that there are more differences among nonwhites than among whites because on top of all their other differences is superimposed a wide range of difference in how many white ancestors they have and what social, educational and financial advantages this white blood may have given their grandfathers. Caste lines among nonwhites are at least as strong as among whites, not just in lands like Haiti and Jamaica whose population is nearly 100 percent nonwhite but in this country too.

College-educated nonwhites (and there are more Negroes in U.S. colleges today than white men in English universities) have the same aspirations as college-educated whites, and have good reasons for feeling they should be accepted for what they are, instead of being rejected for what their great-grandfathers were. Middle-class nonwhites (and nonwhites have to work a lot harder to achieve middle-class incomes and values) have the same aspirations as middle-class whites, only more so. After long years of frustration they are more eager for status; market surveys show that they spend more of their incomes to be nicely dressed, spend more for "personal care," buy more expensive shoes, spend more for their home entertainment equipment. They limit their families to fewer children, work harder on their lawns and planting, and seem to have made good neighbors in every tract where they are accepted, from Levittown on the East Coast to Eichler on the West.

These people do not need special relief or special subsidies. They do not need special schools for their children, for their children have little trouble keeping up with white classmates. What they need now is recognition of their past achievements, freer access to better-paying jobs (Negro incomes still average 47 percent lower than white), a wider door to escape their present segregation on the edges of the nonwhite slums, and a better chance for further progress toward assimilation into the rest of our social and economic life.

These nonwhites moving up have little in common with the poor nonwhites sunk in the slums except their color and their common resentment of segregation. They have so little in common that when New York tried to speed desegregation by moving poor Negroes out of Harlem's slums into new public housing in middle-class areas, the middle-class Negro owners of nearby homes protested as angrily as their white neighbors.

Most of the Negroes now crowded into urban slums are newly arrived fugitives from the farm mechanization that wiped out a million field hands' jobs in the South, and sent them fleeing to the cities to seek jobs for which they had neither skills nor training. On top of this came a mass migration of 700,000 penniless Puerto Ricans, mostly to New York, and a mass migration of Mexican peons that made Los Angeles the world's sixth largest Spanish-speaking city. For this huge and sudden influx, the cities–north, south, east and west–were completely unprepared, without jobs, housing or schools ready to receive them.

The newcomers were equally unprepared for urban living. Old established urban Negroes welcomed the Negro newcomers with little enthusiasm, and the Spanish-speaking newcomers with even less. Poor whites greeted them with open bitterness and hostility, for they threatened their low-pay unskilled-labor employment just at a time when automation was eliminating millions of cheap-labor jobs.

Poor nonwhites need much better housing, but the sad fact is that as long as there are 6 million fewer decent homes in the urban housing inventory than there are urban families in need of homes, it is inevitable that 6 million urban families will have to live crowded into substandard units. Most of these 6 million victims of the urban housing shortage are bound to be the poor, and a disproportionate number of the very poor are nonwhite.

So we agree with HUD Secretary Weaver that the best answer to the nonwhite slum problem and the housing segregation problem is to build enough good housing so there will be a good home available for everyone. Some of this new housing will have to include building new low-rent units, but most of the low-rent need could be met better by trickle-down work, just as the auto needs of low-income families are better met by second-hand cars than by cheap new models. With today's land costs, today's building-trades wages and today's code and labor restrictions, private enterprise cannot hope to build good enough new homes cheaply enough for poor people to buy or rent without big subsidies. Two of the wisest contributions government could make to better housing for the poor would be to help finance the purchase and resale of sound used dwellings, and to help finance low-cost modernization.

But more good enough housing is only a small part of the answer.

Poor nonwhites need freedom to move out of their racial ghettos and live closer to available jobs—but when all restrictions are ended, most nonwhites still will prefer living with their own people, just as almost every other ethnic group has tended to stick together for a generation or more; often for three generations.

Poor nonwhites need better schools and better education, but bussing white children to nonwhite-neighborhood schools cannot be a good enough answer, when it means holding white children back because poor nonwhite parents cannot give their children the advantages needed to start even and stay even. School buildings in nonwhite-neighborhoods are notoriously inferior, partly because they are old buildings in old neighborhoods; teaching in nonwhite-neighborhoods averages below the white-neighborhood level, mostly because the teacher's work is harder and the pay no more.

But in all fairness it should also be realized that New York, for example, spends as much per pupil (well over $1,000) to educate nonwhite children in the public schools of Harlem as the tuition charged by the city's most exclusive private schools—quite a bit more money than most lily-white suburbs pay to educate their own. Furthermore, in Philadelphia and elsewhere the drive for school desegregation is tending to turn segregation upside down, with more and more white children taken out of public school, and more and more desegregated public schools getting to be almost 100 percent Negro. How will this affect the willingness of the white population, which carries some 95 percent of the local tax load, to pay increased taxes for better schools that few of their own children will be attending?

Nonwhites need more human contact with the rest of the community. The primary cause for the trouble in Watts was not that the housing in Watts is so bad (it isn't; not so long ago Watts was a fairly good middle-class white neighborhood). It was not because the area is overcrowded (it isn't; the density in Watts is not much more than 20 per acre). The primary cause of the trouble in Watts is the fact that it had been allowed to become an island apart. Not enough people outside had any contact with their fellow citizens walled off inside Watts. So it took a riot that cost $40 million and 34 dead to make outsiders realize that Watts had no good hospital for 87,000 people, no modern schools for more than 30,000 children, no movie house, only one public swimming pool and almost no public transportation to let people get to the kind of jobs they could hold. No wonder 30 percent of all the job seekers in Watts are unempoyed; no wonder its residents felt forgotten, bitter and almost hopeless.

But most of all, poor nonwhites desperately need more money, more jobs and more job opportunities, particularly more jobs for male heads of families and for young people, both boys and girls. Everybody knows that unemployment among nonwhites is more than twice as heavy as among whites, averaging out to 8.2 percent, but too few people seem to understand the peculiar pattern hidden behind the 8.2 percent average—a pattern which helps explain the bitterness of Negro youth, and also accentuates the matriarchal character of Negro home life which, in turn, accentuates the school problem of poor Negro children. An unemployment rate of 8.2 percent is bad enough, but what the "average" conceals is a jobless rate that often exceeds 30 percent among some of the nonwhites most in need of jobs.

Unemployment among college-educated Negroes is actually much less than among college-educated whites, because so many companies are making special effort to find qualified nonwhites to hire. Unemployment among middle-class Negroes has to be small almost by definition (otherwise they could not enjoy middle-class incomes); unemployment among adult Negroes with less than a grade school education is also low, probably because they seem willing to take menial jobs that nobody else wants. And one-third more Negro women than white have jobs outside the home—despite a 34 percent unemployment rate among teen-age Negro girls (three times the unemployment rate among teen-age white girls).

In other words: Negro unemployment is concentrated among Negro men who were high school dropouts, and is heaviest of all among young Negro men, who are most likely to have young children. In big city slums, their unemployment rate often runs higher than 30 percent.

A tragic consequence of this unemployment pattern is that the No. 1 breadwinner in too many slum-trapped nonwhite families is a working mother, and in some 40 percent of these poor families there is no man at all because the working mother is either deserted or unwed (in Harlem 43.4 percent of the children are illegitimate). So there is no one at home all day to care for and bring up the children. Of all Negro children, 36 percent live in broken homes; in the slums this percentage is much higher.

What all this adds up to is that the hard-core problem of nonwhite segregation is very largely a poverty problem, and it cannot be solved until employers, labor unions and the government (mostly federal) work out a good way to let nonwhites escape from poverty and male unemployment. Says Philadelphia's Joseph V. Baker: "A Negro does not need a college degree to put gasoline in an empty tank, or to turn a wrench as far as the threads have been cut, or to collect tickets on trains."

Desegregation, in the sense of living next door to white neighbors, is mostly for upper- and middle-class nonwhites. For the great mass of poor nonwhites, desegregation means mostly a chance to escape from poverty, slum housing and male unemployment, plus a chance for better education to help their children work their way up.

No local government can solve all the problems of the nonwhite poor, but few of their problems are likely to be solved unless and until local governments take an active part in their solution. For example and specifically:

• Only local governments can deflate the bootleg price of slum housing by code enforcement and/or taxation. Dean Abrams' block-by-block research shows that in Philadelphia, vigorous code enforcement has so deflated central-city housing prices there that a large percentage of the 14,400 row houses new vacant can be bought (or put) in decent move-in condition for $4,000 cash or less. (Compare this with an average cost of $20,-500 for new public housing, and $12,300 now budgeted by the Housing Authority to buy units and do them over completely, regardless of how much fixing up they really need.) If FHA or other special financing is made available, this $4,000 cost would make it possible for even relief clients, black or white, to buy or lease decent used homes.

Pittsburgh, on the other hand, has been fearful that strict code enforcement might leave the 10,000 families homeless, and in New York the mayor's special housing adviser declared in 1961 that "no amount of code enforcement can stop the spread of slums unless and until the profit is taken out of slums by taxation."

• Only local governments can locate some of their own employment centers where they will be easy for the nonwhite poor to reach.

• Only local governments can tear down the obsolete and decaying school buildings found in most nonwhite slums, and replace them with up-to-date plants less likely to encourage high school dropouts (the average nonwhite boy quits school after the ninth grade).

• Only the local government, with financial support from Washington, can provide the nursery schools and the day-care centers needed to keep the preschool slum children of broken homes and working mothers off the streets, giving them some of the care, attention and mental stimulation middle-class children get from their families, so these slum children will be ready to keep up with their classes when they reach school age. This kind of need is already met by the state in Russia (another case where most mothers work outside the home) by including day-care centers, playgrounds, nursery schools and primary schools in the center of every new apartment block. In this respect it is high time for American cities to catch up with Russian ones. In New York, 80 percent of the 600,000 relief recipients whose support costs local, state and/or federal taxpayers $700,000 a year belong to no-male-breadwinner families.

• Only the local government can provide or encourage the kind of bus or jitney service poor nonwhites need to get from where they live to jobs they can hold.

• Local government can provide neighborhood centers to help slum owners who want to improve their property understand and take advantage of all the various state, federal and foundation grants and aids available to them.

• Local governments can pressure the state to stop forcing them to discourage and penalize improvements with increased assessments and taxes. (Personal interview surveys in Newark and elsewhere make it clear that fear of higher assessments is a prime reason why slum property owners won't spend money to maintain or improve their properties.)

• Finally, the job needs of the nonwhite poor will not soon be met until local government cooperates in attracting and encouraging not just high-wage industries but also the kind of lower-wage industries and services in which unskilled workers could expect to find steady jobs.

Racial segregation is the worst kind of segregation because it is so rigid, so hopeless and so humiliating; but we deplore all one-class neighborhoods big enough to segregate their people from the larger community.

Suburbia is the great segregator, segregating not only white from nonwhite but also the lower-middle-class from the middle-middle-class, and the middle-middle-class from the upper-middle-class and the wealthy. We think this is as bad for those who are segregated *in* as for those who are segregated *out*. For example, it makes it harder for those who are segregated *in* to employ the kind and variety of help they need, while at the same time making it harder for many of those who are segregated *out* to get the kind of service jobs they need and could fill.

Small enclaves of people with the same background and about the same income are perfectly natural and no problem at all; there is no reason why millionaires should live next door to relief clients, and no reason why relief clients should want to live between millionaires. But there are many good reasons why rich and poor, white and nonwhite should live close enough together to know how the other half lives, and to share the community of life and the openness of opportunity whose sharing is the first essential of urbanism. Big one-class or one-race neighborhoods frustrate ease of contact and ease of access; they deny variety, opportunity and the exchange of services; and the bigger the one-class or one-race ghetto, the more complete the frustration and denial.

Middle- and upper-income families pay in more ways than one for their flight from the city to one-class enclaves in the suburbs. They pay in travel time and all the extra hours they spend getting to and from the center. They pay in lost leisure, doing household chores they could otherwise find someone else to do. They pay in loss of variety and stimulation because they live too far from town. (Says the former AIA president: "One-class neighborhoods are just plain dull.") And they pay in higher prices and heavier state and federal taxes for supporting on relief millions of people who, in a better-integrated metropolitan society, might be self-supporting and helping to meet the labor shortage and up the gross national product in our full-employment economy.

It is more than a coincidence that the most underprivileged people in urban America must also be the most heavily subsidized (in Philadelphia, for example, 80 percent of the relief clients are nonwhite).

The View from Watts Two Years After the Riot

Jack Jones

Part I

Four thin young Negro men with "natural" hair drink wine near spilled trash cans in the sprawling Jordan Downs public housing project in Watts. "Ain't nuthin changed," one of them says, adding an explosive four-letter word.

Another demands, "What the hell's the good of all them training programs? Ain't no decent jobs anyway."

At the Watts Manufacturing Co. on El Segundo Blvd., the single major new plant in the area, 26-year-old John L. Price works as a cabinet man after two years' "hard time" in prison for forcible rape and five years of joblessness.

"This is a beautiful place if you want to work," he says. "I love to work. Just give me half a damn chance and get off my back."

These differing attitudes point up the impossibility of measuring just how much two years of studies, federal grants, private industry efforts, redevelopment plans and endless discussion have begun to bleach the scars of a fiery August in South-Central Los Angeles.

Do Negro residents of the region—particularly Watts—sense any improvement in employment, housing, education and the white community's willingness to see the most impoverished escape from hopelessness?

Part I of this article appeared in *The Los Angeles Times* on July 16, 1967. Part II appeared on July 17. Reprinted with permission.

It depends on where one looks and whom one asks.

A few general conclusions are possible:

1. To the ever-present question—Is more violence likely?—it can only be said that most of the basic problems underlying the 1965 violence still exist. The real and psychological isolation has been broken only slightly.

2. Physical changes are minimal, with everything hanging on the success of redevelopment plans.

3. The job and training picture has improved, but not particularly for the "hard core" unemployed, the totally unskilled and unmotivated.

4. Education is better, primarily because of federally supported programs. And more parents are communicating with teachers. The question remains as to whether de facto segregation makes remedial programs futile.

5. Housing is little changed, but there are various plans to upgrade it. There are indications that, as they get jobs, some Negroes are moving from the area's heart.

6. Health facilities are better and will improve.

7. Feelings against the police remain high among militant youths, while many other residents sense that the efforts of new Police Chief Tom Reddin are producing better relations.

8. Pride in being black is on the rise, partly inspired by the self-sufficiency stand of

nationalist groups. But some confusion exists in the minds of those who decry the anti-white connotation of "black power."

"Even if we attribute some minor gains in jobs as a result of activities following the 1965 disorders," the area's Negro congressman, Rep. Augustus F. Hawkins (D-Los Angeles), said recently, "conditions today in South Los Angeles are worse than in 1960.

"Median income in down. Segregation is more widespread. Schools, already inferior, are now threatened with cutbacks. Welfare cases have climbed. The number of families headed by women has increased."

If Hawkins bases his conclusion on reports criticized by others as being misleading, certainly there are few visible changes.

Most of the basic problems underlying the 1965 violence are still in existence. The real and psychological isolation has been broken only slightly.

Along 103rd St.–the so-called "Charcoal Alley" of Watts–weed-strewn lots stretch as bleak reminders of the stores and jobs which vanished in flame.

They give witness to prohibitive insurance rates, the difficulty of financing and the reluctance of businessmen to invest until the city and Community Redevelopment Agency complete plans to breathe new life into Watts and surrounding areas.

Only three major chain stores have been rebuilt since August, 1965–and none of these is in Watts itself.

At 103rd and Grape Sts., USC's multipurpose family health clinic finally nears completion after long delays.

Southeast General Hospital, for which a bond issue was turned down by the voters last year, apparently will be built (supposedly by 1970) despite recent opposition to state-federal financing.

The county's South Health District Center recently expanded its clinic facilities at 1552 E. 102nd St.

But outside of the privately built Doctors' Building (under construction before the disorders) and the USC health center, the only significant new structure on 103rd St. is the Bureau of Public Assistance office.

This drew resentment from those who saw it as a prefabricated reminder "that we're on handouts and they can pull it out of here tomorrow if we don't behave."

Ground has been broken for a proposed community art center adjacent to the now-famous Simon Rodia towers of junk but the dirt was easier to turn up than money.

Directors of the various vocational training programs–either federally financed or depending on community and private industry help–agree that in an area of staggering unemployment and compacted poverty, the job ground also is scarcely broken.

But any kind of agreement in the Negro community–just as in the white community–is not always easy to find. "Tell it like it is, baby," may be a constantly heard expression, but just how is it?

Tommy Jacquette, 23, tall and bearded black nationalist, said, "What's happening is nothing. There hasn't been any real change in this community–or in L.A. and the white attitude–since August, 1965.

"A lot of motion has taken place. We've had a lot of festivities–conferences, retreats, training programs, festivals–but nobody has gotten better houses. There's still bad employment and still bad education in the schools."

On the other hand, Ben Peery, former Watts Community Coordinating Council president and conservative figure who says the riots wiped out his real estate business, saw definite improvement:

"There are more people employed than last year. Many people who haven't actually attended any of the training schools have been inspired to seek jobs when they were at the point of giving up."

But Watts and environs never will see the promise of high employment fulfilled until there is significant industry in the area.

"The situation," Peery observed, "has become a political football. It will be years before anything is done . . . unless people take the attitude of the pioneers and do it themselves."

Here, it would appear, his viewpoint closes with that of black nationalists who stress black pride, self-help and self-determination.

"But he's going the individualistic route while we're going the collectivistic route," Jacquette said.

Many Negroes point out that arguments swirling around community redevelopment, the Southern Pacific Railroad's suggestion for an industrial park and other proposals are no different from disputes which would arise over similar projects in white communities.

"I don't think there's the frustration in the average person's mind that there was prior to August of 1965," commented Willard Murray, Mayor Sam Yorty's Negro assistant who has maintained close contact with all kinds of groups.

"But counterbalancing that, there are more people who have developed the ability to articulate the problems that do exist. The noise level is probably greater now, but it comes from fewer people."

Never before, he pointed out, have there been so many meetings, so many reporters and survey-takers prowling around Watts and the rest of South-Central Los Angeles asking Negroes what they think.

"It used to be that no one wanted to lead. Now everyone does."

How much effect has black nationalism had on most Negroes in South-Central Los Angeles?

Like everything else, this is difficult to assess. Many of those who have not given up on integration, as black nationalists have, concede that the movement has helped heighten pride in being black.

This, they say, is a positive aspect widely overlooked by whites.

"Natural" hair is a common sight, especially among the young men and women who are disgusted by the thought of straighteners and bleach creams.

Ron Karenga's US group stresses the wearing of "bubas" and "kangas," African-style clothes, and argues that without his own culture, the black man will never really escape slavery.

Because so much of what happens in the Negro community is in the hands of the youth, it is important to know what teen-agers think about black power. Here are comments from several Fremont High School students:

"It makes us equal . . . more powerful in elections."

"It can hurt the cause. I believe in making my own way, the individual way."

"Black power is a coming together of Negroes."

"Those who advocate black power are the radicals. They're against the whites, but they're a small group."

Certainly there are a number of organizations expressing all these viewpoints and suddenly visible since the fires of August made Watts known throughout the world as a symbol of urban Negro discontent.

They range from Society for Leadership All Nationalities Today (SLANT) and US (stressing black culture and distrust of whites) to neighborhood improvement groups.

The latter generally support strong law enforcement and reject the separatist movement which prompted the short-lived push for "Freedom City" as an independent municipal entity.

As an indirect outgrowth of the war on poverty's community action phase, small groups such as the Mothers of Watts have sprung up—primarily in the housing projects–to press for better schools and upgrade other conditions.

If some of these organizations are viewed by their detractors as agitative, it must be remembered that life in Watts is abrasive to start with.

Watts Positive, a campaign headed by Mrs.

Eva Bradford-Rock, was launched to improve the image of Watts, to point out that there are pleasant neighborhoods populated by responsible, law-abiding people.

And to echo resentment that Watts problems get more attention than those in white communities.

Black nationalists, too, resent the stress on Watts, but their concern is with the oversight of problems in other black communities–in Pacoima, Venice, Pomona, etc.

If Watts has become a social welfare laboratory more popular with federal and local agency program developers than Pacoima or Venice, it has become also–in the minds of some, at least–a study in frustration.

"Watts," goes an often-repeated epigram, "is no longer a place, but a state of mind."

Announcements come almost daily of programs designed to raise the level of education, employment, housing, recreation and opportunity to share in the affluence of American society.

Some of these programs get off the ground after many slow months of confusion, deliberation and red tape. Others, after initial flurries of publicity, die quietly.

Few–if any–deliver on what the community feels are promises of immediate change.

To the jobless youths standing at the corner of 103rd and Beach Sts., any statement that H. C. (Chad) McClellan's Management Council has spurred private industry to hire thousands of Negroes from the curfew area is a lie.

No report from any source in the white community will convince them otherwise.

Dr. Paul Bullock, who has studied hard-core poverty in Los Angeles during several projects by UCLA's Institute of Industrial Relations, said:

"The fact that all these publicized programs are happening so slowly only increases frustration. Few agencies are really prepared to make a frontal attack on the hard core–the totally unskilled, unmotivated guy who has just given up."

As for the poverty programs, including job training and other life betterment designs:

"The goal so far has been simply to put out fires–crash programs, anti-riot measures. There is no real continuity."

Hiring figures cannot be taken at face value, Bullock said, because "we never get the figures on people being displaced by automation and other factors."

Census figures–both from 1960 and the special 1965 South Los Angeles count–cannot be trusted, he said, because too many people were missed. Thus, unemployment percentages are meaningless.

The McCone Commission Report estimate that there were 25,000 unemployed Negroes in Central Los Angeles at the time of the riots Bullock called "the wildest kind of a guess."

At 103rd St. and Central Ave., where an abandoned insurance office has been turned into a headquarters for the second annual Watts Summer Festival, committee co-chairman Billy Tidwell agreed that things are not so hopeful as some would like to think.

The festival itself, which last summer marked the anniversary of violence with a successful exhibition of community pride, has been going through financial difficulties.

Tidwell, with his neat goatee and powder-blue vest, is a Jordan High School graduate with a master's degree from UC Berkeley in social welfare.

It was he who helped turn a gang of idle young men into the Sons of Watts Improvement Assn., active for a time in trying to clean up the community.

About 70 of the Sons got jobs after Chad McClellan responded to their challenge to prove that industry and the state employment service were really trying.

But, Tidwell said, most of the 70 are out of work again. Some of the jobs were temporary in nature and others folded in routine cutbacks affecting short-term employes.

Tidwell said the positive attitude of Watts that crested during the first festival last summer "still exists–but in a different way. The last festival lifted the community spirit. There was pride and hope for the future."

What has happened to temper that hope?

"The election of Ronald Reagan, the Adam Clayton Powell thing, problems over getting the hospital, the antipoverty cutbacks ... all have had tremendous effect.

"People feel that the power structure doesn't really want us to see things improve."

Any discussion of individual problems facing the urban Negro—housing, jobs, education—is impossible without considering all the other problems at the same time. Each grows out of the other and each compounds the other.

"There is only one problem," SLANT's Tommy Jacquette said with bitterness, "and that's the white problem. Without discrimination from white, racist America, there wouldn't be no problems."

There would not be, he implied, any Watts.

Part II

Jessie Powell, 46-year-old Negro laborer with a wife and two children, was out of work four months before he heard about the Watts Skill Center.

Today, at the U.S. Labor Department-supported training project operated by Los Angeles City Schools at 840 E. 111th Place, he is being taught auto body work, and his enthusiasm is irrepressible:

"I know I'm learning a lot," he grins gripping your hand and holding on to be certain you understand.

"When I leave here I'll be able to tackle anything. It's a good feeling. I'm going to make it."

But Powell happens to be one of those in the Negro community who has not allowed the generations-long compaction of poverty and a myriad of dead ends to grind down his spirit.

To grasp the odds against swift, significant results from the collection of post-riot training and job programs in South-Central Los Angeles, one also must listen to the "unreachables":

"That damn Skill Center just take who they want to take. I went over there and they say, 'Come back some other time.' "

"They don't teach nuthin' I want to learn."

"You keep hearin' about guys go through there and still can't get no job."

"Sure, I been to the State Service Center. They send you to some damn job way cross country and when you get there it don't pay a damn thing."

"Westminster [Neighborhood Assn.] got this youth training program, but they only give you this $20 a week. How do you get along on that? I can do better other ways."

No one—all the Labor Department, McCone Commission, State Employment Service and university reports notwithstanding—can say accurately how many persons were unemployed in South Los Angeles two years ago and how many remain jobless today.

Thousands of persons, it is now conceded, were overlooked in the 1960 census and in the 1965 special census.

They were mostly the real hard-core—the always jobless, the drifters, the people who simply exist somehow without showing up on welfare lists or job applications.

Based on studies admittedly two and three years old, the U.S. Department of Labor has estimated that one out of every three persons in the South Los Angeles slum area probably is underemployed.

This term was used because the standard measures of unemployment fail to include those working part-time while looking for full-time jobs, those working full time for substandard wages, those labor force dropouts who have given up looking for work and those invisible persons who do not show up in any survey.

In "traditional" terms, the Labor Department reported:

1. That 63.8% of unemployed Negro

women and 14.5% of unemployed Negro men in South-Central Los Angeles earned less than $60 a week at their last jobs.

2. That 27% of the area's families reported annual incomes under $3,000.

3. That 36% of unemployed Negro men and 16% of the unemployed women were receiving unemployment insurance while 14% of the men and 29% of the women received public assistance.

If, indeed, traditional measurements do not begin to tell the story, the situation in South Los Angeles has been much worse than those figures show.

In fact, since the surveys on which the report was based, welfare caseloads in South-Central Los Angeles have risen dramatically, hardly indicative of any significant improvement in the job picture.

On the other hand, the State Department of Employment reports a slight drop in the number of South-Central requests for unemployment insurance benefits since 1965.

It must be noted, however, that this reflects the general countywide employment rate and, in the case of Negroes, application percentages run a bit higher than for whites.

Also, these figures deal only with those Negroes who had jobs in the first place.

H. C. (Chad) McClellan, whose Management Council was set up after the 1965 rioting to bring private enterprise efforts to bear on the unemployment problem, challenges the Labor Department "subemployment" report on the grounds that the surveys are too old to be meaningful.

But McClellan concedes that the much-maligned figure of nearly 18,000 curfew-area job placements (based on reports to his Management Council from cooperating firms last November) also fails to give a true picture.

Such reports, he agrees, do not include those Negroes who worked briefly and quit or were fired, or those counted two or more times at various jobs.

But he was enthusiastic about a report from USC's graduate school of business administration which (based on "a random sample . . . of 100 Negroes placed in jobs from the Watts Service Center") showed two-thirds still on their jobs.

Of the remaining one-third, the report said, half had gone on to better positions.

It is obvious that if the McCone Commission–McClellan estimate of 25,000 unemployed in South-Central Los Angeles at riot time (called the "wildest kind of a guess" by Dr. Paul Bullock of UCLA) and the total of 18,000 hired were both correct, job troubles in the area would be virtually over.

Another estimate that seems to conflict with the report of soaring welfare rates is that of Arthur Morgan, area manpower administrator for the State Employment Service, that 29,000 South-Central area persons have received some kind of job training since the riots.

This total includes products of the Skills Centers, Manpower Development and Training Act (MDTA) on-the-job training contracts with private companies, Job Corps, Neighborhood Youth Corps, work-training programs for welfare recipients and a variety of other projects.

"The only thing we can really say," commented Morgan, "is that 85% of the graduates from the Skills Centers have gone on to jobs. But even this is misleading because the other 15% may include people who have had to drop out of the labor market for various reasons."

Actually, if 29,000 have been trained and a certain number have gone to work, why is the problem still so acute in South-Central Los Angeles?

"As people get jobs, they move out of the area," said Morgan. "But we have a constant influx. As fast as you get someone trained, someone else takes his place."

It appears, then, that what we are dealing with is guesswork at best and that the old metaphor "shoveling snow into a furnace" could never be more suitably applied.

The assault on a situation which had been allowed to stagnate for too many years is still in its formative months and complaints are many that labor unions and industry are yet to show a meaningful commitment.

The Watts branch of the National Assn. for the Advancement of Colored People (NAACP) has charged, as have others, that unions have discriminated against Negroes in apprenticeship programs.

(The Legislature recently passed a bill making such discrimination a misdemeanor.)

The building trades unions, targets of many such complaints, point out that unemployment in their industry is higher than in any other.

The NAACP branch has said also that Skills Centers and other MDTA projects are inadequate and unrealistic, that there is a need for "a complete restructuring and reorganization of all vocational education in California."

The Management Council, which has been pressing private industry to help Skills Centers design practical curricula, also is working with the city schools to make vocational courses match industry needs.

But the McCone Commission itself pointed out that MDTA programs "skim the cream of the unemployed . . . and seldom include the most disadvantaged."

Only now is the Labor Department's Concentrated Employment Program, designed to reach out and pull in the persons at least likely to seek training and work, getting under way in Los Angeles.

At most, it probably will make 1,700 training spots available in South Los Angeles.

Nearly 2,000 of those who went into various training programs last year were processed through the State Service Center in Watts, according to employment section manager Bud Bylsma.

Although Skills Centers aren't expected to produce journeyman workers, only entry-level employees, Bylsma concurs with Morgan that 85% of the graduates have been placed on jobs after training.

But the Service Center's waiting list for training averages 5,000, which makes it clear that the need is constantly greater than the availability of facilities.

Bylsma said his staff has listed many jobs it can't fill because of the tremendous lack of trained people. There just aren't many jobs available for the totally unskilled.

But here he differs with the theory that constant immigration compounds the situation.

"People who come in from other states ordinarily have a pretty good work record and we can usually place them," he said.

"It's the people who have been here a long time, who haven't worked, who are the problem. Employers generally want a work record."

Another thing "that gives us fits," added Bylsma, is that many applicants have police records.

"Even though many companies and the government are saying this shouldn't matter, employers still aren't buying this too much."

Aircraft companies do the major hiring, he pointed out, and they require security clearances—"especially in the type of jobs that many people in Watts would become very proficient in."

The attitudes of workers would change markedly, he said, if they could hope for the better jobs.

"If you get $3 an hour, you have an entirely different feeling than if you get $1.40."

Bylsma concluded, "We're not making any huge dents, but we are doing things that haven't been done before."

The number of better jobs, said Cornelius Gray, acting director of the Service Center, "has subsided noticeably."

The center receives requests for day laborers and other temporary workers, and by 11 A.M. these jobs are all gone.

The meaningful jobs—with futures—are in

short supply, but so are those unemployed trained well enough to fill them.

Most of those administering and working in the various training programs agree that no huge dent is being made. Their outlooks differ as to whether there is any dent at all.

The Rev. Morris (Father Sam) Samuel, bearded white Episcopal minister working in job placement at Westminster: "All the programs are just scratching the surface.

"Some of the jobs out there are so far above the achievement level of the kids that there's got to be some give on the part of free enterprise.

"We call a guy to get a job for a kid and the first thing he wants to know is has he worked before and has he been arrested.

"It's a fantastically expensive thing to take a kid 17 or 18 who's been culturally and academically deprived and shape him to society's standards.

"Look how long it takes the middle-class person with mental or emotional problems to get out of that bag."

Fred Grant, job placement man at Westminster: "The kid in the street wearing his 'natural' is defying the middle-classism, wanting dignity on his own basis.

"But if he goes to the employer that way, he's X'd out."

Stan Myles Jr. of the Westminster Staff: "There are more programs in the community, but what are they doing? The same people unemployed two years ago are unemployed today.

"Many of our young men are beyond help. You learn you can't save everybody.

"You'll be teaching basic English, talking about verbs, and you forget to think, 'Is this guy hungry?' He's thinking, 'Can I eat that verb?' and the instructor wonders why he isn't paying attention.

"This environment teaches you not to stay in class if you don't feel like it."

T. D. Kimbrough, supervisor of the Watts Skill Center: "The MDTA skill centers are a step in the right direction, but there has to be a real marriage between industry and the centers.

"Maybe 3 or 4% of industry is really working with us. You can't blame them for wanting to make money, but they have a great responsibility to take on a few people who may be a deficit to the company as their share of the job.

"We have employers who still call in and want to hire janitors, dishwashers or domestics. We're talking about skills here, not dishwashers.

"But a nurse's aide, for example, after training here and then on-the-job training, probably would end up earning $1.60 an hour. She might do better on county aid. How do you tell somebody it's worth it?"

Harold Tolin, training supervisor for Community Skill Center: "A lot of industry is leaning over backward. Some big firms know our graduation schedules and wait for them."

Howard Morehead, Community Skill Center staff member: "Our biggest problem is trying to get industry to judge the individual and overlook some police records. Maybe the guy got a ticket, had no money to pay, so it went to warrant."

Oliver Childs, executive-director of Opportunities Industrialization Center: "It has taken this program some time to overcome community skepticism. But during our fundraising drive, $5,000 came from the community itself in a door-to-door solicitation.

"The trainees really demonstrate an involvement. They've organized student councils and have raised money for emergency situations. They feel that here is a vehicle that can really reach those in need."

Richard Steverson, South-Central Youth Training and Employment Project staff: "We've had to drop many of our programs because of the hang-ups in federal funding. As kids are turned away from here, they have no place to go but the streets.

"They're right at the point where they could either become productive citizens or drift into the criminal life."

Robert Hall, of Operation Bootstrap: "Government programs as a whole are a total failure. They're not really reaching the people on the street, the hard-core unemployable, the man with a police record.

"Bootstrap has had excellent rapport with some companies, but overall private industry isn't doing enough. It could get more involved . . . relax their standards on things like jail records."

Ted Watkins, executive director of the Watts Labor Community Action Committee —"There's been as much change in some of our kids as night and day. A lot of the hate and animosity are gone.

"One problem is that kids don't want to leave the area. A lot of them have been offered jobs somewhere else making $1.70 an hour. The next day they're right back here where they feel safe . . . have some identity.

"It's amazing how much love and attention these kids want. They don't have this father and it's killing them."

UCLA's Paul Bullock, noting the rash of new programs in a speech before the Industrial Relations Research Assn., observed:

"It would be oversanguine to conclude from this evidence that the Negro poor have finally secured the recognition they have lacked.

"The special programs can generate meaningful and permanent change only as they affect the relationship between the residents of the poverty ghetto and the central institutions of society—the schools, law enforcement agencies, the employment services, governmental and private welfare organizations, employers, unions, politicians and the like.

"There is little reason to believe as yet that this relationship has been fundamentally altered by the multitude of ad hoc measures."

The institutions, he said, "remain inflexible and unimaginative disciplinarians, either converting the poor to their standard or (more frequently) punishing them in overt or subtle ways for their failure to conform."

One of the basic arguments concerning many training programs hinges on the "new careers" concept being applied to the anti-poverty war by Congress.

Entry level positions such as teacher aides, nurse aides, office helpers, etc., are fine for women, said a Negro city official. "But what about the man with a family? He wants to feel manly. He wants to do the kind of work he is capable of doing now."

Thus, the feeling by some that the hard-core unemployable and untrainable remain overlooked. That they can only be put to work through massive WPA-type programs requiring little or no skill.

There are, of course, countless training projects—many of them federally subsidized —conducted by companies, unions and agencies to upgrade the skills of potential dishwashers and janitors, injecting some small measure of dignity with titles like "floor maintenance mechanic."

But the expressed objection is that the main thrust of the "new careers" concept— in the absence of simultaneous make-work projects for illiterate, untrained men—will serve to perpetuate the dominant status of women.

Although some private firms have cooperated by hiring Negroes from the curfew area, basically seeking qualified workers and in many cases getting MDTA funds to help train others, there has been little inclination to move into the region with plants and easily reachable jobs.

It is apparent this situation will not change noticeably until redevelopment and insurance problems are solved.

The lone exception is the Watts Manufacturing Co., formed by Negro businessmen as a subsidiary of Aerojet-General Corp., with a rapidly expanding plant at 1901 E. El Segundo Blvd. (not actually in Watts).

After six months of operation the company now has four buildings and more than 200 employes (double the number planned at this stage).

It began with a $2.5 million government contract to make military tents. It already has begun to diversify, turning out wooden packing cases and loading pallets as well as a 6.5-mile-long conveyor belt for the new Oakland Post Office.

"We're operating at a profit already," said Leon G. Woods, the company's general manager, "which we hadn't expected for a year."

The firm hopes to get up to 500 employes and to set up a stock ownership plan for them. "We've got tremendous spirit," Woods said. "Among our workers there is great identification with the company."

Most of those hired have had no significant work experience, so the company trains them on the job, with some federal fund help through the Urban League, Youth Training and Employment Project and the Department of Vocational Rehabilitation.

"We're getting many boys through the Youth Authority," Woods reported. "I'd like to find more. They have trouble getting jobs and they appreciate the hand."

Predictably, it hasn't all been smooth. There was a high turnover at the outset, "because we went from a standing start to 130 employes in 30 days and we hired many we wouldn't have hired if we hadn't been in a hurry."

Too, absenteeism continues to be a major problem, especially on Monday mornings.

"That's one of the habitual troubles of the area," admitted Woods. "We have to keep pointing out that if they want advancement, they have to make it to work regularly."

If there is any conclusion to be drawn from seemingly conflicting representations, it is that the magnitude of unemployment in South-Central Los Angeles is yet to be accurately pictured.

And, too, that traditional methods of erasing that joblessness, in an area where generations of children have never seen fathers going off to regular jobs each day, are next to futile.

Roots of Riot—Call to Battle Newsweek

In the sulphurous aftertaste of last summer's [1967] ghetto explosions, President Johnson's appointment of a commission to study riots seemed a master stroke of redundancy. Never had the dimensions and imperatives of a national emergency been more evident to every sentient man on the street, and the call for one more government study struck many as a confession of government's inability to act. Then last week the National Advisory Commission on Civil Disorders released the results of a vast study that appeared to justify the effort after all.

In four sections and 250,000 often searing words, the commission traced the history and effects of the American way of prejudice, and concluded: "Our nation is moving toward two societies, one black, one white–separate and unequal." That drift, said the report, has been accelerated by the strife of recent summers. And though it sharply condemned rioting, it directly implicated white Americans in the existence of the ghetto: "White institutions created it, white institutions maintain it, and white society condones it . . . White racism is essentially responsible for the explosive mixture which has been accumulating in our cities since the end of World War II."

Here was the formal ethic for action missing conspicuously from recent proclamations of the Congress and the President himself: an indictment of the System, by a top-level organ of the System, that might ring louder and clearer than all the thunder of the ghettos themselves.

In unsparing detail, the report sketches the pattern of economic exclusion, unresponsiveness by local government, abrasive police tactics and "pervasive discrimination" that has left the Negro uniquely isolated and embittered. Its conclusion: to reverse the damage done "will require a commitment to national action–compassionate, massive and sustained . . . From every American it will require new attitudes, new understanding and, above all, new will."

Among scores of recommendations for action on the national and local levels, the commission urged:

• Creation of 2 million jobs in the public and private sector in the next three years, with Federal subsidies for training to make the unskilled employable.

• Provision of a "basic allowance" to families and individuals as a step toward a guaranteed minimum income.

• Bringing 6 million new and existing dwelling units within reach of low- and moderate-income families.

The alternative to wide-scale positive action, the commission warned, would be con-

This article appeared in *Newsweek,* March 11, 1968.

tinued polarization of blacks and whites leading to a garrison state.

Created by Presidential order last July 28 on the heels of the Newark and Detroit blowups, the commission set a furious pace, delivering its report four months ahead of schedule, for whatever it might be worth in generating action before the 1968 riot season begins.

Meeting usually in a former snack bar in the Senate building, the commission (chairman and vice chairman: Illinois's Gov. Otto Kerner and New York's Mayor John Lindsay) held 44 regular sessions, innumerable night sessions, and took time out for visits to eight urban ghettos that left most of the eleven members "shocked" by what they saw. Staffers under the direction of Washington lawyer David Ginsburg conducted simultaneous studies of 24 civil disorders in 23 cities, taking testimony from more than 1,200 witnesses.

There were few special services in the cramped commission meeting room—aside from a steadily flowing coffee urn and a bottomless supply of Coca-Cola, the latter requested by police chief Herbert Jenkins of Atlanta, home base for Coke. At times the members would have welcomed stronger drink. "We tried to tell it like it is," said liberal Oklahoma Sen. Fred Harris. But there were occasional differences over how it was: tussles over whether to plump for a broad or limited open-housing law (it came out broad), whether to specify politically and economically practical programs or take a more sweeping moral approach (the sweepers won out).

But though the talk was heavy it rarely waxed hot. There was a cordial give-and-take between the liberal faction led by Lindsay, Harris, Massachusetts Sen. Edward Brooke and the NAACP's Roy Wilkins and moderates like Ohio Republican William McCulloch. In the end, all eleven members agreed to sign the hard-hitting report.

The Record of Riot

As its first order of business, the commission reviews the course of rioting in the first nine months of 1967. Of the 164 civil disorders recorded, the study profiles the eight classified as major. What emerges is not simply a chronicle of Negro rioting but a shattering picture of ineptness and, often, panic by law-enforcement agencies; in one instance in an unsupervised Detroit station house, a nearly total breakdown of discipline occurred, with police beating prisoners and stripping and fondling a female suspect.

Extremist agitation may have helped set the mood for rioting, but the panel said it found no evidence of an organized conspiracy. "Widespread misunderstanding and exaggeration" characterized all the ghetto explosions, the report says—most notably, "the belief, widely held across the country last summer, that riot cities were paralyzed by sniper fire." In fact, says the commission, though some sniping probably did take place, the best evidence is that "most reported sniping incidents were demonstrated to be gunfire by either police or National Guardsmen." In Newark, when a National Guardsman fired a random shot and then a prankster set off a string of firecrackers, nervous guardsmen and state troopers opened up on a housing project with massive fire. Two mothers and a grandmother were killed. The sound of one richocheting bullet might whang through a mile of ghetto blocks, causing half a dozen reports of sniper fire for the same bullet. The result was general panic with nonrioting Negroes randomly killed or wounded. "As a matter of fact," Newark police director Dominick Spina told the commission, "it was so bad that, in my opinion, guardsmen were firing upon police and police were firing back at them."

The study reported instance after instance of "excessive and indiscriminate shooting" by law officers. Fusillades were loosed at the sound of bottles breaking, unidentified cars were riddled. During the Detroit riot an accidental shot by a soldier swiftly escalated into an Army barrage on an empty building. A Negro store guard fired a shot in the air to drive off a trio of Negro looters and was promptly cut down by a hail of police bullets.

But hysteria fed the flames on both sides. Routine arrests triggered wild accounts of Negroes being beaten or murdered by police. Rumors aggravated tensions in 65 per cent of the 1967 ghetto disorders, the report declares, and in Tampa and New Haven such false rumors were the direct cause of full-scale riots. Usually there was no single cause but an accumulation of incidents and grievances real or imagined in which any encounter with the law could touch off an explosion.

The Challenge of Control

The report offers no handy formula for cooling riots, except the standard suggestion of a "sufficient display of force." Too often, the report says, there are too few police on hand in the initial stages. In one major city with a 5,000-man police force, only 192 patrolmen were on duty when a major riot erupted. In any case, the study notes, most police are trained to work alone, with little supervision, while riot situations call for them to team up in units: "Thus a major civil disturbance requires a police department to convert itself suddenly into a different organization . . ." Performance of National Guardsmen, however, especially in Newark and Detroit, "raised doubts regarding their capabilities for this type of mission," and "brought into question the caliber and competence of certain guard officers." The most disciplined, efficient riot fighters were the Army troops finally summoned to Detroit.

Weapons of mass destruction have no place in the cities, says the report. Instead it urges the Defense Department to help develop new "middle range" weaponry, like the wooden pegs fired at Hong Kong rioters by British troops. It commends the "discriminating" use of tear gas as preferable to firearms, and urges "Rumor Central" clearinghouses in the ghettos to sort fact from fantasy.

The Plight of the Cop

The typical rioter is described as a young Negro male (more than half were between the ages of 15 and 24), raised in the North, a lifelong resident of the riot city, a high-school dropout but better educated and more politically aware than his nonrioting neighbor, and usually underemployed or employed in a menial job. And against him stands the cop as the symbol of white authority.

The commission is genuinely sympathetic to the policeman's plight. With city agencies unresponsive to slum problems, the cop in effect becomes the repository of burgeoning ghetto grievances. Reluctant broker and ombudsman, he shoulders the ghetto resident's anger over dirty streets, bad housing, poor services, exploitative shopkeepers. And he carries the burdensome discretion of arresting a Negro lawbreaker or looking the other way. Often he is baselessly accused of brutality in the course of enforcing an arrest, and in the edgy summer even the most routine incident becomes a challenge to his judgment.

But the cop on the beat seems singularly ill-equipped for his sensitive role. "The average police officer," says the report, "has little knowledge or understanding of the underlying tensions and grievances that exist in the ghetto." Frequently he harasses, bullies and humiliates. Special roving task forces of ghetto cops often exacerbate the tensions they are supposed to avert. The report identified a high percentage of bigotry among white cops assigned to Negro precincts.

The report stresses the urgent need for clearly and forcefully stated departmental policy on orders to citizens on their movement, handling of minor disputes, arrests for certain offenses which do not involve victims, use of firearms. It urges the hiring of more

Negro policemen (in 28 departments the proportion of Negro cops ranged from less than 1 per cent to 21 per cent), establishment of service battalions of young Negroes and independent police review boards.

The Conditions for Disorder

The commission traces the deep-rooted sources of the present crisis to Negro slavery, exploitation, segregation and, finally, migration to the North. Currently, says the report, 15 million Negroes live in Northern metropolitan areas, where they incorporate a bleak catalogue of statistics: 40.6 per cent live below the poverty level, nine out of ten young ghetto males have an arrest record. A young ghetto adult is more than twice as likely to be unemployed as a young white, more than three times as likely to be working at a menial job. Most hard-core jobless are Negro males between 18 and 25; indeed, one of the most pervasive ghetto grievances is unemployment (topped by police practices).

Virtually every major riot in 1967, says the panel, "was foreshadowed by... unresolved grievances... against local authorities" and usually no authority was around to hear the grievances. The ghetto resident, unlike the middle-class citizen, has no access to authority, no one to turn to. As Negroes migrate in, whites migrate out of the cities and as the gulf between city government and ghetto widens, the Negro feels a "profound sense of isolation" and powerlessness. From the ghetto, "city government appears distant and unconcerned, the possibility of effective change remote... The explosion comes as the climax."

A Time to Begin

For all its sense of urgency and sweeping recommendations, the commission insisted that there is little new in its findings, "no unique insights, no simple solutions." But, it adds, "We have provided an honest beginning." Race prejudice has shaped American history "decisively," the panel points out, and the plea it addresses to "the minds and hearts of each citizen" is that race prejudice should not be allowed to shape the American future as well. It concludes: "The destruction and the bitterness of racial disorder, the harsh polemics of black revolt and white repression have been seen and heard before in this country. It is time now to end these things... not only in the streets of the ghetto but in the lives of people."

It was a stirring exhortation. But would it stir swift compliance? First reactions to the report brought a trickle of praise and a torrent of caution. Said militant CORE director Floyd McKissick: "We're on our way to reaching the moment of truth. It's the first time whites have said, 'We're racists'." From others there were promises of action. But from the White House itself only a bland assurance that "the report will be carefully evaluated." Privately a top Presidential aide conceded, "It's an impressive piece of work, a vast piece of goods. Its aims are desirable—but some of it just can't be done." And that note of doubt was echoed on the powerful appropriations committees of Capitol Hill.

The commission had decided that cost estimates were beyond the scope of its study. And so too, apparently, was any explicit reference to the failures of national leadership. Still, the report commissioned by the President had gone as far as it could, and that was far indeed. It had made the government signatory to an unflinching essay of national self-criticism—and, not incidentally, to a bold call to battle against the prime social ill of the age.

Rx for Action: Key Points

Only a commitment to national action on "an unprecedented scale" can effectively deal with the pathology which spawns racial tension in America, the riot commission concluded. The panel made recommendations in four major areas:

Jobs: Pervasive unemployment and underemployment are the most persistent grievances in the Negro ghetto. More than 20 per cent of the rioters in cities surveyed were jobless–and many who were employed had only intermittent, low-status jobs which they considered below their education and ability. The report recommends:

- Creation of 1 million new government jobs, another million in the private sector.
- Consolidation of Federal, state and city manpower programs, emphasizing on-the-job training with the extra cost to private employers borne by the government.
- A full-scale Federal campaign to remove artificial barriers to employment.

Welfare: The present welfare system is designed to save money instead of people, "and tragically ends up doing neither." Not only does it exclude great numbers of needy Americans, it also fails to provide a minimum decent standard of living to those covered, and imposes restrictions that encourage continued dependency and undermine self-respect. The panel recommends:

- Establishment of a national standard of assistance at least as high as the "poverty level" income set by the social security administration, abolishment of all residency requirements and Federal assumption of at least 90 per cent of all welfare payments.
- Requirement that states receiving Federal welfare contributions participate in child-assistance programs that allow both a mother and a father to live in the home–thus buttressing family stability.
- Development of a national system of income supplements.

Schooling: Another persistent source of resentment in the ghetto is the failure of public education to provide the educational experience that could overcome discrimination and deprivation. And the resulting hostility of Negro students and their parents generates increasing tension in many school districts. The panel recommends:

- Sharply increased Federal efforts to eliminate segregation North and South.
- Greater Federal funding of remedial-education programs for disadvantaged children.
- Extension of early-childhood programs to every needy child and expanded opportunities for higher education.

Housing: More than 30 years of "grossly underfunded" Federal housing programs have left nearly 6 million substandard housing units in this country with the problem most acute in the ghetto. The panel recommends:

- Enactment of an open-housing law that covers all sales and rentals.
- Placement of more low and moderate housing outside ghetto areas.
- Provision of 6 million new or existing units of decent housing for low- and moderate-income families through lower interest rates on loans to spur construction and expanded rent and ownership supplements to the needy.
- Expansion of the urban-renewal, public-housing and model-cities programs,

Chapter 6

THE ECOLOGICAL CRISIS

One generation ago, one of the most satisfying of fall household chores in many parts of the country was raking and burning the leaves that fell in the yard. The heat from the piles of burning leaves provided a pleasant warmth in the chilly air, and the smoke, rising lazily into the afternoon sky, gave a pleasant smell to the neighborhood. In most communities today this pleasant task is against the law. Burning leaves in the back yard can lead to a court appearance and a fine. What has happened?

The world has not grown smaller, but it has become more crowded. Population has become more and more concentrated, particularly in suburban metropolitan areas. With ever-increasing numbers of people on earth, mankind is polluting his world at an alarming rate. He has killed off hundreds of species of birds and animals, and he may be causing permanent changes in the earth's atmosphere, its oceans, and its land. He is running out of places to discard his refuse, the enormous daily accumulations of human wastes and trash.

As late as the nineteenth century there was no such thing as a central sewage treatment disposal plant, as we know it, in any part of the world. Today, even with such plants to denitrify raw sewage, we are polluting our waters to the point where we have killed most of the fish in our major rivers, and in some of our major lakes. Even the oceans have suffered severe damage. By the year 2000 there will be more than twice as many people as there are now and more than twice as much waste. Not only can environmental pollution do permanent damage to the ecological balance in nature, but it can do permanent damage to human beings. There are few, if any, people in this country who do not already have measurable amounts of DDT and other poisons in their systems as a result of the agricultural chemicals we use. There are few people alive who have not suffered some degree of lung deterioration from the air we breathe. The Egyptian obelisk in New York City, which stood unmarred for more than 3,000 years in Egypt, has clearly visible signs of erosion brought about by its exposure to the air of New York for the equivalent of a human lifetime. How can we fail to be concerned about the effect that the minute-by-minute inhalation of such air has on live human tissue?

We need to look at the problem of pollution in both immediate and long-range terms. It may be all right today to talk about burying the world's trash in a large hole in the ground, but a time will come when this solution will no longer work: we must develop ways to avoid producing trash.

There are many kinds of pollution. The first to come to public attention was smog ("Menace in the Skies"). One of the most recent is noise ("The Jet Noise Is Getting Awful"). In *Silent Spring,* one of the most powerful books on environmental pollution, Rachel Carson pointed out the terrible damage already done by pesticides ("And No Birds Sing"). Man must also be concerned about his water supply and about industrial encroachment upon his natural resources ("Precedent on the Hudson"). Is industry alone to be blamed for our polluted atmosphere—or has the shortsightedness of individuals contributed to the problem? And who will have to pay for cleaning up the mess ("Air and Water")?

Menace in the Skies Time

On the morning of Oct. 26, 1948, at Donora, Pa., the skies delivered a deadly warning that man had poisoned them beyond endurance.

As workers trudged to their jobs, a heavy fog blanketed the bleak and grimy town. It hung suspended in the stagnant air while local businesses–steel mills, a wire factory, zinc and coke plants–continued to spew waste gases, zinc fumes, coal smoke and fly ash into the lowering darkness. The atmosphere thickened. Grime began to fall out of the smog, covering homes, sidewalks and streets with a black coating in which pedestrians and automobiles left distinct footprints and tire tracks. Within 48 hours, visibility had become so bad that residents had difficulty finding their way home.

Donora's doctors were soon besieged by coughing, wheezing patients complaining of shortness of breath, running noses, smarting eyes, sore throats and nausea. During the next four days, before a heavy rain washed away the menacing shroud, 5,910 of the town's 14,000 residents became ill. Twenty persons–and an assortment of dogs, cats and canaries–died.

Investigating the tragedy, meteorologists concluded that it had been triggered by a temperature inversion, an atmospheric phenomenon that prevents normal circulation of air. Ordinarily, warm air rises from the earth into the colder regions above, carrying much of man's pollution with it. Occasionally, a layer of warmer air forms above cooler air near the ground; the inversion acts as a lid, preventing the pollutants at lower altitudes from rising and dispersing. Inversions are no novelty, but what happened at Donora shocked public-health officials into an awareness that such layers pose a deadly threat to an increasingly industrialized and pollutant-producing society.

Sulky Sun. On Dec. 5, 1952, a thick fog began to roll over London. Hardly anyone paid any attention at first in a city long used to "pea-soupers." But this fog was pinned down by a temperature inversion, and was steadily thickened by the soot and smoke of the coal-burning city. Within three days, the air was so black that Londoners could see no more than a yard ahead. Drivers were forced to leave cars and buses to peer closely at street signs to find out where they were. Policemen strapped on respiratory masks. The Manchester Guardian reported that London's midday sun "hung sulkily in the dirty sky with no more radiance than an unlit Chinese lantern."

Hospitals were soon filled with patients suffering from acute respiratory diseases; deaths in the city mounted. The British Committee on Air Pollution finally estimated that during the five days that the smog smothered London, there were 4,000 more deaths than would have occurred under normal circumstances. During the next two months, there were another 8,000 excess deaths—most of them apparently caused by respiratory disease—that scientists suspected were a direct result of the killer smog.

Extreme air pollution again darkened London in 1956, killing 1,000, and in 1962, claiming more than 300 lives. In 1953, a ten-day temperature inversion over New York City trapped so much air pollution that 200 excess deaths were attributed to the smog by Dr. Leonard Greenburg, then New York's commissioner of air pollution. Another New York smog in 1963 killed more than 400, and there were 80 excess deaths recorded in New York during a four-day siege over the last Thanksgiving Day weekend. Scientists suspect that thousands of deaths each year in cities all over the world can be linked to air pollution. Says U.S. Assistant Surgeon General Dr. Richard Prindle: "It's already happening. Deaths are occurring now. We already have episodes in which pollution kills people. And as we build up, we're going to have an increasing frequency of episodes."

"Take a Deep Breath." Such warnings, added to the widely publicized New York and Los Angeles air-pollution alerts and open bickering between politicians and industry over pollution controls, have made the U.S. suddenly aware that smog is a real and present danger. The belching smokestacks that long symbolized prosperity have now become a source of irritation: the foul air that had come to be accepted as an inevitable part of city living has suddenly become intolerable. "Tomorrow morning when you get up," reads a recent magazine ad placed by New York's Citizens for Clean Air, Inc., "take a nice deep breath. It'll make you feel rotten." Indeed, ... the U.S. city dweller has only to look at his skyline ... to see the startling and ominous inroads that smog has made.

Air pollution has become a world-wide preoccupation. Some 230 miles southwest of Tokyo, for example, school yards in the port city of Yokkaichi are filled with children running and playing games. But their shouts and laughter are muffled by yellow masks impregnated with chemicals to protect them against air polluted by nearby petrochemical plants. In Tokyo, where smog warnings were issued on 154 days last year, policemen in ten heavily polluted districts return to the station house to breathe pure oxygen after each half-hour stint on traffic duty in order to counteract the effects of breathing excessive amounts of carbon monoxide.

"Sitting on the hill of Lycabettus, overlooking the valley of Athens," writes Greek City Planner Constantinos A. Doxiadis, "I can see early Monday morning the first dark clouds building in the lower part of the valley, where the industries are. It grows, it covers the middle and lower parts of the city. Gradually it reaches the eastern part, and by expanding in height it covers the rock of the Acropolis and the Parthenon. By then everybody in the city of Athens has had to breathe the polluted air."

Authorities in the German state of North Rhine–Westphalia are so concerned about the dangers of smog in 15 Ruhr districts that they have posted warning signs that will bar traffic from roads in the event that air pollution becomes extreme. And out in space last September, after other astronauts had repeatedly failed to photograph Houston because of the dense brown disk of smog that usually hangs above it, Gemini 11 Command Pilot Pete Conrad finally shot a picture of the city on one of its better days. Discussing the photograph after his return to earth, Conrad pointed to the reduced but ever present pall over the city. "Notice the air pollution drifting out there," he said, "in case anybody thinks we don't have it."

Smog disintegrates nylon stockings in Chicago and Los Angeles, eats away historic stone statues and buildings in Venice and

Cologne. Rapidly industrializing Denver, which for many years boasted of its crystalline air, is now often smogbound. In Whiting, Ind., a concentration of fog and pollution from an oil refinery produced a chemical mist that one night last year stripped paint from houses, turned others rusty orange, and left streets and sidewalks covered with a greenish film.

Pollution's First Victim. Air pollution, commonly thought to be a result of the industrial revolution, actually preceded man himself. Nature has long contaminated the air with sand and dust storms, with forest fires and volcanic eruptions, that spew tons of particles and gases into the atmosphere. When Krakatoa, a volcano in the East Indies, blew up in 1883, the debris and dust it hurled into the air spread around the globe, darkening daytime skies for hundreds of miles. Krakatoa dust, suspended in the atmosphere, produced spectacularly ruddy sunsets and sunrises the world over for months after the blast.

Nature even produces its equivalent of smog. Over large fir forests, there is a continuous bluish haze produced by terpenes—volatile hydrocarbons that are emitted by the trees. Decaying animal and vegetable matter give off gases. Flowers saturate the nearby air with pollen that causes such allergic reactions as hay fever in man. It was natural air pollution rather than the man-made kind that claimed the man who is probably the first recorded human victim; Pliny the Elder died in 79 A.D. after breathing in an overdose of sulphur oxides emanating from erupting Vesuvius.

Once man mastered fire, however, he was superbly equipped to surpass nature's contribution to air pollution. The burning process—combustion—powers most transportation in the U.S., plays a vital role in its manufacturing, generates electric power, heats homes and buildings, and consumes much of its refuse. But this year it will also pour 140 million tons of pollutants into the air. And as population, industrial production, number of automobiles, and other indices of U.S. prosperity increase, the upward flow of contaminants will increase correspondingly.

Colorless Contamination. The most obvious component of polluted air is the smoke that pours from millions of home chimneys, power-plant and factory smokestacks, incinerators and garbage dumps. It consists of tiny pieces of carbon, ash, oil, grease, and microscopic particles of metal and metal oxides. Some of these particles are so large that they settle rapidly to earth, but many are small enough to remain suspended in the atmosphere until they are removed by rain or wind. Though the particulates, as they are called, are highly visible and often the first target of antipollution officials, they constitute only about 10% of the pollution in the air over the U.S.

Cities such as Pittsburgh and St. Louis, which after World War II enforced vigorous and successful campaigns to clear smoke from their skies, have now discovered that their drives against pollution have only just begun. A full 90% of U.S. air pollution consists of largely invisible but potentially deadly gases. More than half of the contamination in the air over the U.S., for example, consists of colorless, odorless carbon monoxide, most of it issuing from the exhaust pipes of automobiles, trucks and buses.

The second most plentiful gas pollutant is composed of oxides of sulphur, produced by home, power-plant and factory combustion of coal and oil containing large percentages of sulphur. More than a tenth of air pollution consists of hydrocarbons, most of them emanating as unburned or only partially burned gaseous compounds from automobile fuel systems. Combustion also produces large quantities of carbon dioxide, nitrogen oxides and other gases.

As if these products of combustion were not unpleasant or dangerous enough by themselves, some also undergo complicated chemical changes in the atmosphere that make them even less attractive. In the presence of sunlight, the hydrocarbons and nitrogen oxides emitted largely by automobile exhausts react to produce the sort of brownish and irritating photochemical smog that blankets Los Angeles for most of the year. "Los Angeles smog" is a highly complex soup containing, among other things, nitrogen dioxide, hydrocarbons, ozone (a highly active and poisonous form of oxygen) and peroxyacyl nitrate (commonly called PAN). "London smog," on the other hand, usually contains high quantities of sulphur oxides that react with moisture to produce a dilute but corrosive sulphuric-acid mist.

Though air conditioners can effectively filter pollutant particles out of the air, the troublesome gaseous contaminants pass through unhindered. Thus city dwellers who feel that they have found sanctuary from the smog in sealed and air conditioned offices and apartments are actually in an atmosphere that may be little better than the foul air of the streets.

$600 for Cleaning. The unwholesome mess that U.S. citizens and corporations spew into that great sewer in the sky costs them dearly —$11 billion a year in property damage alone, according to the Department of Health, Education and Welfare. Air pollutants abrade, corrode, tarnish, soil, erode, crack, weaken and discolor materials of all varieties. Steel corrodes from two to four times as fast in urban and industrial regions as in rural areas, where much less sulphur-bearing coal and oil are burned. The erosion of some stone statuary and buildings is also greatly speeded by high concentrations of sulphur oxides.

Heavy fallout of pollution particles in metropolitan areas deposits layers of grime on automobiles, clothing, buildings and windows; it adds about $600 per year in washing, cleaning, repairing and repainting bills to the budget of a family with two or three children in New York City, according to a study made by Irving Michelson, a consultant in environmental health and safety. Because of fly ash and soot from smokestacks, the main façade of Manhattan's New York Hilton was so badly discolored that it had to be replaced last year, only 3½ years after the hotel was completed. Ozone, a principal component of photochemical smog, discolors and disintegrates clothing and causes rubber to become brittle and crack.

Vegetation, too, suffers from polluted air —even in rural areas that until recently were believed to be out of the range of contamination. Sulphur dioxide causes leaves to dry out and bleach to a light tan or ivory color, kills the tips of grasses and of pine and fir-tree needles.

Scientists are certain that the ozone and PAN in Los Angeles smogs have caused the serious decline in the citrus and salad crops in the area. In one of the many smog experiments they are conducting, they have planted lemon trees in small greenhouses in a grove near Upland. Pure, filtered air is pumped into some of the greenhouses, air containing measured amounts of pollutants into others. When the fruit is finally picked, the scientists will compare the quality and yield of lemons from trees in different greenhouses, hoping to learn more about how each component of smog affects the crop. Some effects of the smog are indisputable. Such diverse plants as orchids and spinach can no longer be grown in metropolitan Los Angeles.

In semi-rural Florida, east of Tampa, large amounts of fluorides emitted from phosphate plants have rained down on nearby citrus groves, ranches and gladiolus farms. Orange and lemon trees that absorbed the fluorides produced smaller yields, and gladioli turned brown and died. A national air-pollution symposium reported that cattle grazing on grass that was contaminated with the fluorides developed uneven teeth that hindered chewing and joints so swollen that many of the animals could not stand. Fluorides have also etched windowpanes, giving them the frosted appearance of a light bulb.

Damage to People. Pollutants that injure plants and erode stone are likely to have a damaging effect on humans too. Motorists who would never contemplate committing suicide by running a hose from their exhaust pipe into the car often unknowingly endanger their lives by exposing themselves to large amounts of carbon monoxide on expressways and in tunnels and garages. Though an hour's exposure to 1,500 parts of monoxide per million parts of air can endanger a man's life, only 120 parts per million for an hour can affect his driving enough to cause an accident. And concentrations of about 100 parts per million have been found in tunnels and garages and on the streets of Chicago, Detroit, New York and London.

Assistant Surgeon General Prindle points out that a heavy cigarette smoker carries a 3% to 4% concentration of carbon monoxide in his bloodstream. Thus it is not surprising, he says, that habitual smokers are the first to turn up at hospitals during periods of extreme air pollution; carbon monoxide concentrations in their bloodstream reach a toxic 25%-30% level before those of nonsmokers.

Chief culprits in the Donora, London and New York smog disasters were probably sulphur dioxide and sulphur trioxide, which, either in gaseous form or converted into sulphuric-acid mist, can irritate the skin, eyes and upper respiratory tract. Extreme exposure, such as might occur in an industrial accident, can do irreparable damage to the lungs—and even attack the enamel on teeth.

Arsenic & Heart Disease. Ozone and PAN produce the eye irritation, coughing and chest soreness experienced by many Los Angeles residents on smoggy days. In laboratory experiments, continuous exposure to ozone shortened the lives of guinea pigs. Scientists have also calculated that a child born in New York City after World War II has now inhaled the pollution equivalent of smoking nine cigarettes per day every day of his life. Like those in cigarettes, some of the hydrocarbons identified in automobile exhausts have produced cancer in laboratory animals.

The particles in pollution are injurious to humans also. Carbon particles that blacken the lungs of residents of London and New York carry gases adsorbed onto their surface. They enable sulphur dioxide, for example, to penetrate deeper into the lungs than it could on its own; without particles to carry it, the gas can be exhaled relatively easily from the upper respiratory tract. Other particulates act as catalysts in the atmosphere, speeding the conversion of sulphur dioxide into more harmful sulphuric acid. Particles of arsenic, beryllium, cadmium, lead, chromium and possibly manganese, discharged into the atmosphere by a variety of man-made processes, may contribute to cancer and heart disease.

Though researchers have not been able to prove a direct cause-and-effect relationship between air pollution and disease, they have found that the incidence of chronic bronchitis among British mailmen who deliver mail in areas with heavy air pollution is three times as high as among mailmen who work in cleaner regions. Researchers also know that there are more deaths from chronic pulmonary disease in high-pollution areas of Buffalo than in other neighborhoods. Boston policemen working around high concentrations of carbon monoxide seem more susceptible to the common cold.

Evolution of Control. Alarmed by ever-murkier skies, increasing property damage, unpleasant odors and more frequent pollution alerts, communities, states and the Federal Government have finally begun to mount a systematic attack on air pollution. They have been able to use as a model the pioneering antipollution program of Los Angeles, which evolved out of sheer necessity. Though the city has frequent temperature inversions and lies in a mountain-rimmed bowl that traps the pollutants, Los Angeles had practically no pollution problem until the 1940s, when it began its explosive growth in population and industry.

Almost overnight, the clear air that had played so important a role in drawing movie-makers to Hollywood was replaced by palls of smoke, a brownish haze and offensive odors that made city life irritating and unpleasant. Concerned Angelenos began to come forward with California-size plans to solve the problem. One suggestion was to bore mammoth tunnels through the surrounding mountains, install huge fans in them and literally suck the smog from the Los Angeles basin into the desert to the east. There was one drawback: operating the fans for a day would require the total annual power output of eight Hoover Dams. A proposal to install giant mirrors to focus the sun's rays, heat the air, and thereby cause it to carry pollution up through the inversion also turned out to be impractical; even if the entire basin were a giant mirror, scientists calculated, not enough heat would be generated to do the job.

Then, backed by aroused citizens, Los Angeles County established a control board and vested it with the authority to control any pollution released into the atmosphere from Los Angeles County, an area of 4,000 sq. mi. Running roughshod over objections from many business leaders, the board established regulations to limit the amount of pollutants released into the air by industry, banned the use of high-pollution fuels and the burning of junked cars and garbage. To further limit pollution, the board even ordered that paint containing volatile, smog-forming chemicals not be sold in containers larger than quart size. It reasoned that such a regulation would discourage large users from purchasing high-pollutant paints.

To prove that it meant business, the board brought to court and won conviction of thousands of pollution violators. It was backed to the hilt by Angelenos. In protest against an oil company that was convicted of a pollution offense, 1,500 residents returned their credit cards issued by the firm. On a single day in 1958, the board closed down $58 million worth of incinerators; instead of burning garbage, the county began hauling it as far as 40 miles away to use as land fill. Aided and goaded by the board, Los Angeles oil refineries developed new techniques to reduce sulphur and to trap and recycle malodorous wastes; the refineries became the cleanest and least offensive in the world. Power companies were ordered to use low-suphur natural gas whenever available, and required to use fuel containing a minimum amount of sulphur the remainder of the time.

Losing Battle. Instead of disappearing, however, Los Angeles' characteristic whisky-brown smog has actually grown worse. The culprits are Los Angeles County's 3.75 million autos, which produce 12,420 of the 13,730 tons of contaminants released into the air over the county every day. (Some of the remainder is contributed by planes; a 4-engine jet expels 88 lbs. of pollutants during each takeoff.) In addition to nearly 10,000 tons* of carbon monoxide, autos exhaust 2,000 tons of hydrocarbons and 530 tons of nitrogen oxides daily, enough to form a substantial brew of irritating smog.

At the urging of the pollution-control board, California decreed that cars sold in the state from 1964 on be equipped with a "blow-by" connection to feed unburned gasoline in the crankcase back into the engine manifold. Another law made it mandatory for all 1966 cars sold in the state to have devices that would reduce carbon monoxide emitted from the tail pipe by 50%, hydrocarbons by 65%. A further reduction in tail-pipe emissions will be required in 1970. Taking its cue from experts, the Federal Government has

*The volume of carbon monoxide produced in one day is computed by multiplying the amount released by the burning of one gallon of gasoline by the average number of gallons consumed in Los Angeles. The weight of this volume of gas is influenced by existing temperatures and pressures, and can be easily calculated.

ordered Detroit to make similar improvements on all of its 1968 cars. But California—and the U.S.—are fighting a losing battle against the autos.

Inspections of California cars that have been driven more than 20,000 miles and are equipped with antipollution devices have shown that as many as 87% fail to meet state requirements for the suppression of hydrocarbons and carbon monoxide; the devices generally become less efficient with age and are improperly maintained. Even if the devices work perfectly, however, they cannot keep pace with the rapid growth of Los Angeles' auto population—which is expected to increase by another 2,000,000 vehicles by 1980. "Even if by then the average motor vehicle is producing only one-half of the pollution of today's average car," says County Air Pollution Control Officer Louis Fuller, "motor-vehicle pollution will be greater than it is now."

Electric Car Research. To solve the dilemma, Fuller believes, legal limitations may have to be placed on the movement of autos into heavily contaminated urban areas. Frank Stead, a top official in the state's public-health department, has a more drastic solution. "It is clearly evident," he says, "that between now and 1980 the gasoline-powered engine must be phased out and replaced with an electric-power package." The only realistic way of bringing about such a change, Stead feels, is to "serve legal notice that after 1980 no gasoline-powered motor vehicles will be permitted to operate in California."

Californians have not overstated the auto-pollution case. In a speech that had ominous implications for Detroit's automakers, HEW Secretary John Gardner suggested that "we need to look into the electric car, the turbine car, and any other means of propulsion that is pollution-free. Perhaps we also need to find other ways of moving people around. None of us would wish to sacrifice the convenience of private passenger automobiles, but the day may come when we may have to trade convenience for survival."

Detroit has responded by talking up its electric-car research, demonstrating new batteries and fuel cells, and driving newsmen around in battery-powered compact cars. And Ford President Arjay Miller insists that a crash program is on to build an electric car. But most auto officials believe that between five and ten years will pass before moderately priced electric cars can be produced in volume. In Washington last week, to emphasize the need for electric cars, New York Democratic Representative Richard Ottinger drove an electric Dauphine, powered by silver-zinc batteries (developed by New York's Yardney Electric Corp.), about 70 miles on trips around the city.

Fines & Prison Terms. While Los Angeles ponders new strategies in its fight against pollution, other cities—aided by increasing federal technical and financial aid made possible by the Clean Air Act of 1963—have begun to take tentative and sometimes faltering steps in the same direction. To reduce New York City's dirty smog, some 50% of which comes from chimneys, smokestacks and open fires (compared with only 10% of Los Angeles' smog), a regulation has recently been passed to limit the sulphur content of fuel burned within the city. It came none too soon; the U.S. Public Health Service describes the sulphur-dioxide concentrations in the New York–New Jersey metropolitan area as "the worst, the most critical" in the U.S.

In heavily polluted New Jersey, which shares high sulphur-dioxide concentrations with New York, a state assemblyman introduced a bill that would empower the Governor to shut down plants and incinerators and prohibit the movement of vehicles and the burning of any fuel during smog emergencies. Private citizens or corporate officers refusing to comply could be fined as much as $100,000 and imprisoned for as long as ten years.

To clear the air in Chicago, the city has launched a campaign to force local steel plants to adopt costly antipollution techniques, and transportation officials are investigating combination diesel-electric buses that would reduce exhaust fumes. An Illinois legislator has gone so far as to introduce a bill that would limit the use of Illinois coal—which has a high sulphur content—in public buildings.

Gradual Suffocation. But with these few exceptions, most communities in the U.S. have still to come to grips with the problems. There is still time to do so, but it is dwindling. U.C.L.A. Meteorologist Morris Neiburger points out that the air that now streams across the Pacific from Asia is clean when it reaches the west coast of the U.S. It picks up pollution over the coastal states, loses some over the Rockies, and becomes dirty again as it moves toward the Eastern Seaboard. "Imagine the smog that would accumulate," he says, "if every one of the 800 million Chinese drove a gasoline-powered automobile—as every Angeleno does."

The Chinese autos and the new factories that produce them will quickly pollute the Asian skies, Neiburger fears, dirtying the air currents even before they reach the U.S. Eventually, if air pollution increases beyond the capacity of the atmosphere to cleanse itself, smog will encircle the earth, he says, "and all of civilization will pass away. Not from a sudden cataclysm, but from gradual suffocation by its own effluents."

Other scientists are concerned about the tremendous quantities of carbon dioxide released into the air by the burning of "fossil fuels" like coal and oil. Because it is being produced faster than it can be absorbed by the ocean or converted back into carbon and oxygen by plants, some scientists think that the carbon dioxide in the atmosphere has increased by about 10% since the turn of the century. The gas produces a "greenhouse" effect in the atmosphere; it allows sunlight to penetrate it, but effectively blocks the heat generated on earth by the sun's rays from escaping back into space.

No Apocalypse. There has already been a noticeable effect on earth—a gradual warming trend. As the carbon dioxide buildup continues and even accelerates, scientists fear that average temperatures may, in the course of decades, rise enough to melt the polar ice caps. Since this would raise ocean levels more than 100 feet, it would effectively drown the smog problems of the world's coastal cities.

The waters, however, need never rise. Within his grasp, man has the means to prevent any such apocalyptic end. Over the short run, fuels can be used that produce far less pollutant as they burn. Chimneys can be filtered so that particulate smoke is reduced. Automobile engines and anti-exhaust devices can be made far more efficient. What is needed is recognition of the danger by the individual citizen and his government, the establishment of sound standards, and the drafting of impartial rules to govern the producers of pollution. Over the long run, the development of such relatively nonpolluting power sources as nuclear energy and electric fuel cells can help guarantee mankind the right to breathe.

The Jet Noise Is Getting Awful Robert Sherrill

To millions of Americans who live near major airports and are being driven frantic by the noise from jet engines, President Johnson must seem the luckiest guy in the world. No planes, propeller or jet, are permitted to fly over *his* home, and when the boisterous world of air transportation intrudes on his private or political life, he can silence the intruder with a command—as he did recently during Carl Sandburg services at the Lincoln Memorial. The commercial airliners landing and taking off from National Airport were interfering with outdoor eulogies and Johnson, not wanting his own speech interrupted, told a Secret Service man to call the airport tower and have the planes temporarily rerouted. They were.

The ordinary jet-noise victim, however, cannot command relief. He can only complain or sue, and neither does him much good. At last count, there were $200-million in lawsuits pending in courts around the country initiated mainly by citizens who felt that aviation noises had destroyed the value of their homes—and sometimes so thoroughly as to constitute actual confiscation of property. In the past, few of these suits have been successful; aviation noise has reigned as one of the era's most privileged nuisances.

This victimization of the public has been very democratic, touching alike all economic classes, from the wealthy homeowners of Playa del Rey, near Los Angeles's International Airport, and the élite of Georgetown, in the path of jets from Washington's National Airport, to the residents of walk-up flats in South Queens.

Congressmen from districts that include major urban airports have files containing many thousands of letters, accumulated over the years, begging for Federal help in muting the engines that make normal life an impossibility. The letters have piled up in a huge snowdrift of despair.

Scoop out a few from the La Guardia and Kennedy airport areas: A Flushing physician complains that "it is sometimes impossible to have a conversation with patients and even less possible to listen to a heart or take the blood pressure of patients." A Flushing music-lover claims he "cannot listen to a complete symphony without 10 to 15 interruptions." A Whitestone father says he cannot talk with his family at the dinner table "without being interrupted every three or four minutes while the parade of jets goes by overhead." A pupil of No. 3 School in Cedarhurst complains: "We cannot hear the teacher's questions and she cannot hear the class's answers. Every two minutes a plane passes over our school." A Rosedale housewife calls the situation "unbearable . . . there are no hours when this horrible shrieking

Mr. Sherrill is a journalist. This article appeared in *The New York Times Magazine,* January 14, 1968.

noise is not overhead . . . my baby cries constantly from the noise." A Floral Park mother, finding conversation impossible, spends two hours counting 76 planes passing overhead.

Congressmen Benjamin Rosenthal and Herbert Tenzer, whose constituents are battered around-the-clock by La Guardia and Kennedy traffic noises, warn that the prevailing mood is not merely one of unhappiness but of desperation, and some of the letters support this. From an East Rockaway housewife: "My nerves have me at the point of a nervous breakdown from the constant noise of the planes passing over my house. I don't know how much more I can stand." A letter signed by Bernard Landers, president of the Woodmere Park Association, and 100 neighbors: "Right now the noise is so bad in some areas that not only the comfort, but also the health and well-being of families are being affected. Many people cannot sleep later than 5:30 in the morning when a continuous volume of noise begins."

Consider the life of Martin Kaplan, 35, a former Air Force and airline pilot whose home in Inwood, L. I., is about half a mile from the northwest runway at Kennedy Airport. Kaplan, who had earlier appealed to Congressman Tenzer, gave me a follow-up report by telephone. He sounded keyed up, as if he were relaying observations from a frontline battle. I almost expected to hear the thumping of mortars in the background.

"They're using the runway tonight! Wish you were here! Ho, man, I wish you could feel the walls. When they take off, it's like they were shooting at us. It's like they were firing guns at us. I really mean it. Everything vibrates. It's vibrating right now. There are cracks in the walls. The beams are giving way in the basement. The floor slants. I'm constantly repairing and plastering the place. If you were here, you could smell the fuel. They've been using the northeast runway for two weeks, and that means we're catching it."

Kaplan admits he isn't *sure* the house is cracking up as a result of the jet-induced vibrations, "but this house is 15 years old and that seems a bit old to be settling from natural causes. It's ridiculous already." Worse, Kaplan believes that he and his family, like the house, are beginning to give under the strain. "I honestly think it's getting to us." When the wind is wrong, the stench from the jet fuel washes over the house and makes his 11-year-old asthmatic son sick. His 8-year-old daughter wakes up with troubled accounts of how the wall by her bed shook all night. Kaplan feels cornered. He may sue. "Either the New York Port Authority moves the airport," he said, "or it moves me."

What is happening in New York is also, of course, happening wherever traffic concentrates. For example, the neighbors of O'Hare Airport in Chicago–it is the busiest field in the world; a jet lands or takes off on the average of every 40 seconds–must put up with what their Congressman, Roman C. Pucinski, recently described as "the unrelenting, unremitting, intolerable boom and whine of tidal waves of sound." Similar Miltonic descriptions of misery are even being heard from such places as Minneapolis that used to be considered way stations.

For more than 15 years, Federal officials have been aware that these things would happen as a result of the urban build-up around airports. If they had not known it before, they received a warning in the Doolittle report, "The Airport and Its Neighbors," which was issued in the last year of the Truman Administration, before the jet age had really begun. But only now is the Federal Government making any measurable effort to coordinate its own regulatory bodies (the Department of Transportation, the Federal Aviation Agency and the Civil Aeronautics Board) with state and local authorities, and with the aircraft-manufacturing and operating industries, to bring relief before the public rebels.

Even now the Government's commitment is questioned by some critics, who point to the fact that the only important legislation pushed by the Administration (and passed by this Congress) pertaining to air transportation was an appropriation of $150-million to begin development of the nation's first commercial supersonic transport (SST), which will generously *increase* the noise.

If the SST is permitted to fly overland instead of being restricted to ocean travel—and Maj. Gen. Jewell C. Maxwell (U.S.A.F.), head of the SST program, says that overland supersonic travel is "inevitable"—the plane will drag along a 50-mile-wide sonic boom, coast to coast, which could reach the ears of 20-million Americans.

It is a possibility that chills even some of the men normally most loyal to President Johnson's programs. Interior Secretary Stewart Udall, concerned about the effects of the sonic boom on wildlife and on geological formations and ancient Indian structures that can be destroyed by the boom's shockwaves, recently acted independently of the Administration to seek the advice of half a dozen scientists on the question of possible damage from the SST. Among White House intimates, however, he is a lonely dissenter. The birth of the SST and its potential monster boom was the Administration's contribution to the noise problem for 1967.

But this year, White House lobbyists have assured some Congressmen, they are going to give top priority to legislation attacking jet noise. They say that if they can just pass a bill giving Department of Transportation Secretary Alan Boyd authority to set noise standards for the industry, he will start setting standards all over the place and that will help a lot.

It sounds good, but it might as well be acknowledged by everyone involved that the victims of airborne chaos cannot look for any relief within a decade. The delay in dealing with the problem has guaranteed that, short of moving the major airports or moving most of the people away from them—neither of which seems likely—the situation will become much worse, if not intolerable, before it gets better.

Air travel is expected to triple in volume by 1975, which means that the noise it creates will also triple. At the same time there will be few pro-public counterforces. The momentum of special interests will continue for much of this period. Aircraft industry spokesmen, most of whom concede that noise is their No. 1 problem, admit that the immediate future is barren of solutions; so do officials of the Department of Transportation. Here are the major traditions and influences working against a quicker solution.

Confusion of regulation by whom of what. Some Congressmen want to give the job of regulating aircraft noise to the Surgeon General and to the Department of Housing and Urban Development on the grounds that they are primarily concerned with people and homes, whereas the Department of Transportation—which the Administration wants to have regulatory authority—is primarily interested in the aviation industry. Inasmuch as Secretary Boyd is on record, as of 1962, in opposition to the idea of Government control of aircraft noise—"the Government ought not to involve itself in matters which are primarily the business of business"—these Congressmen have a good argument, but at this stage the jurisdictional dispute is just a bit sad because technical difficulties as well as the economics of the industry are expected to block the introduction of a quieter engine for at least seven or eight years.

The National Aeronautics and Space Agency (which is doing, or supervising, most of the impressive noise research these days) has contracted with Pratt & Whitney, manufacturers of the engine of the upcoming 747 jumbo jet, to turn out a blueprint for a "quiet engine" within the next few months. After that, the industry will spend the next five or six years building the prototype engine at an estimated cost of $200 million.

But even then (and now we are speaking of 1973 or beyond), there is no assurance that the prototype will in fact be suitable for commercial use. It is not intended to be more than a demonstrator. If a commercial engine is adapted from it, the airlines may not want to use it for a few years anyway because they may still be paying for their current fleet and may not be in a financial position to switch to another engine just because it is quieter.

If all goes well, this prototype engine will be 20 decibels quieter than anything flying today. A decibel is an arbitrary unit of sound measurement (10 decibels for breathing, 70 for heavy traffic, etc.) and the best way to suggest what the 20-decibel reduction will mean is to point out that most big jets taking off today are recorded at 120 decibels and up—about the same loudness as a machine gun at close range. A 20-decibel drop would be very noticeable and doubtless very welcome, but it would still leave the jets of the future making more noise than is considered the maximum tolerable level. Community complaint, which can be expected to begin at 90 decibels, usually boils over at about 105 decibels.

And when the aircraft industrialists talk of a 20-decibel drop, they talk of their ideal. Dropping back to reality, the major manufacturers recently sent Gen. William F. McKee, F.A.A. administrator, a private memorandum saying that after much soul-searching they had concluded that a six-to-eight-decibel drop is all that they can promise, sometime in the nineteen-seventies. So that's that: a commercial "quiet engine" which, in fact, is still a noisy engine is 7 or 8 to 10 years away, and it will be absorbed into the commercial fleet thereafter very gradually.

With these technical obstacles ahead, it is not clear why Secretary Boyd is pressing for immediate jurisdiction. It will be many months before even the most general standards are ready. Some observers fear that Boyd's legislation can only result in shifting the risk of damage suits from industry onto the Federal Government. If that were the effect of the legislation, it might cause the aircraft industry, which now is conscientiously spending millions of dollars seeking a quiet answer, to ease back in its research. As a Senator told Evert B. Clark of The New York Times recently: "If the Department of Transportation would come up here and say, 'We've got to have this new power because Lockheed or American Airlines or so-and-so isn't doing its part,' then we might do something. But there is no point in passing a bill and conning people into thinking we've solved their problems when we know we really haven't."

Some officials think noise protestors are a little odd. Secretary Boyd suspects the mental and nervous balance of people who hate airplane noises. Five years ago, when he was chairman of the C.A.B., Boyd testified at a Congressional hearing on the noise problem that the Government should get the advice of psychologists on how to deal with the protests, which, he said, could probably be traced back to the "anxiety psychosis that seems to dwell over a great many people nowadays." He called for "more tolerance of noise." In a recent interview with a reporter from Science magazine, Boyd said that most of the opposition to the SST's inevitable supersonic boom comes from the "periphery," a statement which the reporter interpreted as Boyd's "euphemism for 'nuts.' " Boyd did not ask the magazine for a correction.

More recently he has given further indication that he thinks the anti-noise forces are composed largely of fanatics who would like to go back to the horse and buggy. In a November appearance before a House committee, Boyd's opening plea was for the committee to disregard those who would "eliminate aircraft in the United States" simply because planes are noisy—a radical suggestion that, in fact, nobody had made.

Boyd is not alone in this fear. General Maxwell told me that the opponents of the supersonic boom give him the impression that they are "little old ladies in tennis shoes who don't think we should travel 1,800 miles an hour when God clearly intended we shouldn't fly faster than 600 miles an hour."

A variation of this attitude finds the bureaucrats convinced that the public can be brought back to normalcy through repeated exposure to aircraft noise. "I think it is fair to say that as one lives with noise one tends to develop a greater tolerance of it," said Boyd, in a statement that has been repeated, in one form or another, by every important official of the Department of Transportation.

It is, somehow, a myth that has survived scientific studies showing the contrary. Dr. Karl D. Kryter of Stanford University, in an often-cited study, showed that the more exposure to noisy flights a community is subjected to, the feebler its tolerance becomes. With one aircraft blast per day, the community will put up with a rating of 115 decibels. But with 128 flights a day, the tolerance level drops to 94 decibels. (And where does that put the neighbors of Kennedy Airport, who contend with about 700 jet flights a day during the peak tourist season?)

A recent experiment at Edwards Air Force Base in California demonstrated that one-third of the people who have worked to the constant accompaniment of airplane noise for several years still find the sonic boom "intolerable." The most famous tests–tests intended to prepare the way for public acceptance of the SST's boom–were conducted in Oklahoma City in 1964, when the area was bombarded with up to eight sonic booms a day over a six-month period. The F.A.A. had been shrewd in choosing Oklahoma City for this test, inasmuch as a third of the city's residents depend for their living on some phase of aviation. Nevertheless, even if Oklahoma City is a hospitable place for aviation, after six months of booming 27 per cent of the people said they could not stand to think of living with the noise indefinitely.

Experience helped very little; only one in five who started out being annoyed with the boom had adjusted in some degree to it by the end of the tests. Most of the population said the noise was more detestable at the end of the test than at the beginning.

A second variation of the crackpot theme holds that the trouble is all in the public's imagination. This theme is especially com-

Boom!

The phenomenon known as "sonic boom," the thunderlike clap that hovers over the future of the supersonic airline like a thundercloud, is caused by aerial shock waves.

All aircraft, as they push through the sky, compress the air ahead of them, causing a pressure disturbance. The pressure rises as a plane's speed increases; but at subsonic levels, since the pressure disturbance travels with the speed of sound, it can move out from the aircraft in all directions and be dissipated without affecting those on the ground.

But when the plane exceeds the speed of sound, the pressure field is forced out behind the aircraft where it assumes the shape of two cones–one extending back from the nose, the other from the tail. The pressure field is thus contracted, and the pressure radiates out in high-intensity shock waves. When the bottom edges of the cones reach the earth, their waves are received by the ear as an explosive sound–usually single, sometimes double.

As long as the aircraft exceeds the speed of sound, it continuously sends forth waves of "boom" intensity. Any one person on the ground experiences only the one boom from a plane passing overhead at supersonic speed but he has the dubious satisfaction of knowing that all those in the shock cones' path will share the experience.

mon among F.A.A. officials when the conversation shifts to property damage from sonic booms and noise vibrations. The test homes in Oklahoma City that were exposed to the sonic boom developed hundreds of cracks. General Maxwell has an explanation: "I think it is an interesting fact that irritation brings with it an *idea* that somebody is doing damage." He laid most of the blame to green lumber and imagination, although he admitted there might be some exceptions. (One resident successfully charged that the booms split his home in two and won a $10,000 damage suit.)

Like Boyd, General Maxwell sees the answer as a fundamental choice between accepting noise or doing away with airplanes altogether, with nothing in between. "If you don't like supersonic airplanes," he said, "you can go back to the good old days and get a horse. You're either going to have to accept the boom, or . . . well, I don't see any probability—I don't want to say anything isn't possible, but right now I don't see anything coming down that is going to rid the airplane of it. Anyway, I've never tried to convince people that the boom is going to be acceptable, and I don't now."

Officials at all levels are oriented to payrolls and profits rather than to public comfort. Local zoning officials continue to permit realtors to build right up to the landing strips, rather than insisting on an empty buffer zone or a commercial-only zone around the airport. More high-density, high-rise apartments are already on the drawing board for the Kennedy Airport area. At Dulles Airport, the semi-ghost facilities serving Washington, Federal officials tried to get county officials to keep the houses away but they were turned down.

People sometimes seem to have a mysterious moth/flame attraction to noise centers. In the early days of railroads, towns were strung out along the tracks as if everyone were trying to get his share of the soot and rattle. But Federal housing officials are convinced that for the most part people buy houses near airports either out of ignorance —"not realizing that within five years the noise will be driving them crazy," as one H.U.D. official put it—or as victims of real estate hucksters who show them the houses during the hours of least traffic and when the wind is blowing favorably.

When Federal officials attempt to exert some corrective pressures, they are often stymied. A perfect example of this was the directive issued by the Federal Housing Administration to withhold F.H.A. financing of new homes within a certain proximity of the New Orleans International Airport. Representative Hale Boggs of Louisiana, testifying at a Congressional hearing recently, boasted of getting that directive reversed, although he went on at once to complain that the homeowners who had built near the airport with his help were now finding life "intolerable" because of the noise.

In a recent letter to Washington officials, Alfred N. Warwick, chairman of the aviation committee of the Queens Borough Chamber of Commerce, recalled proudly how in the nineteen-thirties the chamber had "selected the actual sites for what are today's Kennedy International and La Guardia airports. Our business vision has been more than justified." He ticked off the resulting thousands of jobs and millions in payroll dollars and hailed the two ports as "without question, 'Queens' biggest single industry . . . good for borough, city and state." Only as a kind of second thought did he mention that passage of some noise-abatement legislation might be a good idea for the people who want to live, rather than only work, in Queens.

The embodiment of this philosophy at the national level is Secretary Boyd, who holds that economics and noise "are completely interrelated." He has always taken the position that the best way to "cause people to look at the discomfort of the airport in a somewhat different light" is to remind them of how many jobs air transportation creates and how unpleasant it is to be out of work. Still very much a favorite saying around the F.A.A. is an old slogan of the agency's former administrator, Najeeb Halaby: "What is one man's annoyance is another man's livelihood."

The C.A.B., which certifies airlines for operation, makes its judgments on the premise that the amount of noise and soot and other nuisances created by airplanes is none of its business. If an airline gives good service, that's all the C.A.B. cares about. To it, air transportation is a matter of efficiently launched ledgers and the public is made up only of paying passengers—not of people who sleep, watch TV, sit in their backyards and converse or participate in a variety of other activities that require some quiet.

Congressman Rosenthal once protested that if the Government could build a national aquarium "so that fish could have a quiet place to spawn, I think that for the perpetuation of the race as I know it, at least in my district, my constituents are entitled to the same thing as the fish."

C.A.B. officials would probably sympathize, but when they certify an airline on the basis of "public convenience and necessity," they are thinking strictly in terms of getting people from one place to another safely, on time and for the industry's profit.

The same bookkeeping philosophy brought the SST program into being, but even more so. SST promoters seldom talk of the convenience of faster trips; they talk about the SST's providing the aircraft industry with 50,000 jobs and sales of between $20-billion and $48-billion; they talk of the threat of losing the jetliner market to the French-British supersonic plane, the Concorde, which is expected to be in production by 1971, and they speak of the dangerous outflow of gold if the Concorde and other European-built supersonic jetliners are left without competition.

The SST is strictly a money proposition. The comfort of the public at large has nothing to do with it. The spirit of the SST era was captured in a recent Minnesota Law Review article: "If the national interest in acquiring a cross-continental SST fleet cannot be sacrificed to the interests of a more quiet society, cost balancing not unlike that underlying the general airport noise problems seems in order." Translated, this means: go ahead and break the crockery and let the people sue.

The future, however, is not altogether hopeless for the advocate of moderate quiet. In fact, there is one positive influence that is developing along such healthy lines that it may eventually balance these negative influences. It deserves a title, so let us call it:

The New Environmental Putsch. Two months ago in Anaheim, Calif., M. Cecil Mackey, Assistant Secretary of Transportation for Policy Development, warned a group of aerospace engineers that if something isn't done to make jet noise acceptable, "people will just say, 'Sorry, we don't want airplanes around anymore, we don't want to travel that way.' " That is a far-fetched threat, but Mackey's speech was considered something of a landmark simply because he was the first important official who seemed to be aware of the bitter rebelliousness developing in airport communities.

Just as revolutionary for a bureaucrat was his admission that the airlines and the airport operators and the aircraft manufacturers can no longer be treated as a privileged industry, as they were in the beginning, but must from now on be considered as just another part of the environment and subject to the total environmental goals of the community.

"As a nation we have changed our standards," he said. "We are no longer satisfied to have additional airports, new aircraft, more freeways, modern buildings or new industries. We must have them on *acceptable terms*—even if this means greater costs. And if they are not available on acceptable terms, they may be rejected altogether."

It is doubtful that Mackey spoke for his department as a whole. The idea that air transportation can only be measured by its community impact and can only be considered in its social context, and that the solution to its problems will be political as much as economic and technical—this doesn't sound much like the kind of traditional thought one finds in the F.A.A. and the C.A.B., whose umbilical cords stretch back unfrayed into the good old days when Government regulatory bodies were tied altogether to the market place.

However, the cord-cutting precedents have been established, one of the most famous being the Second Circuit Court of Appeals' ruling that the Federal Power Commission should not have licensed Consolidated Edison of New York to build the Storm King Mountain plant on the Hudson River without considering the total environmental impact of the plant—not just engineering and profiteering questions but also such things as esthetics and the tranquillity of the community.

The courts are beginning to demand that regulatory agencies view the public as more than consumers, and one of these days, probably soon, the same kind of demand is going to be made of the F.A.A. and the C.A.B. There are several organized efforts to hurry that day along. One of the most militant groups is trying to cancel jet operations out of Washington's National Airport. Headed by Frank C. Waldrop, formerly executive editor of the now defunct Washington Times-Herald, the movement includes many Washington notables, such as Justice and Mrs. William O. Douglas, Mr. and Mrs. Dean Acheson and the wives of several Senators. Not only are they outraged by jet noises, they are also (like airport neighbors everywhere) angry about the pollution from jet traffic.

F.A.A. officials protest that the jets are not great polluters. One of the big jets like the Boeing 727 uses 450 pounds of fuel (kerosene) a minute, they say, and only four-tenths of 1 per cent of this comes out in smoke, soot and other debris. It takes a jet about two minutes to clear the area. This means that the plane will deposit only about two pounds of fuel cast-offs on the city. F.A.A. officials insist that this is a negligible amount; but those who live under it contend that it adds up to several thousand pounds of filth each year.

Waldrop, a highly efficient organizer of the militants, feels that the noise and soot have tightened his army's ranks to the point where they are ready to break through the C.A.B.'s defenses.

"Eddie Rickenbacker told the National Press Club recently that 'the public will just have to get used to aircraft noise'," said Waldrop, smiling grimly. "Well, we will not accept it. The mice are rebelling. We're the mice and we intend to be heard. Heretofore, the C.A.B. has dismissed individual protestors as crackpots. Maybe we are crackpots. But crackpots as a *class* deserve to be heard.

"The C.A.B. has so far said they don't have to hear our story, but they only said it by a three to two vote. They're shaking in their boots. If they tell us, 'You have a case but we don't give a damn,' then we'll go down the street to the courts and sue everybody all over the place for damages—including the C.A.B. They have ignored the public as long as they are going to."

Waldrop's assault on the C.A.B.—and on the courts, if it comes to that—will follow a new route that others also are considering: the qualitative route. Heretofore, aviation has had to adhere mostly to quantitative measures: speed, safety, efficiency. But the elusive index of community impact has not been measured, nor even much considered. As Dr. Patrick J. Doyle, not only one of Waldrop's supporters but also chairman of the Community Medicine and International Health Department at the Georgetown School of Medicine, put it recently: "No matter what euphemisms are offered, this is a real physiological and psychological hazard not measureable by noise machines or computers."

It is a fuzzy area, poorly explored, but the C.A.B. is going to be dragged into it one of these days. "The technological age," says Waldrop, "has run smack dab into the esthetic and psychological age."

If airline and airport and Government officials can limit the growing rebellion to legal action, they will be lucky. When Waldrop complains that his opponents "don't understand anything less than a punch in the nose," he is not speaking literally, but it is still a good measure of the kind of emotions that the noise problem has aroused.

Assistant Secretary Mackey believes that "the methods of protest that are becoming rather widespread in areas like civil rights are equally likely to be used in environmental disputes." Already it is being tried. Some groups have blocked access to airports with their autos; some mothers have tried to wheel their baby carriages onto the landing strips; there has been considerable picketing; here and there an irate citizen has actually taken a potshot at a passing plane. Tempers are short.

Increasingly, airport neighbors would agree with Congressman Pucinski that "a lot of the vested interests, a lot of the special interests who have been trying to skirt around this problem are going to face up to the fact that progress does not mean virtually destroying the lives of some 30-million Americans."

But as a matter of fact, laying all the blame on special interests is the very way to delay progress. The reciprocating machinery of capitalism is propelled by the aggression of special interests balanced by the restraint of government. Aviation's special interests have become overbearing only because Pucinski and his political colleagues at all levels of government haven't done their restraining job. If the politicians are ignorant of how to proceed, it is only because they have not listened to their hirelings.

At least eight agencies and an interagency task force have experts working on the problem, and these are some of their better suggestions for making the airplane a more civilized disturbance.

(1) Manufacturers should be induced (subsidized or bought off) to reverse their present emphasis on engine development. Now they design their engines first and try to silence them after; they should design quieter engines first and then modify them upward in power.

(2) If the quieter engines cannot lift as many passengers per load, fares should be increased to make up the difference. If this chases some travelers back to the rails, thus encouraging the development of faster surface transportation, all the better. If it calls for more Government subsidization of aviation, this will scarcely embarrass the industry, which is perhaps already the most subsidized industry we have.

(3) Future airports should be laid out as nearly as possible to imitate the generosity of the one being prepared for Fort Worth and Dallas. It spreads over 18,000 acres (nearly twice the acreage of the second largest field, Washington's Dulles), and this may even be enough to hold back rapacious real-estate developers.

(4) Wherever possible, neighboring homeowners should be bought out along the paths of maximum noise. Los Angeles, often cited as a model on this point, floated a $20-million bond issue, of which some will be used to buy private property bordering the take-off route. (But as 80 per cent of the complaints come from landing noises, this is a limited relief. Around New York City's airports, where hundreds of miles of premium real estate are involved, the cost of buying would be impressive, indeed.)

(5) Airports established in distant suburbs, like Dulles or Baltimore's Friendship (30 miles from Washington), should be made more attractive by servicing them with really high-speed and cheap transportation.

(6) Within earshot of every major airport in the country are dozens of schools and several hospitals; there are 40 schools within noise distance of the Los Angeles airport alone. By 1975, at least 460 cities will be

getting jet service. Schools and hospitals built in these cities in the future should be insulated against noise; the materials have been available for years.

In proposing all these things, the experts are quite correct. The only trouble is, with Government planners the good ideas are almost always canceled out by timidity and by niggardliness. Dorn McGrath, director of metropolitan area analysis for H.U.D., after estimating that $240 million would be needed to insulate the homes most plagued by noise around Kennedy, O'Hare and Los Angeles International airports, said that one should not expect Congress to pick up such a bill.

In saying so, he exposes the operative psyche of Washington's legislators, who are expected eventually to appropriate up to $3 billion to develop the supernoise of the SST but are not interested in spending 1/12th that amount to insulate homes against jet bedlam.

McGrath's pessimistic appraisal is probably justified, just as is Mackey's warning that "the Federal Government *cannot* be looked upon as the principal source of capital" to pay for aircraft reform. The reason is simple: Congress just doesn't care enough. Perhaps 50 to 60 Congressmen are really worked up over the problem, but no more than that. The results are exactly what one would expect.

More than two years ago, the brand-new Housing and Urban Development Department was statutorily ordered to "undertake a study to determine feasible methods of reducing the economic loss and hardship" suffered by people who live near airports. The study was to include "feasible methods of insulating such homes from the noise of aircraft" and it was supposed to be completed within one year. It still isn't complete. In fact, it has hardly been started. Congress refused to supply the money for the job.

The default was symptomatic of why the noise problem will continue for a while. There is nothing metaphysical about it. It is just a matter of buying land, of developing quieter engines, of paying the airlines to use them, of soundproofing homes and schools and hospitals, of *not* filling in more Jamaica Bays to please real-estate operators, of *not* subsidizing the development of noisier SST's.

It all comes down to a matter of budgetary priorities and esthetics—the very things, unfortunately, that politicians understand least and that an exasperated public will probably have to teach them.

And No Birds Sing Rachel Carson

Over increasingly large areas of the United States, spring now comes unheralded by the return of the birds, and the early mornings are strangely silent where once they were filled with the beauty of bird song. This sudden silencing of the song of birds, this obliteration of the color and beauty and interest they lend to our world have come about swiftly, insidiously, and unnoticed by those whose communities are as yet unaffected.

From the town of Hinsdale, Illinois, a housewife wrote in despair to one of the world's leading ornithologists, Robert Cushman Murphy, Curator Emeritus of Birds at the American Museum of Natural History.

Here in our village the elm trees have been sprayed for several years [she wrote in 1958]. When we moved here six years ago, there was a wealth of bird life; I put up a feeder and had a steady stream of cardinals, chickadees, downies and nuthatches all winter, and the cardinals and chickadees brought their young ones in the summer.

After several years of DDT spray, the town is almost devoid of robins and starlings; chickadees have not been on my shelf for two years, and this year the cardinals are gone too; the nesting population in the neighborhood seems to consist of one dove pair and perhaps one catbird family.

It is hard to explain to the children that the birds have been killed off, when they have learned in school that a Federal law protects the birds from killing or capture. "Will they ever come back?" they ask, and I do not have the answer. The elms are still dying, and so are the birds. *Is* anything being done? *Can* anything be done? Can *I* do anything?

Reprinted from *Silent Spring* by Rachel Carson by permission of the Houghton Mifflin Company.

A year after the federal government had launched a massive spraying program against the fire ant, an Alabama woman wrote: "Our place has been a veritable bird sanctuary for over half a century. Last July we all remarked, 'There are more birds than ever.' Then, suddenly, in the second week of August, they all disappeared. I was accustomed to rising early to care for my favorite mare that had a young filly. There was not a sound of the song of a bird. It was eerie, terrifying. What was man doing to our perfect and beautiful world? Finally, five months later a blue jay appeared and a wren."

The autumn months to which she referred brought other somber reports from the deep South, where in Mississippi, Louisiana, and Alabama the *Field Notes* published quarterly by the National Audubon Society and the United States Fish and Wildlife Service noted the striking phenomenon of "blank spots weirdly empty of virtually *all* bird life." The *Field Notes* are a compilation of the reports of seasoned observers who have spent many years afield in their particular areas and have unparalleled knowledge of the normal bird life of the region. One such observer reported that in driving about southern Mississippi that fall she saw "no land birds at all for long distances." Another in Baton Rouge reported that the contents of her feeders had lain untouched "for weeks on end," while fruiting shrubs in her yard, that ordinarily would be stripped clean by that time, still were laden with berries. Still another reported that his picture window, "which often used to frame a scene splashed with the red of 40 or 50 cardinals and crowded with other species, seldom permitted a view of as many as a bird or two at a time." Professor Maurice Brooks of the University of West Virginia, an authority on the birds of the Appalachian region, reported that the West Virginia bird population had undergone "an incredible reduction."

One story might serve as the tragic symbol of the fate of the birds—a fate that has already overtaken some species, and that threatens all. It is the story of the robin, the bird known to everyone. To millions of Americans, the season's first robin means that the grip of winter is broken. Its coming is an event reported in newspapers and told eagerly at the breakfast table. And as the number of migrants grows and the first mists of green appear in the woodlands, thousands of people listen for the first dawn chorus of the robins throbbing in the early morning light. But now all is changed, and not even the return of the birds may be taken for granted.

The survival of the robin, and indeed of many other species as well, seems fatefully linked with the American elm, a tree that is part of the history of thousands of towns from the Atlantic to the Rockies, gracing their streets and their village squares and college campuses with majestic archways of green. Now the elms are stricken with a disease that afflicts them throughout their range, a disease so serious that many experts believe all efforts to save the elms will in the end be futile. It would be tragic to lose the elms, but it would be doubly tragic if, in vain efforts to save them, we plunge vast segments of our bird populations into the night of extinction. Yet this is precisely what is threatened.

The so-called Dutch elm disease entered the United States from Europe about 1930 in elm burl logs imported for the veneer industry. It is a fungus disease; the organism invades the water-conducting vessels of the tree, spreads by spores carried in the flow of sap, and by its poisonous secretions as well as by mechanical clogging causes the branches to wilt and the tree to die. The disease is spread from diseased to healthy trees by elm bark beetles. The galleries which the insects have tunneled out under the bark of dead trees become contaminated with spores of the invading fungus, and the spores adhere to the insect body and are carried wherever the beetle flies. Efforts to control the fungus disease of the elms have been directed largely toward control of the carrier insect. In community after community, especially throughout the strongholds of the American elm, the Midwest and New England, intensive spraying has become a routine procedure.

What this spraying could mean to bird life, and especially to the robin, was first made clear by the work of two ornithologists at Michigan State University, Professor George Wallace and one of his graduate students, John Mehner. When Mr. Mehner began work for the doctorate in 1954, he chose a research project that had to do with robin populations. This was quite by chance, for at that time no one suspected that the robins were in danger. But even as he undertook the work, events occurred that were to change its character and indeed to deprive him of his material.

Spraying for Dutch elm disease began in a small way on the university campus in 1954. The following year the city of East Lansing (where the university is located) joined in, spraying on the campus was expanded, and, with local programs for gypsy moth and mosquito control also under way, the rain of chemicals increased to a downpour.

During 1954, the year of the first light

spraying, all seemed well. The following spring the migrating robins began to return to the campus as usual. Like the bluebells in Tomlinson's haunting essay "The Lost Wood," they were "expecting no evil" as they reoccupied their familiar territories. But soon it became evident that something was wrong. Dead and dying robins began to appear on the campus. Few birds were seen in their normal foraging activities or assembling in their usual roosts. Few nests were built; few young appeared. The pattern was repeated with monotonous regularity in succeeding springs. The sprayed area had become a lethal trap in which each wave of migrating robins would be eliminated in about a week. Then new arrivals would come in, only to add to the numbers of doomed birds seen on the campus in the agonized tremors that precede death.

"The campus is serving as a graveyard for most of the robins that attempt to take up residence in the spring," said Dr. Wallace. But why? At first he suspected some disease of the nervous system, but soon it became evident that "in spite of the assurances of the insecticide people that their sprays were 'harmless to birds' the robins were really dying of insecticidal poisoning; they exhibited the well-known symptoms of loss of balance, followed by tremors, convulsions, and death."

Several facts suggested that the robins were being poisoned, not so much by direct contact with the insecticides as indirectly, by eating earthworms. Campus earthworms had been fed inadvertently to crayfish in a research project and all the crayfish had promptly died. A snake kept in a laboratory cage had gone into violent tremors after being fed such worms. And earthworms are the principal food of robins in the spring.

A key piece in the jigsaw puzzle of the doomed robins was soon to be supplied by Dr. Roy Barker of the Illinois Natural History Survey at Urbana. Dr. Barker's work, published in 1958, traced the intricate cycle of events by which the robins' fate is linked to the elm trees by way of the earthworms. The trees are sprayed in the spring (usually at the rate of 2 to 5 pounds of DDT per 50-foot tree, which may be the equivalent of as much as *23 pounds per acre* where elms are numerous) and often again in July, at about half this concentration. Powerful sprayers direct a stream of poison to all parts of the tallest trees, killing directly not only the target organism, the bark beetle, but other insects, including pollinating species and predatory spiders and beetles. The poison forms a tenacious film over the leaves and bark. Rains do not wash it away. In the autumn the leaves fall to the ground, accumulate in sodden layers, and begin the slow process of becoming one with the soil. In this they are aided by the toil of the earthworms, who feed in the leaf litter, for elm leaves are among their favorite foods. In feeding on the leaves the worms also swallow the insecticide, accumulating and concentrating it in their bodies. Dr. Barker found deposits of DDT throughout the digestive tracts of the worms, their blood vessels, nerves, and body wall. Undoubtedly some of the earthworms themselves succumb, but others survive to become "biological magnifiers" of the poison. In the spring the robins return to provide another link in the cycle. As few as 11 large earthworms can transfer a lethal dose of DDT to a robin. And 11 worms form a small part of a day's rations to a bird that eats 10 to 12 earthworms in as many minutes.

Not all robins receive a lethal dose, but another consequence may lead to the extinction of their kind as surely as fatal poisoning. The shadow of sterility lies over all the bird studies and indeed lengthens to include all living things within its potential range. There are now only two or three dozen robins to be found each spring on the entire 185-acre campus of Michigan State University, compared with a conservatively estimated 370 adults in this area before spraying. In 1954 every robin nest under observation by Mehner produced young. Toward the end of June, 1957, when at least 370 young birds (the normal replacement of the adult population) would have been foraging over the campus in the years before spraying began, Mehner could find *only one young robin.* A year later Dr. Wallace was to report: "At no time during the spring or summer [of 1958] did I see a fledgling robin anywhere on the main campus, and so far I have failed to find anyone else who has seen one there."

Part of this failure to produce young is due, of course, to the fact that one or more of a pair of robins dies before the nesting cycle is completed. But Wallace has significant records which point to something more sinister–the actual destruction of the birds' capacity to reproduce. He has, for example, "records of robins and other birds building nests but laying no eggs, and others laying eggs and incubating them but not hatching them. We have one record of a robin that sat on its eggs faithfully for 21 days and they did not hatch. The normal incubation period is 13 days . . . Our analyses are showing high concentrations of DDT in the testes and ovaries of breeding birds," he told a congressional committee in 1960. "Ten males had amounts ranging from 30 to 109 parts per million in the testes, and two females had 151 and 211 parts per million respectively in the egg follicles in their ovaries."

Soon studies in other areas began to develop findings equally dismal. Professor Joseph Hickey and his students at the University of Wisconsin, after careful comparative studies of sprayed and unsprayed areas, reported the robin mortality to be at least 86 to 88 per cent. The Cranbrook Institute of Science at Bloomfield Hills, Michigan, in an effort to assess the extent of bird loss caused by the spraying of the elms, asked in 1956 that all birds thought to be victims of DDT poisoning be turned into the institute for examination. The request had a response beyond all expectations. Within a few weeks the deep-freeze facilities of the institute were taxed to capacity, so that other specimens had to be refused. By 1959 a thousand poisoned birds from this single community had been turned in or reported. Although the robin was the chief victim (one woman calling the institute reported 12 robins lying dead on her lawn as she spoke), 63 different species were included among the specimens examined at the institute.

The robins, then, are only one part of the chain of devastation linked to the spraying of the elms, even as the elm program is only one of the multitudinous spray programs that cover our land with poisons. Heavy mortality has occurred among about 90 species of birds, including those most familiar to suburbanites and amateur naturalists. The populations of nesting birds in general have declined as much as 90 per cent in some of the sprayed towns. As we shall see, all the various types of birds are affected–ground feeders, treetop feeders, bark feeders, predators.

It is only reasonable to suppose that all birds and mammals heavily dependent on earthworms or other soil organisms for food are threatened by the robins' fate. Some 45 species of birds include earthworms in their diet. Among them is the woodcock, a species that winters in southern areas recently heavily sprayed with heptachlor. Two significant discoveries have now been made about the woodcock. Production of young birds on the New Brunswick breeding grounds is definitely reduced, and adult birds that have been analyzed contain large residues of DDT and heptachlor.

Already there are disturbing records of heavy mortality among more than 20 other species of ground-feeding birds whose food –worms, ants, grubs, or other soil organisms –has been poisoned. These include three of the thrushes whose songs are among the most exquisite of bird voices, the olive-backed, the wood, and the hermit. And the sparrows that flit through the shrubby understory of the woodlands and forage with rustling sounds amid the fallen leaves—the song sparrow and the white-throat—these, too, have been found among the victims of the elm sprays.

Mammals, also, may easily be involved in the cycle, directly or indirectly. Earthworms are important among the various foods of the raccoon, and are eaten in the spring and fall by opossums. Such subterranean tunnelers as shrews and moles capture them in some numbers, and then perhaps pass on the poison to predators such as screech owls and barn owls. Several dying screech owls were picked up in Wisconsin following heavy rains in spring, perhaps poisoned by feeding on earthworms. Hawks and owls have been found in convulsions—great horned owls, screech owls, red-shouldered hawks, sparrow hawks, marsh hawks. These may be cases of secondary poisoning, caused by eating birds or mice that have accumulated insecticides in their livers or other organs.

Nor is it only the creatures that forage on the ground or those who prey on them that are endangered by the foliar spraying of the elms. All of the treetop feeders, the birds that glean their insect food from the leaves, have disappeared from heavily sprayed areas, among them those woodland sprites the kinglets, both ruby-crowned and golden-crowned, the tiny gnatcatchers, and many of the warblers, whose migrating hordes flow through the trees in spring in a multicolored tide of life. In 1956, a late spring delayed spraying so that it coincided with the arrival of an exceptionally heavy wave of warbler migration. Nearly all species of warblers present in the area were represented in the heavy kill that followed. In Whitefish Bay, Wisconsin, at least a thousand myrtle warblers could be seen in migration during former years; in 1958, after the spraying of the elms, observers could find only two. So, with additions from other communities, the list grows, and the warblers killed by the spray include those that most charm and fascinate all who are aware of them: the black-and-white, the yellow, the magnolia, and the Cape May; the ovenbird, whose call throbs in the Maytime woods; the Blackburnian, whose wings are touched with flame; the chestnut-sided, the Canadian, and the black-throated green. These treetop feeders are affected either directly by eating poisoned insects or indirectly by a shortage of food. . . .

From all over the world come echoes of the peril that faces birds in our modern world. The reports differ in detail, but always repeat the theme of death to wildlife in the wake of pesticides. Such are the stories of hundreds of small birds and partridges dying in France after vine stumps were treated with an arsenic-containing herbicide, or of partridge shoots in Belgium, once famous for the numbers of their birds, denuded of partridges after the spraying of nearby farmlands.

In England the major problem seems to be a specialized one, linked with the growing practice of treating seed with insecticides before sowing. Seed treatment is not a wholly new thing, but in earlier years the chemicals principally used were fungicides. No effects on birds seem to have been noticed. Then about 1956 there was a change to dual-purpose treatment; in addition to a fungicide, dieldrin, aldrin, or heptachlor was added to combat soil insects. Thereupon the situation changed for the worse.

In the spring of 1960 a deluge of reports of dead birds reached British wildlife authorities, including the British Trust for Ornithology, the Royal Society for the Protection of Birds, and the Game Birds Association. "The place is like a battlefield," a landowner in Norfolk wrote. "My keeper has found innumerable corpses, including masses of small birds—Chaffinches, Greenfinches, Linnets, Hedge Sparrows, also House Sparrows . . . the destruction of wild life is quite pitiful." A gamekeeper wrote: "My Partridges have been wiped out with the dressed corn, also some Pheasants and all other birds, hundreds of birds have been killed . . . As a lifelong gamekeeper it has been a distressing experience for me. It is bad to see pairs of Partridges that have died together."

In a joint report, the British Trust for Ornithology and the Royal Society for the Protection of Birds described some 67 kills of birds–a far from complete listing of the destruction that took place in the spring of 1960. Of these 67, 59 were caused by seed dressings, 8 by toxic sprays.

A new wave of poisoning set in the following year. The death of 600 birds on a single estate in Norfolk was reported to the House of Lords, and 100 pheasants died on a farm in North Essex. It soon became evident that more counties were involved than in 1960 (34 compared with 23). Lincolnshire, heavily agricultural, seemed to have suffered most, with reports of 10,000 birds dead. But destruction involved all of agricultural England, from Angus in the north to Cornwall in the south, from Anglesey in the west to Norfolk in the east.

In the spring of 1961 concern reached such a peak that a special committee of the House of Commons made an investigation of the matter, taking testimony from farmers, landowners, and representatives of the Ministry of Agriculture and of various governmental and nongovernmental agencies concerned with wildlife.

"Pigeons are suddenly dropping out of the sky dead," said one witness. "You can drive a hundred or two hundred miles outside London and not see a single kestrel," reported another. "There has been no parallel in the present century, or at any time so far as I am aware, [this is] the biggest risk to wildlife and game that ever occurred in the country," officials of the Nature Conservancy testified.

Facilities for chemical analysis of the victims were most inadequate to the task, with only two chemists in the country able to make the tests (one the government chemist, the other in the employ of the Royal Society for the Protection of Birds). Witnesses described huge bonfires on which the bodies of the birds were burned. But efforts were made to have carcasses collected for examination, and of the birds analyzed, all but one contained pesticide residues. The single exception was a snipe, which is not a seed-eating bird.

Along with the birds, foxes also may have been affected, probably indirectly by eating poisoned mice or birds. England, plagued by rabbits, sorely needs the fox as a predator. But between November 1959 and April 1960 at least 1300 foxes died. Deaths were heaviest in the same counties from which sparrow hawks, kestrels, and other birds of prey virtually disappeared, suggesting that the poison was spreading through the food chain, reaching out from the seed eaters to the furred and feathered carnivores. The actions of the moribund foxes were those of animals poisoned by chlorinated hydrocarbon insecticides. They were seen wandering in circles, dazed and half blind, before dying in convulsions.

The hearings convinced the committee that the threat to wildlife was "most alarming"; it accordingly recommended to the House of Commons that "the Minister of Agriculture and the Secretary of State for Scotland should secure the immediate prohibition for the use as seed dressings of compounds containing dieldrin, aldrin, or heptachlor, or chemicals of comparable toxicity." The committee also recommended more adequate controls to ensure that chemicals were adequately tested under field as well as laboratory conditions before being put on the market. This, it is worth emphasizing, is one of the great blank spots in pesticide research everywhere. Manufacturers' tests on the common laboratory animals–rats, dogs, guinea pigs–include no wild species, no birds as a rule, no fishes, and are conducted under controlled and artificial conditions. Their application to wildlife in the field is anything but precise.

England is by no means alone in its problem of protecting birds from treated seeds.

Here in the United States the problem has been most troublesome in the rice-growing areas of California and the South. For a number of years California rice growers have been treating seed with DDT as protection against tadpole shrimp and scavenger beetles which sometimes damage seedling rice. California sportsmen have enjoyed excellent hunting because of the concentrations of waterfowl and pheasants in the rice fields. But for the past decade persistent reports of bird losses, especially among pheasants, ducks, and blackbirds, have come from the rice-growing counties. "Pheasant sickness" became a well-known phenomenon: birds "seek water, become paralyzed, and are found on the ditch banks and rice checks quivering," according to one observer. The "sickness" comes in the spring, at the time the rice fields are seeded. The concentration of DDT used is many times the amount that will kill an adult pheasant.

The passage of a few years and the development of even more poisonous insecticides served to increase the hazard from treated seed. Aldrin, which is 100 times as toxic as DDT to pheasants, is now widely used as a seed coating. In the rice fields of eastern Texas, this practice has seriously reduced the populations of the fulvous tree duck, a tawny-colored, gooselike duck of the Gulf Coast. Indeed, there is some reason to think that the rice growers, having found a way to reduce the populations of blackbirds, are using the insecticide for a dual purpose, with disastrous effects on several bird species of the rice fields.

As the habit of killing grows–the resort to "eradicating" any creature that may annoy or inconvenience us–birds are more and more finding themselves a direct target of poisons rather than an incidental one. There is a growing trend toward aerial applications of such deadly poisons as parathion to "control" concentrations of birds distasteful to farmers. The Fish and Wildlife Service has found it necessary to express serious concern over this trend, pointing out that "parathion treated areas constitute a potential hazard to humans, domestic animals, and wildlife." In southern Indiana, for example, a group of farmers went together in the summer of 1959 to engage a spray plane to treat an area of river bottomland with parathion. The area was a favored roosting site for thousands of blackbirds that were feeding in nearby cornfields. The problem could have been solved easily by a slight change in agricultural practice–a shift to a variety of corn with deep-set ears not accessible to the birds–but the farmers had been persuaded of the merits of killing by poison, and so they sent in the planes on their mission of death.

The results probably gratified the farmers, for the casualty list included some 65,000 red-winged blackbirds and starlings. What other wildlife deaths may have gone unnoticed and unrecorded is not known. Parathion is not a specific for blackbirds: it is a universal killer. But such rabbits or raccoons or opossums as may have roamed those bottomlands and perhaps never visited the farmers' cornfields were doomed by a judge and jury who neither knew of their existence nor cared.

And what of human beings? In California orchards sprayed with this same parathion, workers handling foliage that had been treated *a month* earlier collapsed and went into shock, and escaped death only through skilled medical attention. Does Indiana still raise any boys who roam through woods or fields and might even explore the margins of a river? If so, who guarded the poisoned area to keep out any who might wander in, in misguided search for unspoiled nature? Who kept vigilant watch to tell the innocent stroller that the fields he was about to enter were deadly–all their vegetation coated with a lethal film? Yet at so fearful a risk the farmers, with none to hinder them, waged their needless war on blackbirds.

In each of these situations, one turns away to ponder the question: Who has made the decision that sets in motion these chains of poisonings, this ever-widening wave of death that spreads out, like ripples when a pebble is dropped into a still pond? Who has placed in one pan of the scales the leaves that might have been eaten by the beetles and in the other the pitiful heaps of many-hued feathers, the lifeless remains of the birds that fell before the unselective bludgeon of insecticidal poisons? Who has decided—who has the *right* to decide—for the countless legions of people who were not consulted that the supreme value is a world without insects, even though it be also a sterile world ungraced by the curving wing of a bird in flight? The decision is that of the authoritarian temporarily entrusted with power; he has made it during a moment of inattention by millions to whom beauty and the ordered world of nature still have a meaning that is deep and imperative.

Precedent on the Hudson

Maxwell C. Wheat, Jr.

When I first saw Storm King Mountain ascending 1,340 feet above the Hudson—the *Grande Riviere* to its discoverer, Giovanni da Verrazzano—the stars above the steep Highlands backdrop were sparkling sharply in the clear black sky on a night that was frigidly windy. From where I stood shivering on the deserted east bank at Cold Spring, the riled waters of the river appeared strangely narrower than their three quarters of a mile width because of the almost disproportionately huge, black hump of a mountain looming up toward the heavens like some ancient Leviathan heaved out of its watery depths. This was Storm King—"solemn and wild," as a Revolutionary War chaplain reported—overshadowing the village, the river, and the very night itself.

Cupping an ear I strained to hear, between chill blasts, a faint echo of the thunderous peals rolling off the Highlands that for generations of Hudson folklore have heralded the ghostly charge of some redcoat or continental regiment. Or to hear Henry Hudson's crew—his Half Moon was harbored 300 years ago near Storm King's flanks—again playing ninepins among the mountain tops as Rip Van Winkle heard them.

"Inside us," said New York State's folklorist-historian Carl Carmer about the Hudson recently, "there is a conviction that everything that happens in a place lingers in some form or other."

I wonder if I could have been so haunted that night by the Hudson's beauty and past—by high pooped Dutch sailing ships plying the waters, by pirates lurking in wait for unlucky sailors, by Ichabod Crane and his headless pursuer—if parts of that mountain had been efficiently illuminated by a $162,000,000 pumped storage hydroelectric plant. The Consolidated Edison Company plans to build the biggest pumped storage plant in the world here, blasting a site for it out of the side of Storm King. The plant would be capable of sucking more than one million cubic feet of water per minute from the river and pumping it more than 1,000 feet up the mountain through a tunnel 40 feet in diameter to a 240-acre reservoir—all this to create, in effect, a massive storage battery. At peak demand periods, when New York City's millions are switching on their air conditioners or lighting their Christmas trees, Con Ed would unleash the pent-up water to cascade unnaturally back down the mountain and send 2,000,000 kilowatts surging through transmission lines strung from 100- to 150-foot towers through 25 miles of town and country.

No wonder Carl Carmer demanded "that the time for opposing those selfish interests that would defile the Hudson is now." For this river is deep in myth and tradition, re-

Mr. Wheat is Conservation Chairman of the Federation of New York State Bird Clubs. This article appeared in the 1966 Sierra Club *Bulletin*.

sources necessary to the feeling for one's native land. Who can imagine the picturesque frigates of old navigating up and down the river past a "scenic" view dominated by a powerhouse 800 feet long?

The scenic and historic values of Storm King Mountain and the Hudson River were recognized by the U.S. Court of Appeals in an epoch-making decision handed down December 29, 1965. Setting aside Federal Power Commission orders granting Con Ed a license to construct a powerplant at Storm King, the Court ruled that the FPC had fallen short in failing to concern itself with the fact that the plant was "to be located in an area of unique beauty and major historical significance."

This wasn't all. The Court declared that the FPC had failed to adequately consider the disruption of local planning (transmission lines would march through the site of a proposed junior high school in Yorktown), the inundation of trails maintained by the New York–New Jersey Trail Conference in the proposed reservoir area, and the consequences of locating the hydroelectric plant amidst the spawning grounds of perhaps 88 percent of the river's striped bass..

"Who would have thought that fish would become so important to us in this fight?" asked one impressed conservationist. He was commenting on the varied and sometimes far-away interests–esthetes, sportsmen, historians, garden clubbers–who had joined together to fight the powerplant at Storm King. A small sportsmen's club far up-river voted to donate its entire $47 treasury to the Scenic Hudson Preservation Conference (which, with the towns of Cortlandt, Putnam Valley, and Yorktown, took the matter to court), and a bartender member of the sportsmen's club added $15 from his own pocket. Long Island fishermen who may never have seen Storm King, but who enjoy reeling in fighting 20-pound stripers spawned in the Hudson, passed resolutions of protest and donated funds. They feared that the minute, fragile bass eggs and larvae floating in the tidal river waters would be sucked up and destroyed in the billions of gallons of water drawn in daily at Con Ed's intake.

Ironically, the Court simply told the FPC to do what the Commission itself had stated it was to do under the Federal Power Law of 1920: to decide "whether the project's effect on the scenic, historical, and recreational values of the area are such that we should deny the application." This was the FPC's legal responsibility to the public.

"In this case, as in many others," the Court said, "the Commission has claimed to be the representative of the public interest. This role does not permit it to act as an umpire blandly calling balls and strikes for adversaries appearing before it; the right of the public must receive active and affirmative protection at the hands of the Commission."

The FPC "umpire" called three strikes against fishermen when it rejected as "untimely" warnings by fishery experts of striped bass losses. The Commission affirmed confidently that "the project will not adversely affect the fish resources of the Hudson provided adequate protective facilities are installed." But James McBroom of the Department of the Interior testified before a congressional committee that although screening devices might protect young fish, "practical means of protection of eggs and larvae stages have yet to be devised." This is only one example of the way the FPC disregarded the interests and dismissed the objections of hikers, naturalists, residents, historians and others.

"What's good for Con Ed is good for the country" seems to have been the attitude of the FPC. Unfortunately, there is a pronounced tendency for regulatory agencies to feel more of an identity of interest with the industries they are supposed to regulate than with the public they are supposed to serve. This stems from an obsession with so-called growth and development, which has often transformed the useful concept of "progress" into the horns of a moral dilemma. Armed with the argument that "you can't stop progress," a powerful utility is able to assert intimidatingly: "You are not going to stand in the way of New York's getting more power, *are* you?" With that the person who likes to watch the sun set behind the Hudson Highlands, who likes to wade into the water casting for stripers, or who likes to explore woods that appear much as General Washington might have seen them, is supposed to mutter "I'm sorry" and slink to a seat in the back row.

The Court of Appeals ruled that people who like to hike, watch sunsets, fish, birdwatch, absorb history, or live in scenic surroundings, belong in the front row at hearings alongside the professional experts and public relations personnel of big corporate entities. This court decision affirming the right of all such interests to equal and full consideration is a precedent that will be noted by other courts ruling on conservation controversies involving highway departments or federal agencies such as the Corps of Engineers and the Bureau of Reclamation.

Engineers of highway departments or utilities usually claim that theirs is the only solution, but there are generally alternatives. The Storm King controversy is not a question of whether New York needs and will get more power or not; in contradiction to Con Ed's intransigence about Storm King, alternatives have been urged. A former chief engineer of New York City's Bureau of Gas and Electricity, Alexander Lurkis, has advocated natural gas fueled jet turbines that could be built as needed in the city itself without increasing air pollution. (Such a turbine made Holyoke, Massachusetts, an island of light in the midst of [the 1965] power blackout in the northeast.) The court's opinion states: "Especially in a case of this type, where public interest and concern is so great, the Comission's refusal to receive the Lurkis testimony, as well as proffered information on fish protection devices and underground transmission facilities, exhibits a disregard of the statute and of judicial mandates instructing the Commission to probe all feasible alternatives."

Con Ed's attempt to harness the Hudson at Storm King may prove a blessing in disguise. It has called widespread attention to the ominous power of agencies such as the FPC to determine the fate of scenic areas. (The FPC and at least four other federal agencies are empowered to condemn land for projects regardless of local zoning.) In an encouraging reaction against arbitrary decisions adversely affecting scenic areas, Congressman Richard L. Ottinger of Yonkers, N. Y., introduced a bill that would authorize the Secretary of the Interior to veto projects that federal agencies propose to build on scenic sites. In effect, it is a bill to protect the federal government from itself. The bill, which also would enable the Secretary to negotiate scenic easements, sets a precedent that might well be followed elsewhere.

Court cases and protective legislation don't just happen. They are the result of aroused people demanding and financing action. At Con Ed's threat to Storm King, many organizations for the defense of the Hudson sprang up. Instead of casting about in all directions and dissipating their energies, these organizations affiliated themselves with or coordinated their work with that of the Scenic Hudson Preservation Conference, which is headed by a 75-year-old attorney, L. O. Rothschild. Scenic Hudson's offices (Suite 1625, 500 Fifth Avenue, New York, N. Y. 10036) are so crowded with documents, clippings, letters, research publications and files about Storm King that they tend to produce claustrophobia. The organization has an energetic executive director, Rod Vandivert, who contacts lawmakers and agency officials, testifies at hearings, and does crucial legwork in Washington, Albany, and elsewhere. All of this, of course, requires money. Scenic Hudson depends solely on contributions by individuals and organizations. In a virtuoso performance, it has raised and spent a quarter of a million dollars so far. More will be needed, much more.

The Court's stinging rebuke to the FPC does not end the matter. Con Ed might have appealed the Court's decision, but preferred instead to rest its hopes on renewed hearings before the FPC, which are scheduled to open in late March. As adamant as ever, Con Ed even claims that its 800 foot powerplant would be a scenic adornment. Although the FPC will certainly be wary of inviting another reversal by the courts, it is likely to do everything it can to justify its earlier action and grant Con Ed another license to build a plant at Storm King. The Scenic Hudson Preservation Conference must redouble its efforts to mobilize marine biologists, hydrologists, electrical engineers, lawyers, and others who can speak with authority in defense of Storm King and the Hudson.

Defenders have their work cut out for them, but they can take heart from a significant aboutface that occurred in early February. New York's Governor Nelson Rockefeller, who had earlier endorsed Con Ed's proposal, announced his hope that an alternate power source could be found and that Storm King could perhaps be purchased as a state park. This is in line with recommendations of the state's Hudson River Valley Commission, of which the Governor's brother Laurance is Chairman, calling for pollution control, a network of roads linking the valley's historic landmarks, and the narrowest park in the world–a footpath 32 miles long and 66 feet wide along the Hudson's shore.

All the money and all the effort expended by the Scenic Hudson Preservation Conference will be well spent to save this stretch of river. Asked while scanning the great river valley from a mountaintop what it looked like to him, James Fenimore Cooper's character Natty Bumpo found a word for it.

"Creation!" Natty exulted. "All creation, lad."

Air and Water M. A. Wright

Concern over the quality of the air we breathe and the water we drink has become a public issue of the first magnitude. But like many issues facing society, it is widely misunderstood and susceptible to varying degrees of emotion, alarm, ignorance, and indifference. Because of the confusion and growing urgency of the problem, I believe it is timely to consider some of its most important aspects. Specifically, I would like to offer some thoughts on how serious pollution is, who causes it, and what should be done about it.

Contamination of the air and water dates from the beginning of time. Unpleasant and even poisonous substances found their way into our air and water long before man became an accomplished polluter. Even before the spread of civilization, forest fires, dust storms, and volcanic eruptions poured vast quantities of contaminants into the air. As those with allergy problems can attest, plants have contaminated the air with pollen for hundreds of centuries. In fact, one of the conditions for the earth's existence has been some degree of pollution.

Nor is man-made pollution something peculiar to the 20th Century. It has only become more highly developed in our time. Untold generations of mankind have dumped trash and wastes into our streams. Smoke and soot have contaminated the air ever since Stone Age man first began building fires in unventilated caves. Residents of Ancient Rome complained that the airborne soot smudged their wool garments, and London in 1660 was described as having "her stately head in clouds of smoke and sulphur."

The industrial revolution, however, created new problems and stepped up the contamination process. Along with its new-found wealth came the odors and unsightliness of industrial wastes and factory smokestacks. While industrialization raised man's standard of living, it lowered the quality of his most vital resources–air and water. Now, some 100 years later, it appears that the quality of these resources may be significantly affected merely by living in the manner to which we have become accustomed.

The full extent of America's pollution problem defies accurate measurement. It is increasingly obvious, however, that we have a serious problem on our hands–and one that seems to be growing more serious each year. Though I cannot agree with those who fear that we will be destroyed by our own environment, there are too many locations in the United States where the air or water has become objectionable, unpleasant, and–on occasions–hazardous.

Man's potential for damaging his environment is continually increasing. The U.S. Public Health Service estimated that we

Mr. Wright is Chairman of the Board of Humble Oil & Refining Company. This is the text of a speech delivered to the Houston Chamber of Commerce on December 6, 1966. It was published in *The Humble Way,* First Quarter, 1967.

Americans, in performing our normal activities, release some 360,000 tons of principal pollutants into the atmosphere each day. We also produce nearly 400,000 tons of waste material each day. Enough of this flows into our lakes and rivers to jeopardize their usefulness for recreation or consumption purposes. Secretary of the Interior Udall recently warned that barring effective remedial action parts of the Great Lakes were threatened with an early and unnatural death. And according to New York's Governor Rockefeller, sections of the Hudson River are so contaminated that fish are unable to live in them.

In its most simple terms, pollution results from the daily activities of an increasing number of people. In 1900 the approximately 3 million square miles of the United States accommodated the daily activities of less than 80 million people. Today, that same area—and the same amount of air and water—must accommodate the activities of nearly 200 million people.

Moreover, at the turn of the century our nation was predominantly rural; today it is predominantly urban. In 1900, less than one person in three lived in a major metropolitan area. Today two-thirds of our population live in urban areas, and according to one source, 85 percent of the people live on less than 2 percent of the land.

Pollution is also in many respects an offshoot of progress. As our nation has become more highly mechanized, our ability to contaminate our environment has steadily increased. In 1900, for example, the nation's car population was almost nil. Today it is over 70 million and is projected to approach 120 million by 1980. Not even the boldest of forecasters project this trend to the year 2000.

A hundred years ago, isolation of the sources of air and water pollution was a simpler matter. One could merely point to an industrial smokestack or trace the scum on the water to a manufacturing plant's waste outlet and the question was answered. There was the prime polluter— industry.

Today, however, assigning the responsibility for air and water pollution is not that simple. Although industry still receives most of the blame, it has in recent years become less and less the main offender. In defining the causes of air pollution, a recent report by the National Academy of Sciences said that less than one-third of the principal atmospheric pollutants released in the U.S. comes from manufacturing plants or electricity generating complexes. The remaining two-thirds comes from other sources, mainly individuals and municipalities.

Even in the area of water pollution, where industry continues to be depicted as the main culprit, recent studies indicate that community sewage is an equal and oftentime greater despoiler of our waterways. Murray Stein, federal commissioner for water pollution control, has stated that "The underlying cause of water pollution is that all over the country you have municipal sewage systems that are inadequate for the loads that have been imposed on them in the last few years."

The fact is that the problem of air and water contamination involves all of modern society. Pollutants are released whenever backyard leaves are burned, whenever an automobile is used, whenever apartment or municipal trash is incinerated, wherever inadequate city sewage treatment facilities discharge wastes into rivers. One study early this year revealed that in New York City alone several hundred thousand tons per day of sewage remains untreated, and the city's 11 municipal incinerators contribute more than 35 tons of objectionable matter to the atmosphere each day. In Houston, according to our morning newspaper, the city's own sewage plants have on occasion been singled out as serious offenders. In short, all segments of society have created the pollution problem. And all segments will now have to be parties to the solution.

The best solution to the problem of restoring and maintaining the quality of our air and water lies in a well-coordinated, community-wide effort. No single segment of society is capable of accomplishing the job that lies ahead. But, as in the case of all community programs, some group must take the initiative in getting an effective program under way. In my opinion, this group should be the community's business leaders. If a reasoned and reasonable response to this growing problem is to be forthcoming, business leadership must play an active and consistent role.

I am not suggesting that businessmen have ignored their social responsibility in connection with this problem. This is true of some, but others have made substantial contributions toward improving the quality of air and water. In just the last 10 years, for example, the electric power industry has spent some $750 million dollars on air and water conservation. Over the same period, the chemical and petroleum industries have spent a similar amount on pollution control equipment, and are now spending additional millions of dollars a year to operate, improve and expand this equipment. In all its operations this year, the petroleum industry will spend more than $10 million just on air and water conservation research with the aim of counties, or regions have established anti-pollution programs. Many of these are judged by the Health Service to be grossly inadequate. More than 2000 American communities pour untreated sewage into the nation's lakes and rivers. An additional 700 municipalities in the United States have sewer systems with inadequate refuse treatment facilities. Fewer than half our states have air pollution laws on their books, and most of these are of the antiquated "smoke law" variety.

If the pollution problem is to be solved, and it must be, it is imperative that more state and local governments play an active role. In most cases, the problem is a local responsibility, and we should see that it remains such. But if effective local programs are to be implemented, we may be assured that federal action will be forthcoming. It behooves all of us–local officials, industry and interested citizens–to take the appropriate remedial action, and accept our proper responsibility.

The final responsibility of effective business leadership is to educate the public as to what can be done and how much it will cost. Here again, I believe business has been negligent. Society must be made fully aware that though the prospect of clean, country air and water in the city is pleasant, the cost of achieving this goal may be prohibitive. Society must realize that to achieve this level of clean air and water involves more than just having industry spend money in crash programs.

The average citizen, for example, would have to buy add-on exhaust controls for his car. He would have to pay for at least annual testing to insure their efficient operation. He would be required to pay additional taxes so the city could purchase smoke-free incinerators and vastly improved facilities for the treatment of sewage. He would be forced to collect the leaves in his yard and pay for an inspection system which assures that he doesn't burn them. In some parts of the country his office space or apartment rent might also have to be boosted because of higher electrical costs and higher heating costs resulting from more expensive low-sulfur fuel.

The public must realize that, in the final analysis, the problem of air and water pollution is closely linked to economics. The purity of our air and water depends almost entirely on how much we are willing to pay. Senator Muskie of Maine, Chairman of the Subcommittee on Air and Water Pollution, believes that $100 billion will be required by the year 2000 just to clean up the waterways. A recent article in *Harvard Business Review* estimated that total expenditures of at least $275 billion will be required over the next 34 years to ensure the availability of clean air and water. Of this sum $110 billion will be needed to control and reverse water pollution, $105 billion to abate and control air pollution, and $60 billion for disposing of wastes.

An informed and enlightened public must realize that outlays of this magnitude will be necessary to satisfy its desires for a relatively pollution-free environment. The public must also understand that a large part of this sum will come directly from its own pockets. When these facts are widely known, society can then make the necessary judgments on how clean it wants air and water to be. We can achieve almost any desired level of purity, but we must be willing to pay the price.

Given complete information, the community will probably decide on a course of action somewhere between the extreme positions. The one extreme is that no price is too great to restore our air and water to their natural purity. The other extreme is that no pollution problem actually exists. The first position would result in a waste of capital, and would jeopardize future economic progress. The second position would result in the waste of our two most essential resources. Industry, government, and the individual must decide, on the basis of costs and benefits, what level of purity they wish to attain.

No reasonable person would suggest that man not use his environment, or that he revert to his primitive past. But at the same time no reasonable person can condone the misuse of two resources needed to sustain life.

Society must come to grips with the problem of air and water conservation. We must not do this, however, in a mood of panic. We must develop a reasoned and effective response to the challenge. To be specific, industry must act responsibly—government must act fairly—the public must act with understanding. The time for decision is here.

Chapter 7

TOWARD THE YEAR 2000

In the year A.D. 1000 there were probably fewer than 500 million people in the world–one sixth of today's population. The ordinary man lived and died within an area of 25 miles of his birthplace, and he lived and died in ignorance, poverty, ill-health, and in fear of his neighbor, his lord, his church, and his God. With few exceptions, much of the world's population is still in the same condition.

Mankind's achievements in the past 1,000 years have been dazzling. He has slowly but surely mastered his environment. He has harnessed mighty rivers to supply power to his great cities. He has acquired the knowledge to conquer many of the diseases that scourged mankind in the past. Man today is healthier and he lives longer than ever before. Man has traveled to the moon and returned safely to earth.

Perhaps the history of the third millennium will concern man's struggle to create an ideal world for himself–one that his knowledge and imagination can make possible. Perhaps he can now begin to turn inward and discover himself–while he still has time.

The two final articles in this book ("What's to Come" and "What the Year 2000 Won't Be Like") deal with the world that is immediately ahead of us.

What's to Come Warren R. Young

In just 35 years now, that magic-sounding turn of a millennium: the year 2000! What will urban life in the U.S. *really* be like then? It is difficult for the average person to take literally all the confident talk of garden-covered cities, glistening towns suspended on guy wires and fingertip housekeeping when, as a single depressing reality, we have in the *past* 1,000 years made so little progress in the dreary matter of getting rid of garbage. A thousand years ago townfolk simply threw their refuse into the street; now Americans put it in a bucket and *carry* it down to the street—part of a collection and disposal system which costs us $3 billion a year.

Unfortunately the art of city planning, like the art of garbage disposal, is still in a primitive state. So the typical citizen may be forgiven a little old-fashioned skepticism about the breathtaking blueprints he has so long heard touted for that time. What he wants to know is this: will new skylines, new modes of travel and new technical aids for the home add up to a sensibly planned dream really come true—or to an Orwellian nightmare?

Margaret Mead has pointed out that we still know less about what actually goes on in any American city than we do about the society of most South Seas islands. Our vision of the future lacks crisp definition. We are told that we can expect a doubled population of some 400 million by not long after 2000 A.D., and that four out of five people—a total greater than the entire U.S. population today—will live in cities and towns. Beyond that, there has to be a degree of imprecision in any forecast, starting with the elementary question: Where will all these masses mass?

Demographers at the Stanford Research Institute predict: "Probably in the same areas as those of greatest concentration now, only more so." There will indeed be a fully developed Northeastern megalopolis, but there will be other continuous high-density bands: San Francisco–San Diego; Buffalo–Cleveland–Detroit; Chicago–Minneapolis, and perhaps an urban coastal crescent running 1,288 miles from Miami to Houston.

True, sudden migrations as unpredictable as those of the gold-rush days still happen. Who would have thought, 35 years ago, that the humble desert town of Phoenix, Ariz., (pop. then 48,118) would ever catch mighty Pittsburgh (pop. then 669,817)? Yet today Phoenix has 545,000 people; Pittsburgh is just barely ahead, with 597,000. And the trend over the past 35 years points dramatically to the fact that modern Americans prefer warmer areas of their country. It seems likely that Orange County, Calif., for instance, will become a census rival of New York City, without ever having been a "city" in the traditional sense of the word.

Thus, the architectural historian Vincent

This article appeared in *Life*, December 24, 1965. Reprinted by permission.

Scully poses a disturbing question: "Will we ever again be able, as we speed toward something impressive rising out of an open landscape, to exclaim, 'There it is! The City—what a thing!'?"

Scully's question evokes forebodings, and we are stuck with the knowledge that the old ways just won't serve. The "expert" planners are at least agreed on what we must *not* do. We must not sit on our hands while slum and sprawl make a mockery of the cities we have; nor may we rely on miracle-pill remedies swallowed before: slum clearance, new clutches of high-rise apartment houses and our charmless subsections—urban renewal as it has been done too often in the past. Tearing down filthy tenements is a futile exercise if the space thus created is used to build the shiny slums of the future. Whole new concepts are called for.

Three hopeful concepts may be described as (1) Instant Communities, (2) Megastructures and (3) Platform Cities. Each seeks to bring urban man back into a livable relationship with his natural world by making more sophisticated use of his own mechanical creations.

Proponents of the Instant Community are constructing complete new towns in the open countryside, close enough to the orbit of an existing large city for the new towns to serve, in effect, as city satellites. Far from being mere bedroom communities, however, these new towns will build in all the basic elements of a self-contained community—places to live, to work, to shop, to learn and to find recreation. They aim to restore a kaleidoscopic richness to urban life, using such devices as connected townhouses and tower buildings of modest height which are neatly grouped in village-sized clusters, permitting significant numbers of people to live together. They will be surrounded by hills, forests, cow pastures and streams maintained in—or restored to—a natural state. Children could walk to their schools, mothers to their shops, fathers to work; and everybody could walk or bicycle to woodland trails or to boats moored in the village lagoon.

This satellite-town idea is being tried out right now not far from the District of Columbia, where the country's most advanced regional planning is being done. Known as Washington's "Year 2000" plan, it calls for rapid-transit and expressway routes leading, like the spokes of a wheel, out of the city to serve at least a dozen new towns like Reston, Va., which is already well along; Columbia, Md., which is ready for groundbreaking; and Germantown, Md.

Nobody doubts that thousands of people will rush to live in such creatively scaled new towns. But whether a true sense of community can be synthesized in such surroundings is a question only time can answer. "We are trying to seek out the needs and yearnings of people and respond to them," says James Rouse, the imaginative developer of Columbia, Md. "We are going to produce a beautiful city with a rich culture and green valleys which will grow better, more creative people."

But who can foretell what will happen in the years after the first wave of professional people and rising executives settles in the new towns? In time, if the present job-transfer pattern continues, they will be replaced by new faces, which in turn will keep being replaced by others. What kind of local political structure will emerge in these mobile and necessarily rigidly zoned societies? Happy, close-knit democratic utopias or uneasy little feudal domains? Nobody knows.

The thinkers who look to Megastructures see an exciting bulk solution to the more monstrous problems of today's cities. Struck by the contrast between clogged city streets and the high internal efficiency of large automatic-elevator office buildings, several architectural planners have asked, in effect, "Why not simply design new buildings big enough to qualify as self-contained cities?"

A first stab at erecting such a structure in

the U.S. will be attempted soon in Chicago. A one-third-mile-high, 100-story John Hancock Center, rising from a base covering only three acres, will combine apartments, shops and recreation areas—all within the tapered walls of a truncated obelisk which designer Bruce Graham calls a tumulus. ("The word doesn't really describe the shape, but I got the idea while looking at all those burial monuments in Greece.")

Opinions are mixed on Graham's esthetic success, but visions of even more ambitious Megastructures are already whirring in other audacious minds—*e.g.*, a low-flying "linear city" consisting of a nearly continuous structure which would stretch on and on, perhaps for 20 miles. The linear design would utilize improved transportation techniques—automated trains, plus multitiered channels for cars and trucks, moving sidewalks—to get people and parcels from one point to another within the long complex. However, since lateral walking distances would be short, everybody would still be within a few steps of the dignifying beauties of nature lying on either side.

But would not Megastructures, by their very massiveness, run the risk of creating an institutional climate that would oppress the human spirit? The counterargument runs this way: the same technology that will make the Megastructures possible could, *if* properly used, give birth to light and airy buildings soaring heavenward with elegance and grace.

One school of U.S. thought foresees enormously high buildings suspended in the sky by relatively slender cables draping down from a central mast. Such spidery colossi, the design scientist Buckminster Fuller thinks, would be ideal for Harlem, where cable-hung buildings could be put up *before* the slums underneath were demolished. Fuller points out that today's architects never know what their buildings weigh. "Contrast that," he says, "to the history of naval architects and aeronautical designers, where every ounce of weight must be counted and every part of a ship must contribute to its strength to withstand wind and wave. Now builders on the land must learn to design with the same respect for the materials they use."

Other planners foresee skeletal Megastructures of enormous lightweight "space frames" —grid-works towering high in the air, adapting to any terrain or shape desired, and containing moveable units for living and working, all linked by catwalks and elevators. Another broad-scale idea is that of a city under an enveloping dome. It seems technically feasible, thanks to advances in the use of glass, plastics, energy production and air conditioning. Such a bubble top would promise a climate-controlled atmosphere, maintained at whatever level City Hall thought best, and—in theory at least—do away with overcoats, umbrellas and even roofs. But these domes are probably prohibitively expensive except for specialized areas within a city—*e.g.*, a college campus or an entertainment center.

The third major concept in future urban design, the Platform City, aims most directly at alleviating the degradation of an asphalt-and-concrete existence. It can be grafted onto existing cities or used in combination with either the Instant Community or the Megastructure. In the Platform City the apparent "ground level" of whole towns—and in larger cities the central business districts, at very least—would be given over entirely to green landscape and to uncluttered sidewalks. All or most buildings would be erected on stilts; all or most streets would be tucked "underground," in cavernous areas beneath the gardened platform.

The Platform City thus represents the first realistic challenge to the encroachment of the automobile on our civilization. Autos could be shunted into the underground parking areas, their drivers traveling by escalator or ramp onto the beautiful plateau which stretches through the city's airy Megastructures or to smaller Instant Community buildings. Further, there is a large lagniappe to this plan: essential conduit lines like sewers, power cables, phone lines and waterpipes could be stretched along concealed roadways, easily accessible for maintenance.

Already the Platform City idea has been put to work in the rebuilt center of Hartford, Conn., and with stunning effect. Connecting pedestrian platforms will also cover about 10 blocks next to Pennsylvania Avenue in Washington. Indeed, the influential American Institute of Architects has put its stamp of approval on the platform as *the* essential starting point for nearly all city planning. Says AIA President Morris Ketchum, "The Platform City will give architects free rein to strive for esthetic marvels. I would think, if the leading cities of today don't keep up with this trend, they'll be just like the ghost towns of the Rockies by the year 2000. But if they do, we can build gemlike cities, surpassing any before seen on earth."

Nobody should be deluded into thinking that even the most clever sculpturing of city shapes will stem the urges and needs of Americans to keep in motion. Provision for the mobility of people within and between cities is simultaneously a distinguishing feature of urban life and a vexing urban problem.

It is today's life-sized reality that national spending for highways and streets is $14 *billion* this year, almost one third as much as that for defense; that in Los Angeles 48% of the real estate, and in Boston 38%, is already taken up for roads and parking; that raising speed limits from 60 mph to 100 mph would increase safe traffic flow by a mere 6%. So the hired dreamers of industry, government and campus have begun a sporadic assault on the problems of urban mobility which may very well result in an exotic mixture of transportation modes by 2000 A.D.

To begin with, all the planners realize that, as far as mobility goes, a park-and-walk philosophy simply is not enough. Beyond moving sidewalks, escalators and elevators (perhaps capable of moving at odd angles), electric vehicles—ranging from the size of golf carts to miniature buses—are likely to find extensive use. They may be powered by rechargeable batteries (improved versions of those now used in electric toothbrushes, although the best idea so far for a vehicle-size battery requires $2,000 worth of silver plate) or fuel cells, like those used in space satellites and already tried by the Allis-Chalmers Company in experimental golf carts and tractors. Not only will such vehicles be silent, but they will give off no noxious exhaust.

City skies will be more crowded than ever with flying machines. Hypersonic airliners, cruising at speeds of 2,000 mph, will wing by on the long journeys, and smaller aircraft for short trips will take off straight up from midcity.

Certain old, neglected ideas are due for resurrection. The ill-used advantages inherent in railroad tracks soon may be exploited better. One set of tracks, after all, has a carrying capacity right now more than equal to that of 20 freeway lanes. And regular passenger trains are expected to make 125-mph test runs on conventional tracks between New York and Washington as early as 1966, suggesting that the death of the iron horse has been greatly exaggerated.

What of the long-publicized and long-ignored monorail? Currently limited to speeds under 100 mph by its balancing-act engineering, it may find use in special situations and probably over dense population areas. An odd hybrid monorail, which lowers built-in elevator cars to the ground and lifts passengers into its belly, is soon due to make the rounds between terminals at Houston International Airport. But the city planners are not entranced by the esthetic problem the monorail intrudes.

Deciding how the urban multitudes can and should move city-to-city in the year 2000 is part of a U.S. Commerce Department project for which $90 million already has been authorized as a beginning. Some of the prospects which the engineers conducting the research have cited as worth exploring involve high-speed ground transportation vehicles that are radically different from what we regard as a proper railroad train. Even primacy of the wheel, for 5,000 years very nearly the most essential transportation tool of man, may be doomed by swift craft floating by means of high-pressure jets of air, perhaps an inch above a hard runway. Some versions of these craft retain vestigial wheels for stopping and starting. But in a system into which the Ford Motor Co. has already invested huge sums, even these would be replaced by devices called levapads–skids clamped loosely around a pair of guide rails and punctured with holes. Air squirting out the holes would produce a nearly friction-free clearance. Other ideas for really fast ground transit call for aerodynamical designs–in effect, an aircraft flying along a controlled circuit at an altitude of less than one inch.

Such concepts assume that, to compete with the airplane and eliminate the advantage-cancelling hours spent in getting to and from large urban airports, truly high speeds are needed for transportation by land–perhaps 350 to 1,000 mph. But zipping along the countryside at these rates, vehicles would stir up a considerable wind wake and create artificial tornadoes, mingling dust, debris, ice and snow, leaves and dead skunks. For this and other reasons involving efficiency and safety, a number of schemes for the roadway itself are, in effect, 1,000-mile-long elaborations of the old covered-bridge idea.

Enormous tubes, sometimes called "pipelines for people," might thread between cities like oversized, above-ground plumbing. But if automatic machinery can be perfected to bore through bedrock, rapidly and cheaply, like great mechanical moles, tunnels as far as half a mile down can carry high-speed transit lines with vast savings in right-of-way compensation costs and in unspoiled landscape. A Commerce Department task force at M.I.T. has recommended some thoughtful experiments on human adaptation to such matters as "long duration confinement in a windowless vibrating seat with intermittent and sustained acceleration." Yet, simulated scenery is possible–murals moving along the sides of the tubes at a familiar ground speed.

High-speed intercity trains may be pushed along by conventional electric motors; blown along by propellers; sucked pneumatically through tubes like the vacuum-borne money containers long used to connect clerks with cashiers in department stores; or powered by "linear-induction motors." The last type named is, in many eyes, the most promising while at the same time probably the farthest from being perfected. It would contain no moving parts at all, thus being the last word in reducing engine wear and tear, a matter even more important to safety than to economy. In one design, a series of electrically charged coils would be buried along the right-of-way and energized in sequence to induce an electromagnetic wave, which would surge down the line. The magnetism thus generated would "grasp" metal plates attached beneath the train-vehicles, throwing them forward at a speed limited only by the level which would endanger craft or passengers. It may be possible to eliminate slowing down for intermediate station stops by casting off cars via feeder tracks leading to their destination and picking up cars by having them jackrabbit out to hook onto the train at running speed.

But while the automobile may lose some of its 90% share of intercity travel to such systems, the family car–or something very much like it–is almost sure to be with us. Americans, more than any other people in history, are accustomed not only to speed and comfort but to personal flexibility in getting around. They want to travel as individuals or as families, not as elements of huge masses, and without fixed timetables.

The automobile, therefore, really is the most marvelous "individualized transportation instrument" since the discovery of the horse.

However, thinking about the year 2000–or even earlier–many urban planners hope to combine the personal efficiencies of the automobile with the efficiencies of mass transit. One reasonable scheme is an automotive piggyback train. The family car would be driven onto extra-wide rail conveyors, then borne effortlessly to a distant station.

Another concept, proposed as part of a transportation net envisioned by the Cornell Aeronautical Laboratory, would accomplish the same goal without special railroad cars. Structurally reinforced automobiles would simply be gripped from above by magnets attached to overhead tracks (supported by pillars in the throughway dividers), hoisted several feet above the ground-level roadways where "slower" drivers would be cruising under their own control at 100 mph, and whisked to faraway places at even higher speeds.

And electric "Urbmobiles"–small two- or four-passenger rented vehicles–could carry commuters from the suburbs on future rail lines, with concrete pathways. Guided and powered by a third rail down the middle of the path, the Urbmobile would zoom along under automatic control. Upon reaching his destination, the Urbmobilist would push a button or set a dial and take hold of the steering wheel, be switched off to the street for battery-powered operation, then drive to a check-in station. For the return trip, he would pick up an identical Urbmobile–a friendly, flexible, fume-free, forgettable car and on-time train rolled into one.

How it will feel to live in the Megastructure parlors above the Urbmobile line is going to depend on many more factors than architectural designs and mobility machines. The physical quality of life will be dictated in good part by the availability of a gallery of devices and systems which, though they sound today like just so much science fiction gadgetry, are actually already well beyond the invention stage in their working parts. They exist in the laboratories of all branches of industrial science, where commercially minded men are pondering how fast to push their final development. Engineering wrinkles in most of these devices still would require expensive ironing-out. But the timing of their public appearance will be determined mainly by advance estimates of consumer interest.

If any single item of hardware is destined to take command of the look and lilt of urban life over the next 35 years, as the ubiquitous automobile did during the past 35, that item almost surely is the electronic computer. First, and unquestionably, the computer will complete its take-over as the central nervous system of municipalities, businesses, libraries and other storage centers for information. Later, for better or worse, its nerve ends at least will invade the home.

'Right now we face the same problem as General Motors did back in 1939," says L. M. Gottlieb, manager of marketing, planning and research for International Business Machines' data-processing division. "We have most of the technology now to make computers that could be put into robots which literally could take care of housework better than human employes, and it looks as if, by about 2000, such developments could become economically feasible for the consumer. . . . Predicting how much change people will accept and how much novelty they will demand is the hard part."

Only the briefest sally at trying to tell what a typical city family's routine may be like in the 21st Century can be justified as reportorial. But let us take the liberty, in the hypothetical account that follows, of putting a few of the now-known pieces of semideveloped hardware into the household of Mr. and Mrs. Sample living in Megalopolis, U.S.A. in the year 2000. Individual firms, where names appear in parentheses, are seriously investigating the concepts described.

Father and Mother Sample may be able to remember a few exciting details of their primitive childhood back in 1965, such as black-and-white TV, legally permitted gasoline-fueled engines and the New Haven Railroad. But reminiscences of the good old days generally wait for the annual Thanksgiving trip to Grandmother Sample's house.

This trip still takes several hours by ground train, since Grandmother's house is at the other end of the U.S. It is a low-cost but pleasant and roomy one-piece shell, woven during off-season time by the missile-making machines of an aerospace firm (Aerojet-General), out of resin-wrapped fibers of glass, a new material so light and strong that it needs no internal supports. When Grandmother first moved into it, the house had been perched by helicopter cranes (United Aircraft) on a steep, 4,000-foot California hilltop, thus leaving the handsome landscape unscarred by construction roads. But Grandmother Sample, being old-fashioned, never did quite get used to riding on the bias in the inclinator between her house and the parking lot down in the draw. So her house was airlifted and now is neatly plugged into a 200-foot steel column (Quinton Engineers) bristling with similar houses in mid-Los Angeles.

The view is still a marvelous reminder of her girlhood back in Denver, and she delights in the fact that all of the electric wall-sockets in her house have disappeared, except for one recharging plug. Every lamp and appliance, from washing machine to deep freeze, is a cordless, battery-packed model. "None of them solar-power sails on the roof or piped-in nuclear juice," she says, "for me."

Mother and Father Sample themselves have only recently moved with the children into their new house on the seventh level of an East Coast Megastructure. When ordering it they sat down in the office of a Managing Erector, who vaguely reminded them of a cross between an old-time general contractor and a high-class automobile salesman. After choosing a home manufacturer with plenty of space-arrangement and appliance options (Whirlpool), they selected a model with the number of room-units they wanted, then equipped it with all the accessories they preferred.

The Samples pondered a while before deciding against a curvy, freeform, one-piece bathroom made of foam plastic (Chemstrand) which incorporated odd swirls here and there for wash-basins and tubs. They did opt for an inflatable sofa (Chemstrand) which could be kept folded in the closet until needed, then pumped up at the flick of a switch. They stipulated that the walls, floors and built-in furniture be left bare so they could apply do-it-yourself spray-on fabrics (Thiokol). They agreed, of course, to the few extra dollars for hingeless, knobless doors mounted on pneumatic air-tubes (Chemstrand) and locks opened not by a key but by recognition of any family member's voice (IBM).

After designing their home, the Samples made a final decision on its location. The geographical choice open to them was far broader than previous generations would have thought possible, due to transportation improvements. They had toyed briefly with locations in woodland villages, apartment towers in old cities and the side of a new machine-made rocky cliff. But they settled on a Megastructure area. The neighborhood use of computers there seemed more complete.

They knew that every telephone could report fires by itself (Western Electric), that firemen had instant access to a central memory bank with a complete run-down on entranceways and hazards in every part of every building (IBM); and that police could use the two-way radios in their helmets to obtain from the headquarters computer a complete, nationwide dossier corresponding to any suspect's name, license plate or criminal characteristics (IBM). Computers were also running the traffic signals as well as controlling completely the speed and spacing of vehicles on the electronic highways, the

Urbmobile commuter tracks (Alden staRR-car) and high-speed people pipelines.

Once installed in their home, the skein of living wove together. Mother Sample quickly adapted herself to using the home radar set which keeps track of a special reflective object sewn into Baby Sample's clothing. The child-minder works anywhere within what once would have been called a 10-block radius (GE). Because they have chosen a highly mechanized area, automated, conveyor-belt delivery of mail, food and all other essential goods is provided (IBM). Laundry and dry-cleaning are automatically shunted into closets, though the Samples passed up the option of a closet which dry-cleans garments every time they are hung in it (Chemstrand).

Mrs. Sample's favorite machine, inevitably, is the household robot (they named it Betsy), a self-moving appliance not much bigger than a large TV set with all manner of telescoping arms, fingers, brushes, suction tubes, optical and audio receivers and an impressive panel of control switches built into her decidedly utilitarian anatomy. Betsy's secret, of course, is that she contains her own small but powerful computer (GE), a souped-up version of those which were designed down to desk-top size back in 1965.

Every night about 2 A.M., the hour for which Mrs. Sample programmed her, Betsy slides open the door of her storage closet, rolls out and patrols the entire house. She vacuums the floors (and once a week the walls and ceilings), picks up fallen objects from the floor and sets them in a predetermined place without breaking them, empties all ash trays, straightens furniture and stops with a gentle purring whimper whenever she encounters an object beyond the scope of her electromagnetic orders. When the Samples leave for the evening, Betsy can be programmed to serve as an excellent watch-dog, sounding an alarm directly or through the telephone if there is any untoward disturbance. And she empties the garbage can into an aperture in the wall.

Since the year 1970, when 80 percent of A.T.&T.'s subscribers had "Touch-Tone" phones, with a numbered keyboard instead of dials, the basic element of a nearly perfect "input" device for feeding information into big computers at central locations had been present in home, office and street-corner phone booth. So, for some time now, Mr. Sample has rarely written a check. Mrs. Sample pays all the bills by dialing a special code number for each business they patronize, plus another number for the amount owed and still another identifying their bank. The bank's computer automatically transfers the right amount of credit from the Sample account to that of the grocer. Money is rarely exchanged, even when the family goes out to shop. Mr. and Mrs. Sample each carry a magnetically coded credit-charge device; when it is placed against a special attachment on a computer-connected cash register in a store, an automatic transfer of funds for a "cash" sale is made in the banking system's memory unit (IBM).

"Picturephone" sets, telephones with TV tubes (A.T.&T.), have long been common, and the Samples have these, with an electric typewriter tied into the unit, as well as devices to record the tube's pictures—using film (Polaroid) and electrostatic copying techniques (Xerox).

The older Sample children go to school for only part of their education and for the rest receive televised instruction directly from a central computer. In the same way libraries, by now fully automated, are important targets for queries from all the Samples at home.

The family even has an emergency medical kit near its computer-input station, containing a number of diagnostic devices. A modification of medical ethics, made necessary by the scarcity of doctors, permits diagnosis by telephone. The family M.D., in his office and with a medically-coached computer on the same hookup, gets his data by phone via the family's electronic diagnostic kit (IBM) and prescribes accordingly.

Improbable? Not exactly. How much of this actually materializes in the next 35 years depends less on technological capacity than on factors like cost and consumer taste—especially the latter. "Now we have the capacity," says furniture designer Darrell Landrum, "to make technology serve our spiritual and biological needs—if we also pause to analyze introspectively what we really want."

Professor Sim Van der Ryn, head of the Design Research Laboratory at the University of California (Berkeley) agrees: "We are, in effect, consumers of our environment and we ought to have more realistic ways to choose what aspects we want to consume. . . . The concept of relative cost . . . is not restricted to money, and we have an enormous amount of work ahead to learn how to measure the so-called intangibles."

Says Architect Philip Johnson: "We in America have always done exactly what we wanted. We've never had any trouble at all. And so we can make over our culture physically into something that we can enjoy looking at, and we can be remembered in history as the greatest builders of all time. We can if we want to. But are we going to want to?"

"I think the pessimists who view scientific progress as wholly detrimental to human values are just as far wrong as the optimistic manufacturers and avid purchasers who see no hazard at all in a computerized life," says Dr. West Churchman, head of programs in space and social sciences at Berkeley. "But I must say I don't think enough people are worrying about all the implications."

It may be that the most frightening implication is already contained in the studies of Dr. Richard L. Meier of the University of Michigan's Mental Health Research Institute. They suggest we should all be worrying right now about the capacity of institutions, officials and ordinary human beings to digest the inevitable enormous glut of information coming our way. And so, the ultimate question about urban existence in the 21st Century: Will the *mind* of man be able to cope with the complexity of living in a digit-directed world?

What the Year 2000 Won't Be Like

Joseph Wood Krutch

The end of a millennium doesn't come around very often. When the last one approached, many people are said to have believed that the world would come to an end in the year 1000. It didn't. But now that 2000 is only thirty-two years away, prophecy is again an active business—and it is upsetting to realize that had these prophecies been made in 1900 rather than in 1967, they would have been far less disturbed by problems then undreamed of. Neither World War I—in 1900 only fourteen, not thirty-two years away—nor World War II would have been anticipated, much less their consequences. Those of us who were alive then did not realize that we were living in a brief Indian summer, and this fact does not encourage confidence in the prophecies now being made.

Unless some of the more extravagant predictions concerning the near-abolition of death are fulfilled, I personally have no stake in any world even thirty-two years away. If, therefore, I have spent two or three weeks examining and comparing a number of serious prophecies, it is only out of curiosity—reinforced by such concern as one can have for that posterity which, as a cynic once remarked, "never did anything for me."

The prophecies are surprisingly numerous and elaborate, some from interdisciplinary teams, some from one or two bold individuals. Among the first are the ambitious symposium published in the Spring 1966 issue of *American Scholar* and the even more ambitious one reported in the 300 pages of the Summer 1967 issue of *Daedalus,* the journal of the American Academy of Arts and Sciences. Also known to me, though only in summary, are contributions from the American Institute of Planners. Notable among individual pronouncements are those by Buckminster Fuller in both the *American Scholar* and the *Saturday Review;* by René Dubos of the Rockefeller Institute; by Robert Sinsheiner, professor of biophysics at California Institute of Technology; by Vladimir Engelhardt, director of the biology section of the Russian Academy of Sciences; and a substantial volume by Anthony J. Wiener and Herman Kahn.

At a less sophisticated level there are the perennial articles in the women's magazines promising such contributions to the good life as cooking by electronic ovens and telephones with TV attachments. There is also the assurance given by an avant-garde magazine that we won't have to wait until the year 2000 for "festivals of pornographic films at Lincoln Center"—which the magazine promises to achieve by 1970. Nevertheless, I had best say right here that, having listened to the confident voices of at least a score of intelligent and informed men, I am no more sure than I was before what the future has in store for

This article appeared in the *Saturday Review,* January 20, 1968. Reprinted by permission.

us. There are so many conflicting forces making for so many possibilities that there are a dozen possible futures, no one of which seems certain enough to justify saying, "This is what it is going to be like."

Almost without exception, these prophecies depend upon projections or extrapolations which consist essentially of prolonging the curve with a dotted line on some chart. And though each prophet tends to concern himself almost exclusively wtih trends observable in his own field of study–with very little attention to the possibility that they will be increasingly influenced by other trends in other fields–I suppose that the majority would accept the list of those tendencies expected to continue as it was drawn up by a contributor to *Daedalus*. It includes the following: "an increasingly sensate (empirical, this-worldly, secular-humanistic, pragmatic, utilitarian, hedonistic) culture; world-wide industrialization and modernization; increasing affluence and (recently) leisure; population growth; urbanization and (soon) the growth of megalopolises; increased literacy and education; increased capacity for mass destruction."

Undoubtedly, these are, at the moment, trends which nearly anybody could have listed. But as soon as one begins to consider them critically, it becomes apparent that they are far from a reliable basis for predicting the future. The method itself disregards the fact that–fortunately–trends do not always continue. If they did, we would be justified in concluding, for instance, that smog and water pollution have obviously been increasing at a rate which makes it inevitable that we will either suffocate or die of intestinal disorders by the year so-and-so. Maybe we will, but possibly we won't. Conscious determination to resist the trend can be effective, though most of the prophets leave that out of consideration. In the second place, even if some of these trends continue to follow the curve drawn by the past and even if no new ones develop, the fact still remains that one trend may collide so disruptively with another that both cannot possibly continue. Surely, the consequences of "increased capacity for mass destruction" might reverse several of the other trends–including that toward population growth. And if certain other prophets are right in assuming that we will not use our increased capacity for mass destruction, then population growth might reverse other trends –for instance, the trend toward affluence.

Consider for a moment the contradictory estimates of the extent to which population pressures are a dominating factor. Secretary of the Interior Stewart Udall, in the article "Our Perilous Population Implosion," protested eloquently against the fatalism which considers only how an overpopulated earth might be fed and housed, rather than how it might be controlled. Paul Sears pointed out several years ago that the most important problem in connection with space is not how to get to the moon but how to avoid running out of it here on earth, and he warned that "no known form of life has been observed to multiply without bumping up against limitations imposed by the space it occupies." Then he added that those who brush the problem aside by assuring us that technology will solve it forget that "the limitations involve not only quantity but quality."

All the projections of the population curve give us stupefying numbers expected to be reached even before the year 2000. A recent study of animal behavior proved that overcrowding produces psychotic behavior and certainly suggests that the reaction of human beings is probably similar–even that the crime explosion may be the result of the overcrowding to which we are already subject. René Dubos, microbiologist and experimental psychologist, warns us that survival depends not so much on our ability to avoid famine and sustain a minimal standard of living as on the quality and diversity of our urban environment. "Just as important [as physical requirements] for maintaining human life is an environment in which it is possible to satisfy the longing for quiet, privacy, independence, initiative, and open space. These are not luxuries but constitute real biological necessities." Yet not a single prophet that I have heard predicts that there will be any successful effort to contain population growth in the near future.

Just to add to our worries, Jean Bourgeis-Pichat, director of the French National Institute of Demographic Studies, declares that medical science will certainly raise problems other than increasing population pressures:

> We are on the eve of an era in which society will have to decide who will survive and who will die. The new medical techniques are becoming so expensive that it soon will be impossible to give the benefit of them to everybody, and society will certainly not let money decide the issue. We will soon be confronted with a problem of choice, and when we say choice we mean a moral problem. Is our cultural state ready for that? I think this is open to doubt.

Compare these thoughts with Bernard Shaw's *Doctor's Dilemma.* On the other hand, all this is waved aside by one of the contributors to the *American Scholar's* symposium with the casual pronouncement that "in hedonic potential, megalopolis is no more and no less a natural environment for man than Athens or a peasant village," and in the same issue of the magazine an assistant dean at Carnegie Tech assures us that the abundance produced by the "productivity revolution" is an assurance that the prospect for world-wide abundance and leisure "will not be delayed by more than a few generations by the population explosion." Buckminster Fuller makes this even simpler by assuring us that "the only real world problem is that of the performance per pound of the world's metals and other resources."

The probable incompatibility of the recognized trends is enough to make them a very shaky basis for predictions that claim to be more than a guess, but there is another reason why existing trends do not necessarily—in fact, very often do not—define the future. How safe is it to assume that something totally unexpected will not create some trend of the times more important than any now recognized? Would anyone have predicted Pasteur's great discovery thirty years before he made it—or insulin, or penicillin? Very few physicists would have predicted thirty-two years before Pearl Harbor that atomic fission would be achieved so soon. Yet this last development was probably the most fateful of all the events of the twentieth century—as well as, perhaps, one of the most horrible of all of the possible solutions of the population problem.

And what of the so-called conquest of space? To some, including educator and writer Willy Ley, it promises the solution of most of our problems. Others may be more inclined to agree with Loren Eiseley that the wealth and creative intelligence being invested in it may constitute a public sacrifice equal to the building of the pyramids. They may then remember that the pyramids were responsible for the otherwise incomprehensible fact that, though what we would now call the national income of Egypt was very great, the majority of its people lived in abject poverty. On the other hand, it is perhaps equally probable that the recognition of the economic burden, or even simple disillusion with the results, may, even before the year 2000, make the obsession with outer space remembered only as a temporary folly.

For all I or anybody else can know, the increasing taste for violence, both public and private—both for gain and for fun—may tell us more about the future than any of the other trends, though I do not remember that it was ever cited as being significant by any of the prophets I read. What of LSD as an invention possibly as important as Pasteur's discovery or penicillin or insulin? The prophets, moreover, for the most part take no account of those intangibles—mental, moral, or emotional—which some are probably quite apt to dismiss as mere by-products of economic and social conditions. Are McLuhanism and the hippie philosophies only, as I assume, fleeting phenomena? If they are not, who can measure the possible effect of the hippies' rejection of society or the McLuhanites' scorn for the word?

Based on most of the prophecies I have consulted, one would hardly suspect the existence of such phenomena as the existentialist's denial of meaning in the universe and of external sanctions for any moral code. Neither, to descend to a lower level, would one meet with any recognition of the possible significance and consequences of that enormous appetite for pornography, the mere existence of which seems to me to be more important than the question of whether it should or should not be regulated by law. Nevertheless, the quality of life in the year 2000 may depend as much upon such beliefs, attitudes, and faiths as it does upon the trends recognized by most of the prophets.

The quality of life—that is precisely what seems to be almost entirely left out of consideration in many prophecies. In many of them, the nearest that one comes to even a reference to the concept of a good life is that declaration previously quoted concerning the "hedonic potential of megalopolis," and, even in this case, the acceptance of such a term as more meaningful than, say, either "the prospect for happiness" or "the possibility of a good life" seems to me in itself likely to have an influence upon the kind of life we are preparing for the future.

So, too, I suspect, might be the persistence of two trends which I have observed in the majority of the prophets which are often characteristic of those who are afraid of being accused of unscientific attitudes unless they assume: (1) that the past not only suggests but actually determines the future; and (2) that, although one may attempt to describe that future, one should avoid judging it. These two assumptions lead, sometimes unintentionally, to a sort of fatalism. Since the future is going to be determined by certain known factors, one is compelled to say simply that what will be will be.

Many of those who use the method of projection talk about planning for the future. Probably at least some of them would reject rigid determinism. Yet planning does not mean planning a main outline for the future, but merely planning ways of meeting and perhaps alleviating what cannot be avoided. So far as I can recall, the only direct and adequate recognition of this necessary result of the method of projection was by two of the participants in the *Daedalus* symposium. The first, Lawrence Frank, social psychologist and retired foundation official, remarked that whereas our ancestors often accepted a theological fatalism, "today we seem to be relinquishing this theological conception as we accept a new kind of fatalism expressed in a series of trends." The second, Matthew Meselson, professor of biology at Harvard, suggested that he would prefer "normative forecasting" to the kind which most of his fellow members of the *Daedalus* symposium seemed to practice. The last session reported is, therefore, headed: "The Need for Normative Studies." But the speeches seem for the most part to suggest postponing that for a future meeting.

Normative is a word which many—perhaps most—scientists are more than merely suspicious of, for it implies a rejection of complete relativism and it accepts the distinction they refuse to make between the normal and the average, between what is and what ought to be. But there seems little reason for wanting to know what the future threatens to be like unless there is some possibility of changing it and some willingness to assume that some futures would be better than others.

If sociology seems somewhat too completely content to describe and predict without attempting either to judge or control, that is certainly not a charge which can be leveled against some of the biologists, who also have been inspired to prophecy by the approaching end of a millennium. The Russian biochemist, Vladimir Engelhardt, is relatively unsensational compared to at least some of his American colleagues. He assures us only that science, having moved on from its concern with the management of the inanimate, has now learned how to apply the same successful methods to living creatures, including man. By the year 2000, he says, we will have pep pills which have no after-effects and which banish fatigue entirely; cancer will be no more serious than a nose cold; and defective organs will be replaced by spare parts as routinely as is now the case with other machines.

Perhaps even Dr. Engelhardt is somewhat guilty of that hubris to which many scientists are prone, but he is humility itself compared to Robert Sinsheiner, professor of biophysics at Cal Tech, who declared before his institution's 75th anniversary conference that the scientist has now in effect become both Nature with a capital N and God with a capital G. Until today, he stated, prophecy has been a very chancy business, but now that science has become "the prime mover of change," it is not unreasonable to hope that the race of prophets employing its method may have become reliable. Science has now proved beyond question that there is no qualitative difference between the animate and the inanimate, and though we don't yet know exactly how the inanimate becomes conscious, there is every reason to believe that we will soon be rid of that bothersome mystery also. "It has become increasingly clear," Professor Sinsheiner said, "that all the properties of life can be understood to be simply inherent in the material properties of the complex molecule which comprises the cell." Already we make proteins; soon we will make viruses, and then living cells—which will be, as he calls it, "the second Genesis."

In their new book, *The Year 2000,* Anthony J. Wiener (formerly of the Massachusetts Institute of Technology) and Herman Kahn (formerly of the RAND Corporation) issue a solemn warning against just such unlimited confidence in the benefits of mankind's increasing power and such blindness to the threat inherent in its lagging wisdom:

> Practically all of the major technological changes since the beginning of industrialization have resulted in unforeseen consequences. . . . Our very power over nature threatens to become itself a source of power that is out of control. . . . Choices are posed that are too large, too complex, important, uncertain, or comprehensive to be safely left to fallible humans.

Sinsheiner, on the other hand, has no such doubts. He is willing to entrust "fallible human beings" with powers, not only over man's physical and social environment, but over his physiology and his personality. Now that we are beginning to understand the role of DNA, he says, we are masters not only of the human body, but also of the future human being. "Would you like to control the sex of your offspring? Would you like your son to be six feet tall? Seven feet? . . . We know of no intrinsic limits to the lifespan. How long would you like to live?"

How would *you* like to be able to determine this or that? To me, it seems that a more pertinent question would be: "How would you like *someone else* to answer these questions for you?" And it most certainly would be *someone else.* Is there—will there ever be—a someone who should be entrusted with that ultimate power which Sinsheiner then goes on to describe as follows?

> Essentially we will surely come to the time when man will have the power to alter, specifically and consciously, his very genes. This will be a new event in the universe. No longer need nature wait for the chance to be patient and the slow process of selection. Intelligence can be applied to evolution.

Does the use made by man of the powers he has achieved suggest that he is ready to merit another such stupendous development? Should we not wait until he has become a little wiser before he holds the whole future of mankind in his hands? Not long ago I was told that the October 1967 issue of the British journal *Science* predicts that within half a century we will be breeding unusually intelligent animals for low grade labor. Wouldn't unusually stupid human beings prove more useful and easier to create?